汉英对照

国学经典选读

A CHINESE-ENGLISH ANTHOLOGY
OF TRADITIONAL CHINESE CLASSICS

主编

俞森林

上海三联书店

前　言

　　五千年华夏文明,孕育了博大精深的国学,其中蕴藏着华夏儿女世代智慧之精华和深厚的中华文化之根基,亦给予今日中国人以自信。"国学",亦称国故,以先秦经典及诸子学说为根基,涵盖两汉经学、魏晋玄学、隋唐佛学、宋明理学和同时期的汉赋、六朝骈文、唐宋诗词、元曲与明清小说,以及历代史学等,是中华民族共同的血脉与灵魂,为连接炎黄子孙的文化之桥、心灵之桥、血脉之桥。"每一部名著都是一个广阔的世界,一个浩瀚的海洋,一个苍莽的宇宙"(刘白羽语),阅读中国国学经典,不仅能增加常识,提高修养,而且能从中获取智慧,陶冶情操,充实人生。在实现中华民族伟大复兴的"中国梦"时代,传承中华民族优秀传统文化精华日益重要。它关乎中华传统文化的发扬光大,关乎中华民族素质的提高,关乎青少年的健康成长。

　　随着中国在世界政治、经济地位的提高,世界对中国的关注亦越来越多,中国已进入世界舞台的中央。开放的21世纪给世界文化交流提供了更为有利的条件。中外文化的交流与融会,正引导着国学经典阅读与传播向更深更广的层次发展。面向世界推广国学,正是继承和弘扬中华民族优秀传统文化,提升中华文化软实力,扩大中国国际影响,实现中华民族伟大复兴的重要门径。

　　《汉英对照国学经典选读》选取从先秦两汉至明清时期最具影响、最具代表性的国学经典中的精彩篇章或段落,同时选取国内外汉学家及翻译大师的经典英文译文,并辅以详尽的注释,在满足中国读者了解中国国学需求的同时,助益西方读者了解和学习中国国学。中外读者一册在手,对中国主要国学经典的脉络了然于胸,欲深入了解中国国学之全貌,推荐阅读为其重要的阅读指引。

本书参考梁启超、胡适、汪辟疆、蔡尚思及屈万里五位国学大师的八种国学书目,即,《国学入门书要目及其读法》(梁启超)、《最低限度之必读书目》(梁启超)、《一个最低限度的国学书目》(胡适)、《实在的最低限度书目》(胡适)、《读书举要》(汪辟疆)、《中国文化基础书目》(蔡尚思)、《哪些书最能代表中国文化》(蔡尚思)及《初学必读古籍简目》(屈万里),从推荐频率最高者之中选取 15 种,再从中西方著名汉学家或翻译家所翻译的经典英文译本中选取学界公认的权威译本与汉语原文对照编排,辅以导言、精要的注释、推荐阅读书目,以期达到窥一斑而见全豹之效。

《汉英对照国学经典选读》所选英文译文均为世界汉学家或著名翻译家的经典英译。阅读《汉英对照国学经典选读》不仅有助于国学常识的普及,还有助于提高读者的中英文阅读能力。读者在阅读《汉英对照国学经典选读》的同时,模仿大师经典翻译之作,亦有助于提高读者的汉英翻译能力,对有志于中国经典外译,传播中华文化的读者亦将大有裨益。

本书可作为汉英国学经典阅读教材,供一学期通识课教学之用,亦可作为译作赏析课程的参考教材。除此之外,本书亦可作为大中学生及国学爱好者的国学普及读物、大中学生及英语爱好者的课外英文读物、对中国语言文化有兴趣的国外读者学习中国语言,了解中国传统文化的双语读物、有志于中国国学研究者的入门读物、有志中国经典外译及中国文化对外传播者的参考读物。

全书选文如下:

序号	类别	书目	汉语节选	英译者
1		《礼记》	《大学》	James Legge
2	经部	《诗经》	《氓》	Bernhard Karlgren
3		《论语》	《学而第一》《为政第二》	Epiphanius Wilson

续　表

序号	类别	书目	汉语节选	英译者
4		《孟子》	《告子章句(上)》 (一)(二)(三)(四)(五)(六) (十)(十一)(十二)(十三) (十四)	James Legge
5	史部	《史记》	《项羽本纪》(节选)	Burton Watson
6	子部	《老子》	《道德经》 (第 1、3、8、25、42、51、76、80章)	James Legge
7		《庄子》	《逍遥游》	Herbert A. Giles
8		《荀子》	《性恶篇》	Burton Watson
9		《孙子》	《孙子兵法》(第一、六、八篇)	Lionel Giles
10		《六祖坛经》	《行由品第一》	Wong Mou-lam & Christmas Humphreys
11		《黄帝内经》	《阴阳应象大论篇》	Paul U. Unschuld & Hermann Tessenow
12	集部	《楚辞》	《离骚》(节选)	David Hawkes
13		《乐府诗集》	《木兰诗》	Arthur Waley
14		《李太白集》	《将进酒》	W. J. B. Fletcher
15		《苏东坡集》	《前赤壁赋》	Herbert A. Giles

论中国学术思想变迁之大势（节选）（代序）

梁启超

　　学术思想之在一国，犹人之有精神也，而政事、法律、风俗及历史上种种之现象，则其形质也。故欲觇其国义野强弱之程度如何，必于学术思想焉求之。

　　立于五洲中之最大洲，而为其洲中之最大国者谁乎？我中华也。人口居全地球三分之一者谁乎？我中华也。四千余年之历史未尝一中断者谁乎？我中华也。我中华有四百兆人公用之语言文字，世界莫能及。（据一千九百年之统计，欧洲各国语之通用以英为最广，犹不过一百十二兆人耳，较吾华文，仅有四分之一也。印度人虽多，而其语言文字，糅杂殊甚。中国虽南北闽粤，其语异殊，至其大致则一也。此事为将来一大问题，别有文论之。）我中华有三十世纪前传来之古书，世界莫能及。（《坟》《典》《索》《邱》，其书不传，姑勿论。即如《尚书》，已起于三千七八百年以前，夏代史官所记载，今世界所称古书，如摩西之《旧约全书》，约距今三千五百年，婆罗门之《四书陀论》亦然，希腊和马耳之诗歌约在二千八九百年前，门棱之《埃及史》约在二千三百年前，皆无能及《尚书》者。若夫二千五百年以上之书，则我国今传者尚十余种，欧洲乃无一也。此真我国民可以自豪者。）西人称世界文明之祖国有五：曰中华，曰印度，曰安息，曰埃及，曰墨西哥。然彼四地者其国亡，其文明与之俱亡。今试一游其墟，但有摩诃末遗裔铁骑蹂躏之迹，与高加索强族金粉歌舞之场耳。而我中华者，屹然独立，继继绳绳，增长光大，以迄今日,此后且将汇万流而剂之,合一炉而冶之。於戏,美哉我国! 於戏! 伟大哉我国民! 吾当划此论之始,吾不得不三熏三沐,仰天百拜,谢其生我于此至美之国,而为此伟大国民之一分子也。

深山大泽而龙蛇生焉。取精多、用物宏而魂魄强焉。此至美之国,至伟大之国民,其学术思想所磅礴郁积,又岂彼崎岖山谷中之犷族,生息弹丸上之岛夷,所能梦见者! 故合世界史通观之,上世史时代之学术思想,我中华第一也;(泰西虽有希腊梭格拉底、亚里士多德诸贤,然安能及我先秦诸子?)中世史时代之学术思想,我中华第一也;(中世史时代,我国之学术思想虽稍衰,然欧洲更甚,欧洲所得者,惟基督教及罗马法耳,自余则暗无天日。欧洲以外更不必论。)惟近世史时代,则相形之下,吾汗颜矣。虽然,近世史之前途,未有艾也,又安见此伟大国民不能恢复乃祖乃宗所处最高尚最荣誉之位置,而更执牛耳于全世界之学术思想界者! 吾欲草此论,吾之热血如火如焰,吾之希望如海如潮,吾不自知吾气焰之何以溢涌,吾手足之何以舞蹈也。於戏! 吾爱我祖国,吾爱我同胞之国民。

生此国,为此民,享此学术思想之恩泽,则歌之舞之,发挥之光大之,继长而增高之,吾辈之责也。而至今未闻有从事于此者,何也? 凡天下事,必比较然后见其真,无比较则非惟不能知己之所短,并不能知己之所长。前代无论矣,今世所称好学深思之士有两种:一则徒为本国学术思想界所窘,而于他国者不屑一厝其意也。夫我界既如此其博大而深赜也,他界复如此其灿烂而蓬勃也,非竭数十年之力,子欲乎,于此乎,一一撷其实,咀其华,融会而贯通焉,则虽欲歌舞之,乌从而歌舞之! 区区小子,于四库著录,十未睹一,于他国文字,初问津焉尔,夫何敢摇笔弄舌,从事于先辈所不敢从事者! 虽然,吾爱我国,吾爱我国民,吾不能自已。吾姑就吾所见及之一二,杂写之以为吾将来研究此学之息壤,流布之以为吾同志研究此学者之筚路蓝缕。天如假我数十年乎,我同胞其有联袂而起者乎? 伫看近世史中我中华学术思想之位置何如矣。

且吾有一言,欲为我青年同胞告者:自今以往二十年中,吾不患外国学术思想之不输入,吾惟患本国学术思想之不发明。夫二十年间之不发明,于我学术思想必非有损也。虽然,凡一国之立于天地,必有其所以立之特质。欲自善其国者,不可不于此特质焉,淬厉之而增长之。今正当过渡时代苍黄不接之余,诸君如爱国也,欲唤起同胞之爱国心也,于此事必非可等闲视矣。不然,脱崇拜古人之奴隶性,而复生出一种崇拜外人、蔑视本族之奴隶性,吾惧其得不偿失也。且诸君皆以输入文明自任者也,凡教人必当因其性所近而利导之,就其已知者而比较之,则事半功倍焉。不然,外国之博士鸿儒亦多矣,顾不能有裨于我国民者何也?相知不习,而势有所扞格也。若诸君而吐弃本国学问不屑从事也,则吾国虽多得百数十之达尔文、约翰弥勒、赫胥黎、斯宾塞,吾惧其于学界一无影响也。故吾草此论,非欲附益我国民妄自尊大之性,盖区区微意,亦有不得已焉者尔。(节选自梁启超:"论中国学术思想变迁之大势"总论,《饮冰室文集之七》(第 1—3 页),北京:中华书局,1988 年版。)

目　录

第一单元　国学概说

何谓国学?

"国学"之名古已有之。《汉语大辞典》《汉语辞海》《现代汉语词典》等的"国学"条下均有两个义项,一是指古代国家设立的学校,如《周礼·春官·乐师》有"乐师掌国学之政,以教国子小舞";《宋书·臧焘徐广傅隆传赞》云"高祖受命,议创国学";唐韩愈《窦公墓志铭》言"教诲于国学也,严以有礼,扶善遏过";清和邦额《夜谭随录·庄鬴松》载:"吉州庄寿年,号鬴松。乾隆初年,贡入国学";等等。

"国学"的第二层涵义是指"我国传统的学术文化,包括哲学、历史学、考古学、文学、语言学等"。这第二层涵义才是我们现代意义上的"国学"。这一概念的提出始于 19 世纪末 20 世纪初,"西学东渐"之风盛行之际,张之洞、魏源等人提出"中学"这一概念,主张"中学为体,西学为用",一方面学习西方文明,同时又恢复两汉经学。维新变法时期称中国传统学术为"旧学",以别于称为"新学"的西洋学术。国学大师章太炎最初称其为"国粹",后改称"国故",并作有《国故论衡》,晚年亦称其为"国性"。作为中立概念,指对中国固有的传统文化学术的研究的"国学"二字盛行于 20 世纪初至 40 年代,期间涌现出一批诸如章太炎、胡适、梁启超、陈寅恪、王国维、赵元任等著名的"国学大师"。此后约 50 年间,"国学"一度走入沉寂。1993 年 8 月 16 日,《人民日报》第三版刊登了毕全忠的署名文章《国学,在燕园又悄然兴起——北京大学中国传统文化研究散记》,《人民日报》编者按指出:

> 在社会上商品经济大潮的拍击声中,北京大学一批学者在孜孜不倦地研究中国传统文化,即"国学"。他们认为研究国学、弘扬中华民族优秀传统文化,是社会主义精神文明建设的一项基础性工作。北大学者以马克思主义为指导,继承北大的好传统,使国学研究进入了一个新阶段,开辟了不少新的研究领域。国学的再次兴起,是新时期文化繁荣的一个标志,并呼唤着新一代国学大师的产生。

　　从此,"国学"一词常常见诸国内新闻媒体,国学研究机构在国内许多大学相继建立,许多高校亦陆续开设国学课程,"国学热"再次兴起。进入21世纪,随着中国越来越接近世界舞台的中央,随着中华民族伟大复兴的加速推进,国学的"复兴"呈加速之势。此时的国学所处的环境亦发生巨大变化,当今的国学被赋予新的历史使命,它不再仅仅是"发思古之幽情",而是为了继承和弘扬中华优秀传统文化,是应中华文化走向世界的大势所需,是建设中国特色社会主义新文化之所需。

　　国学是"中国固有的文化学术"这一点几无争议,但其具体内涵为何,到目前为止,学术界尚未做出统一明确的界定。一般而言,国学是指"以先秦经典及诸子学为根基,涵盖两汉经学、魏晋玄学、隋唐佛学、宋明理学、明清实学和同时期的先秦诗赋、汉赋、六朝骈文、唐宋诗词、元曲与明清小说并历代史学等一套特有而完整的文化、学术体系"。

　　张岱年先生认为,国学除了包括传统意义上的义理之学(哲学)、考据之学(史学)、词章之学(文学)及经世之学(政治学、经济学)之外,还包括天算之学(天文学、数学)、兵学(军事学)、法学、农学、地学、水利学、医学等,而且当代中国的学术思想亦属国学范围。[①]

　　改革开放后,特别是进入21世纪以来,国学已经被赋予新的内涵。除上述传统的思想内容之外,还应该增加新时期中国特色社会主义新的内容,即中华优秀传统文化与马克思主义相结合的新内涵。

　　总之,国学是中国文化之精粹,是中华民族精神文化的重要组成部分,是中华民族的核心价值理念和追求,是数千年来中华民族思维方式、行为方式、生活方式、生产方式的高度总结,五千年来生生不息,塑造、影响着中华民族的性格,融入了一代代中华儿女的血脉、精神和灵魂。在实现中华民族伟大复兴,构建人类命运共同体的大背景下,蕴含"中国智慧""中国方案"的国学,亦需走向世界。

---

① 张岱年:《说"国学"》,胡道静主编,《国学大师论国学》(上),上海:东方出版中心,1998年,第161—163页。

国学的分类

汉代刘向所著《别录》是中国第一部有书名、有解题的综合性的分类目录书,其子刘歆据此序录删繁就简编成《七略》,将书目分为辑略、六艺略、诸子略、诗赋略、兵书略、术数略、方技略七类。

东汉班固依《七略》著《艺文志》,魏郑默著《中经》,晋荀勖因《中经》而著《新簿》,分为甲乙丙丁四部:甲部记六艺小学等书,乙部列古近子家及兵书术数,丙部有《史记》《旧事》《皇览簿》《杂事》,丁部有诗、赋、图、赞。

梁代王俭撰《七志》,阮孝绪撰《七录》,包括经典录(纪六艺)、纪传录(纪史传)、子兵录(纪子书兵书)、文集录(纪诗赋)、技术录(纪术数)、佛录和道录。

唐代长孙无忌撰《隋书·经籍志》,亦采四分法,始称经、史、子、集四部:

经部:《易》《书》《诗》《礼》《乐》《春秋》《孝经》《论语》《图纬》《小学》,共 10 类;史部:正史、古史、杂史、霸史、起居注、旧事、职官、仪注、刑法、杂传、地理、谱系、簿录,共 13 类;子部:儒家、道家、法家、名家、墨家、纵横家、杂家、农家、小说家、兵法、天文、历数、五行、医方,共 14 类;集部:《楚辞》、别集、总集,共 3 类。

清代《四库全书》也依《隋书》的分类方法,分为经、史、子、集四部,每部下分若干类,类下有属:

经,指古籍经典,主要是儒家经典和注释研究儒家经典的相关著作。《四库全书》经部之下又分易、书、诗、礼、春秋、孝经、五经总义、四书、乐、小学 10 类,其中礼类又分周礼、仪礼、礼记、三礼总义、通礼、杂礼书 6 属,小学类又分训诂、字书、韵书 3 属。《诗经》《尚书》《礼记》《乐经》《周易》《春秋》《论语》《尔雅》等均入经部。

史,即历史著作,包括通史、断代史、政事史、专详文物典章的制度史、方志等各种体裁的历史著作。《四库全书》史部之下又分正史、编年、纪事本末、别史、杂史、诏令奏议、传记、史钞、载记、时令、地理、职官、政书、目录、史评 15 类,其中诏令奏议类分诏令、奏议 2 属,传记类分圣贤、名人、总录、杂录、别录 5 属,地理类分宫殿疏、总志、都会郡县、河渠、边防、山川、古迹、杂记、游记、外记 10 属,职官类分官制、官箴 2 属,政书类分通制、典礼、邦计、军政、法令、考工 6 属,目录类分经籍、金石 2 属。《史记》《汉书》《后汉书》《三国志》《春秋左传》《资治通鉴》《续资治通鉴》《越绝书》《吴越春秋》《晋书》《清稗类钞》《山海经》《水经注》《唐六典》《通典》《史通》《文史通义》《战国策》《永乐大典》等均入史部。

子,指历史上创立了各种学说或学派的人物文集,包括诸子百家著作和类书。《四库全书》子部之下分为儒家、兵家、法家、农家、医家、天文算法、术数、艺术、谱录、杂家、类书、小说家、释家、道家,共 14 类,其中天文算法类分推步、算书 2 属,术数类分数学、占侯、相宅相墓、占卜、命书相书、阴阳五行、杂技术 7 属,艺术类分书画、琴谱、篆刻、杂技 4 属,谱录类分器物、食谱、草木鸟兽虫鱼 3 属,杂家类分杂学、杂考、杂说、杂品、杂纂、杂编 6 属,小说家类分杂事、异闻、琐语 3 属。《老子》《庄子》《列子》《淮南子》《抱朴子》《孟子》《荀子》《孙子》《墨子》《管子》《韩非子》《公孙龙子》《坛经》《黄帝内经》《艺文类聚》等均入子部。

集,指文人学者的诗文词总集和个人专集,收入历代作家的散文、骈文、诗、词、散曲集子和文学评论、戏曲著作等。《四库全书》集部之下分为楚辞、别集、总集、诗文评、词曲等 5 类,其中词曲类分词集、词选、词话、词谱词韵、南北曲 5 属。《楚辞》《全唐诗》《全宋词》《乐府诗集》《文选》《李太白集》《杜工部集》《韩昌黎集》《柳河东集》《白香山集》《苏东坡集》等均入集部。

治国学的方法

关于治国学的方法,章炳麟、胡适、梁启超、张岱年等国学大师均有过论述。

章炳麟先生指出,研究国学第一步是要辨书籍的真伪,如果以假为真,就会陷入迷途;第二是"通小学",研究小学有通音韵、明训诂、辨形体三法;第三要"明地理",否则就会犯"臆测的错误""纠缠的错误(相同地名纠缠不清)"以及"意会的错误(以此地为彼地)";第四要"知古今人情变迁",既不可以古论今,也不可以今论古;第五要"辨文学应用",应知诗文之异,骈体散体之别。[1]

胡适先生在"研究国故的方法"[2]一文中指出"不得不注意"的四种方法:

一是历史的观念。把旧书当作历史看,知它好到什么地步,或是坏到什么地步,是研究国故方法的起点,是"开宗明义"第一章。

二是疑古的态度。疑古的目的在于"得其真",一要疑古书的真伪,二要疑真书被弄伪之处,不能"一味迷信","做古人的奴隶",甚至"引旁人亦入于迷途",要"宁可疑而错,不可信而错",要"打破砂锅问到底"。

三是系统的研究。无论研究什么书籍,须从历史方面着手,去寻找它的脉络,研究它的系统,要从"从前没有系统的文学、哲学、政治里边,以客观的态度,去寻出系统来"。

四是整理。整理国故虽不能算是学识上的"创造者",但可当作"运输人",可以从形式方面加上标点符号,分开段落,从内容方面加上新的注解,折中旧有注解,并加上新的序跋和考证,讲明书的历史和价值。其目的在于"使从前少数人懂得的"变为"人人能解的"。

梁启超先生提出研究国学应走的"两条大路"[3]:

一是文献的学问,应该用客观的科学方法去研究;二是德性的学问,应该用内省的和躬行的方法去研究。梁先生提出,六经、诸子、诗文集、小说中"一字一句都藏有极可宝贵的史料",是"世界第一个富矿穴",应该借用科学的方法进行研究。一个人一生的精力非常有限,因此,研究国学需要分工合作,要"合起一群人在一个共同目的共同计划之下,各人从其性之所好以及平时的学问根柢,各人分担三两门做窄而

---

① 章炳麟:《治国学的方法》,胡道静主编,《国学大师论国学》(上),上海:东方出版中心,1998年,第3页。
② 胡适:《研究国故的方法》,胡道静主编,《国学大师论国学》(上),上海:东方出版中心,1998年,第13页。
③ 梁启超:《治国学的两条大路》,胡道静主编,《国学大师论国学》(上),上海:东方出版中心,1998年,第26页。

深的研究"。梁启超进而提出做文献学问的三个标准:

第一求真。研究一种客观的事实,须先要知道它"的确如此",才能判断它"为什么如此"。

第二求博。要明白一件事物的真相,不能靠单文孤证便下武断,所以要将同类或有关系的事情网罗起来贯串比较,愈多愈妙。一是"好一则博",从极狭的范围内生出极博来,不能件件要博,否则连一件也博不成。二要"以浅持博",面对丰富的资料须先求得个"一以贯之"的线索,才不至"博而寡要"。

第三求通。专门一种学问,做到"好一"固然重要,但要注意别门学问和这门学问的关系以及本门学问各方面相互之关系。能常常注意关系,才可以成"通学"。

张岱年先生指出,治国学应牢记司马迁的两个原则,一是"好学深思、心知其意",二是"信则传信,疑则传疑";研究国学不但要整理前人已经做出的成绩,还应该推陈出新,在前人成果的基础之上更向前进①。

---

① 张岱年:"说'国学'",见胡道静主编,《国学大师论国学》(上).上海:东方出版中心,1998年,第163页。

【推荐阅读】

蔡尚思编.中国文化史要论(人物·图书).长沙：湖南人民出版社，
　　1979 年。

曹伯韩.国学常识.北京：生活·读书·新知三联书店，2008 年。

辜鸿铭.辜鸿铭讲国学.长春：吉林人民出版社，2009 年。

胡道静主编.国学大师论国学.上海：东方出版中心，1998 年。

胡适.胡适讲国学.长春：吉林人民出版社，2009 年。

梁启超.国学入门书要目及其读法.《饮冰室合集：专集七十一》.北京：
　　中华书局，1989 年。

梁启超.梁启超讲国学.长春：吉林人民出版社，2008 年。

梁启超.要籍解题及其读法.长沙：岳麓书社，2010 年。

林语堂.林语堂讲国学.长春：吉林人民出版社，2009 年。

鲁迅.鲁迅讲国学.长春：吉林人民出版社，2009 年。

钱基博.国学必读.上海：上海古籍出版社，2011 年。

钱穆.国学概论.北京：商务印书馆，1997 年。

屈万里.屈万里全集·古籍导读.上海：上海辞书出版社，2015 年。

汪辟疆.汪辟疆文集.上海：上海古籍出版社，1985 年。

王国维.王国维讲国学.长春：吉林人民出版社，2009 年。

王敏时编著.国学概论.上海：上海新亚书店，1931 年。

闻一多.闻一多讲国学.长春：吉林人民出版社，2009 年。

章太炎.章太炎讲国学.长春：吉林人民出版社，2008 年。

第二单元　《大学》

【导言】

《大学》与《中庸》《论语》《孟子》合称"四书",为中国古代阐述"修身、齐家、治国、平天下"思想的重要著作。《大学》出自《礼记》,原为《礼记》四十九篇中的第四十二篇。其著作年代及作者历代学者说法不一。班固认为《礼记》各篇作于战国初期至西汉初期,为"七十子后学者所记也";程颢、程颐言"大学,孔氏之遗书,而初学入德之门也";朱熹云:"经一章,盖孔子之言而曾子述之。传十章,则曾子之意而门人记之",但朱氏之言亦"属意度,羌无实证";清人崔述认为"计其时当在战国"。当今学界大多认为其为战国初期曾参所作。

宋代以前,《大学》的注疏大都附于《礼记》之中:东汉经学大师郑玄将当时流传的《礼记》诸本相互参校,并为之作《注》,题曰《三礼注》;唐代孔颖达作《礼记正义》,以解决由于语言文意变迁造成的理解困难等问题。宋代朱熹将《大学》从《礼记》中单列出来,独自成书,作《大学章句》,与《中庸章句》《论语集注》《孟子集注》一起,称为《四书章句集注》,自此,《大学》的"四书之首"地位得以确立。有明一代,《大学》注疏逐渐丰富,较有影响者有,《大学章句大全》(胡广)、《大学古本旁释》(王阳明)、《大学全文通释》(崔铣)、《大学指归》(魏校)、《大学石经古本旁释》(王文禄)等。清代有《大学证文》(毛奇龄)、《大学翼真》(胡渭)、《大学古本说》(李光地)、《大学古义说》(宋翔风)等。

《大学》在西方的译介历史悠久。19世纪前,其译本多为拉丁文和法文,译者多为耶稣会传教士。1593年,利玛窦(Matteo Ricci)将儒家"四书"的主要部分译成拉丁文呈给梵蒂冈教皇,以备后来的耶稣会士利用其译文学习《四书》。1662年,意大利传教士殷铎泽(Prospero Intorcetta)和郭纳爵(Ignatius de Costa)将《大学》译成拉丁文在建昌刻印,题曰"中国的智慧"。进入19世纪,英国汉学家理雅各(James Legge)前后用20余年时间将包括《大学》的《四书》《五经》译成英文陆续出版,对后世影响甚大。其他英译者有马礼逊(Robert Morrison)(1812)、马士曼(Joshua Marshman)(1814)、辜鸿铭(1915)、林语堂(1938)等。

大学①

大学之道②,在明明德③,在亲民④,在止于至善⑤。

知止而后有定⑥,定而后能静,静而后能安,安而后能虑,虑而后能得。

物有本末,事有终始。知所先后⑦,则近道矣。

古之欲明明德于天下者,先治其国;欲治其国者,先齐其家⑧;欲齐其家者,先修其身⑨;欲修其身者,先正其心;欲正其心者,先诚其意;欲诚其意者,先致其知⑩;致知在格物⑪。

物格而后知至,知至而后意诚,意诚而后心正,心正而后身修,身修而后家齐,家齐而后国治,国治而后天下平。

---

① 中文原文依据理雅各中英文对照本中的中文底本,参校王夫之.船山全书(之四)·礼记章句.长沙:岳麓书社,1996 年。
② 大学之道:大学的宗旨。"大学"在古代有两种含义:一为"博学";二为相对于"小学"而言的"大人之学"。古代八岁入小学,学习"洒扫应对进退、礼乐射御书数"等文化基础知识和礼节;十五岁入大学,学习"穷理正心,修己治人"的学问。"大学者,大人之学也。大人者,成人也。十五而入大学,乃学内圣外王之道。"大学"一词,理雅各译为 The Great Learning;辜鸿铭译为 The Higher Education,意为"高等教育",林语堂认为后者更为正确,他指出,"以前中国适于读'大学'的年龄,似乎相当于读美国的'专科学校'(Junior College)"。
③ 明明德:前一个"明"为动词,意为"使……彰明";后一个"明"为形容词,意为清明、光明。明明德:使光明正大的品德显明。
④ 亲:"亲"应为"新",动词,"使……革新"。亲民:即新民,使人弃旧图新、去恶从善。
⑤ 至善:人的道德修养所能达到的最高境界。
⑥ 知止:知道目标所在。
⑦ 知所先后:能够知道和把握道德修养的先后次序。
⑧ 齐:治理。家:家族。齐其家:使家族齐心协力,和睦平安。
⑨ 修其身:修养好自身的品德。
⑩ 致知:汉郑玄认为"致知"是使人"知善恶吉凶之所终始";宋朱熹认为"致,推极也;知,犹识也。推极吾之知识,欲其所知无不尽也";王守仁则认为"致知"即"致吾心之良知"。
⑪ 格物:研究事物,探寻其本原。朱熹云:"言欲致吾之知,在即物而穷其理也。"

The Great Learning

Translated by James Legge[①]

What the Great Learning teaches, is-to illustrate illustrious[②] virtue[③]; to renovate the people; and to rest in the highest excellence.

The point where to rest being known, the object of pursuit is then determined; and, that being determined, a calm unperturbedness[④] may be attained to. To that calmness there will succeed a tranquil[⑤] repose[⑥]. In that repose there may be careful deliberation[⑦], and that deliberation will be followed by the attainment of the desired end.

Things have their root and their branches. Affairs have their end and their beginning. To know what is first and what is last will lead near to what is taught in the Great Learning.

The ancients who wished to illustrate illustrious virtue throughout the kingdom, first ordered well their own states. Wishing to order well their states, they first regulated their families. Wishing to regulate their families, they first cultivate their persons. Wishing to cultivate their persons, they first rectified[⑧] their hearts. Wishing to rectify their hearts, they first sought to be sincere in their thoughts. Wishing to be sincere in their thoughts, they first extended to the utmost their knowledge. Such extension of knowledge lay in the investigation of things.

----

① 译文选自 Legge, J. Trans. *The Chinese Classics*（Volume VI）. London: Trubner, 1898。

② illustrate/ˈɪləstreɪt/ v. 说明，阐明；illustrious 为 illustrate 的形容词形式　辉煌的，明亮的 *adj*. 著名的 /ɪˈlʌstrɪəs/

③ virtue/ˈvɜːtʃuː/ *n*. 美德

④ unperturbedness/ˌʌnpəˈtɜː bdnɪs/ *n*. 平静，镇静，镇定

⑤ tranquil/ˈtræŋkwɪl/ *adj*. 平静的，安宁的

⑥ repose/rɪˈpəuz/ *n*. 歇息，睡眠

⑦ deliberation/dɪˌlɪbəˈreɪʃn/ *n*. 熟思，从容

⑧ rectify/ˈrektɪfaɪ/ *v*. 净化，纠正，调整

Things being investigated, knowledge became complete. Their knowledge being complete, their thoughts were sincere. Their thoughts being sincere, their hearts were rectified. Their hearts being rectified, their persons were cultivated. Their persons being cultivated, their families were regulated. Their families being regulated, their states were rightly governed. Their states being rightly governed; the whole kingdom was made tranquil and happy.

自天子以至于庶人①,壹是皆以修身为本②。其本乱而末治者否矣③。其所厚者薄,而其所薄者厚④,未之有也。

右经一章⑤,盖孔子之言。而曾子述之⑥。其传十章⑦。则曾子之意而门人记之也。旧本颇有错简⑧,今因程子所定,而更考经文,别为序次如左。

第一章

《康诰》曰⑨:"克明德⑩。"
《大甲》曰⑪:"顾是天之明命⑫。"
《帝典》曰⑬:"克明峻德⑭。"
皆自明也。

右传之首章,释明明德。

---

① 庶人:西周称农业生产者。春秋时,其地位在士之下,工商皂隶之上。秦汉以后泛指没有官爵的平民。
② 壹是:一切,都是。
③ 本乱而末治者:修身为本,而家、国、天下为末。否:不对,不行。
④ 所厚者薄:该重视的不重视。所薄者厚:不该重视的却加以重视。
⑤ 右:指前面。古代的书籍是从右至左翻阅,故右为前。
⑥ 曾子:指曾参(前505—前436年),字子舆,山东武城(今山东枣庄)人,孔子的学生。
⑦ 传:音 zhuàn,指解释经书的文字。
⑧ 错简:古代的书是写在竹简上按次序串联编成的,竹简前后次序错乱叫错简。后来古书文字颠倒错乱亦称错简。
⑨ 《康诰》:《尚书·周书》中的一篇。《尚书》为"五经"之一,称为"书经",分为《虞书》《夏书》《商书》《周书》四部分。《康诰》是周公封康叔时所作的文告。周公在平定三监(管叔、蔡叔、霍叔)武庚所发动的叛乱后,封康叔于殷地。此为康叔上任前,周公对他所作的训辞。
⑩ 克:能够。
⑪ 《大甲》:即《太甲》,《尚书·商书》中的一篇。"大"读作 tài。太甲,商代国王,商汤之嫡长孙,太丁之子。太甲即位后,因破坏汤法,不理国政被伊尹放逐。太甲在放逐期间,深入民间,广泛了解了人民疾苦,复位后励精图治,使"诸侯归殷,百姓以宁"。
⑫ 顾:思念。是:此。明命:光明的禀性。说,圣明的命令,特指帝王的命令,诏旨。
⑬ 《帝典》:即《尧典》,《尚书·虞书》中的一篇。主要记叙尧、舜二帝的事迹。
⑭ 峻:《尚书》作俊。峻:大也。

From the Son of Heaven down to the mass of the people，all must consider the cultivation of the person the root of everything besides.

It cannot be，when the root is neglected，that what should spring from① it will be well ordered. It never has been the case that what was of great importance has been slightly cared for，and at the same time，that what was of slight importance has been greatly cared for.

The preceding chapter of classical text is in the words of Confucius，handed down by the philosopher Tsang. The ten chapters of explanation which follow contain the views of Tsang，and were recorded by his disciples②. In the old copies of the work，there appeared considerable③ confusion in these，from the disarrangement of the tablets. But now，availing myself of the decisions of the philosopher Ch'ing，and having examined anew the classical text，I have arranged it in order，as follows：

COMMENTARY OF THE PHILOSOPHER TSANG

Chapter I

In *the Announcement to K'ang*，it is said，"He was able to make his virtue illustrious."

In *the Tai Chia*，it is said，"He contemplated④ and studied the illustrious decrees⑤ of Heaven."

In *the Canon of the Emperor（Yao）*，it is said，"He was able to make illustrious his lofty⑥ virtue."

———————————

① spring from 源自

② disciple/dɪˈsaɪpl/ *n*. 弟子,门徒

③ considerable/kənˈsɪdərəbl/ *adj*. 相当的,重要的,可观的

④ contemplate/ˈkɔntempleɪt/ *v*. 注视,打算,冥思苦想,深思熟虑

⑤ decree/dɪˈkriː/ *n*. 教令,赦令,天意,天命

⑥ lofty/ˈlɔftɪ/ *adj*. (指思想、目标等)高尚的,崇高的

These passages all show how those sovereigns made themselves illustrious.

The above first chapter of commentary explains the illustration of illustrious virtue.

第二章

汤之盘铭曰①:"苟日新,日日新,又日新。"

《康诰》曰:"作新民②。"

《诗》曰③:"周虽旧邦,其命维新④。"

是故君子无所不用其极。

　　右传之二章。释新民。

第三章

《诗》云⑤:"邦畿千里⑥,惟民所止。"

《诗》云⑦:"缗蛮黄鸟⑧,止于丘隅⑨。"子曰:"于止,知其所止,可以人而不如鸟乎?"

《诗》云⑩:"穆穆文王⑪,於缉熙敬止⑫!"为人君,止于仁;为人臣,止于敬;为人子,止于孝;为人父,止于慈;与国人交,止于信。

① 盘:沐浴之盘。铭:盘上的铭文。

② 作新民:激励民众自新。

③ 《诗》:指《诗经·大雅·文王》。

④ 其命:指周朝所禀受的天命。维:语助词。

⑤ 《诗》:指《诗经·商颂·玄鸟》。

⑥ 邦畿:都城及其周围的地区。

⑦ 《诗》:指《诗经·小雅·绵蛮》。

⑧ 缗蛮:鸟鸣声。

⑨ 丘隅(qiū yú):犹丘阿,山丘的曲深僻静处。

⑩ 《诗》:指《诗经·大雅·文王》。

⑪ 穆穆:仪表美好端庄。

⑫ 於:叹美辞。缉熙:光明。敬止:言其无不敬而安所止。

Chapter II

On the bathing tub① of T'ang, the following words were engraved: "If you can one day renovate② yourself, do so from day to day. Yea, let there be daily renovation."

In *the Announcement to K'ang*, it is said, "To stir up③ the new people."

In *the Book of Poetry*, it is said, "Although Chau was an ancient state, the ordinance④ which lighted on it was new."

Therefore, the superior man in everything uses his utmost endeavor⑤.

The above second chapter of commentary explains the renovating of the people.

Chapter III

In *the Book of Poetry*, it is said, "The royal domain⑥ of a thousand *li* is where the people rest."

In *the Book of Poetry*, it is said, "The twittering yellow bird rests on a corner of the mound." The Master said, "When it rests, it knows where to rest. Is it possible that a man should not be equal to this bird?"

In *the Book of Poetry*, it is said, "Profound was King Wan. With how bright and unceasing a feeling of reverence did he regard his resting places!" As a sovereign⑦, he rested in benevolence⑧. As

---

① tub/tʌb/ *n.* 桶,浴盆
② renovate/'renəveɪt/ *v.* 修复,整修……如新
③ stir up 激起,挑起
④ ordinance/'ɔːdɪnəns/ *n.* 法令,法规
⑤ endeavor/ɪn'devə/ *n.* 努力,尽力
⑥ domain/dəu'meɪn/ *n.* 领地,势力范围
⑦ sovereign/'sɔvrɪn/ *n.* 皇帝,君主
⑧ benevolence/bɪ'nevələns/ *n.* 仁慈,善意,善心

a minister, he rested in reverence①. As a son, he rested in filial②
piety③. As a father, he rested in kindness. In communication with
his subjects, he rested in good faith.

---

① reverence/ˈrevərəns/ *n*. 尊敬,敬重
② filial/ˈfɪlɪəl/ *adj*. 孝顺的
③ piety/ˈpaɪətɪ/ *n*. 虔诚,孝行

《诗》云①："瞻彼淇澳②，菉竹猗猗③。有斐君子，如切如磋，如琢如磨④。瑟兮僩兮，赫兮喧兮⑤。有斐君子，终不可諠兮⑥！""如切如磋"者，道学也；"如琢如磨"者，自修也；"瑟兮僩兮"者，恂慄也⑦；"赫兮喧兮"者，威仪也；"有斐君子，终不可諠兮"者，道盛德至善，民之不能忘也。

《诗》云⑧："於戏，前王不忘⑨！"君子贤其贤而亲其亲，小人乐其乐而利其利，此以没世不忘也⑩。

右传之三章，释止于至善。

第四章

子曰⑪："听讼，吾犹人也⑫，必也使无讼乎！"无情者不得尽其辞⑬。大畏民志⑭，此谓知本。

右传之四章，释本末。

---

① 《诗》：指《诗经·卫风·淇澳》。
② 淇：河名，淇水，在今河南北部；澳(yù)：水边弯曲处。
③ 菉：通"绿"。猗猗：美丽茂盛的样子。
④ 斐(fěi)：文质彬彬的样子；切、磋、琢、磨："切以刀锯，琢以椎凿，皆裁物使成形质也。磋以鑢锡，磨以沙石，皆治物使其滑泽也。治骨角者，既切而复磋之。治玉石者，既琢而复磨之。皆言其治之有绪，而益致其精也"。将骨、角、玉、石一类磨制成器物。好像把骨角玉石加工成器物那样。比喻共同商讨，互相砥砺。
⑤ 瑟(sè)：庄严、严密的样子，僩(xiàn)：勇猛的样子。赫：盛大的样子。喧：显著的样子。
⑥ 諠(xuān)：通"谖"，忘记。
⑦ 恂慄(xún lì)：恐惧战栗。
⑧ 《诗》：指《诗经·周颂·烈文》。
⑨ 於戏(wū hū)：叹词。前王：指周文王、周武王。
⑩ 此以：因此。没世：死；一辈子，永久。
⑪ 出自《论语·颜渊》。
⑫ 听讼：听理诉讼，审案。犹人：不异于人。
⑬ 无情者不得尽其辞：使隐瞒真实情况的人不能够花言巧语。情：实。
⑭ 民志：民意，民心。

In *the Book of Poetry*, it is said, "Look at that winding course of the Ch'i, with the green bamboos so luxuriant①! Here is our elegant and accomplished② prince! As we cut then file; as we chisel③ and then grind: so has he cultivated himself. How grave is he and dignified! How majestic and distinguished! Our elegant and accomplished prince never can be forgotten." That expression — "As we cut and then file," indicates the work of learning. "As we chisel and then grind," indicates that of self-culture. "How grave is he and dignified!" indicates the feeling of cautious reverence. "How commanding and distinguished!" indicates an awe-inspiring deportment④. "Our elegant and accomplished prince never can be forgotten," indicates how, when virtue is complete and excellence extreme, the people cannot forget them.

In *the Book of Poetry*, it is said, "Ah! The former kings are not forgotten." Future princes deem worthy what they deemed worthy, and love what they loved. The common people delight in what delighted them, and are benefited by their beneficial arrangements. It is on this account that the former kings, after they have quit the world, are not forgotten.

The above third chapter of commentary explains resting in the highest excellence.

Chapter IV

The Master said, "In hearing litigation, I am like any other body. What is necessary to cause the people to have no litigation?" So, those who are devoid⑤ of principle find it is impossible to carry

---

① luxuriant/lʌɡˈʒuəriənt/*adj.* 繁茂的；肥沃的；浓密的

② accomplished/əˈkʌmplɪʃt/*adj.* 有教养的，有才能的，学识渊博的

③ chisel/ˈtʃɪzl/*v.* 凿，雕

④ deportment/dɪˈpɔːtmənt/*n.* 行为，举止

⑤ devoid/dɪˈvɔɪd/*adj.* 全无的，缺乏的

out their speeches, and a great awe would be struck into men's minds; -this is called knowing the root.

The above fourth chapter of commentary explains the root and the issue.

第五章

此谓知本。此谓知之至也①。

　　右传之五章盖释格物致知②之义,而今亡矣。閒尝窃取程子之意以补之曰:

　　"所谓致知在格物者,言欲致吾之知,在即物而穷其理也。盖人心之灵莫不有知,而天下之物莫不有理,惟于理有未穷,故其知有不尽也。是以《大学》始教,必使学者即凡天下之物,莫不因其已知之理而益穷之,以求至乎其极。至于用力之久,而一旦豁然贯通焉,则众物之表里精粗无不到,而吾心之全体大用无不明矣。此谓物格,此谓知之至也。"

---

① 本章原文只有"此谓知本。此谓知之至也"两句。朱熹认为,"此谓知本"一句是上一章的衍文,"此谓知之至也"一句前面又缺了一段文字。所以,朱熹根据上下文关系补充了一段文字。以下为朱熹补充的文字。
② 格物致知:穷究事物原理,从而获得知识。格:推究;致:求得。

Chapter V

This is called knowing the root. This is called the perfecting of knowledge.

The above fifth chapter of the commentary explained the meaning of "investigating things and carrying knowledge to the utmost extent[①]*," but it is now lost. I have ventured*[②] *to take the views of the scholar Ch'ang to supply it, as follows: The meaning of the expression, "The perfecting of knowledge depends on the investigation of things," is this-if we wish to carry our knowledge to the utmost, we must investigate the principles of all things we come into contact with, for the intelligent mind of man is certainly formed to know, and there is not a single thing in which its principles do not inhere*[③]. *But so long as principles are not investigated, man's knowledge is incomplete. On this account, the Learning for Adults, at the outset*[④] *of its lessons, instructs the learner, in regard to all things in the world, to proceed from what knowledge he has all their principles, and pursue his investigation of them, till he reaches the extreme point. After exerting himself in this way for a long time, he will suddenly find himself possessed of a wide and far-reaching penetration*[⑤]. *Then, the qualities of all things, whether external or internal, the subtle or the coarse*[⑥], *will all be apprehended*[⑦], *and the mind, in its entire substance and its relations to things, will be perfectly intelligent. This is called the investigation of things. This is called the perfection of knowledge.*

---

① to the utmost extent：最大程度
② venture/'ventʃə(r)/ v. (谦虚语)冒昧
③ inhere/ɪn'hɪə/ v. (in)固有,具有
④ outset/'autset/ n. 开始,开端
⑤ penetration/ˌpenɪ'treɪʃn/ n. 穿透,洞察力
⑥ coarse/kɔːs/ adj. 粗略的,劣等的,不精确的
⑦ apprehend/ˌæprɪ'hend/ v. 领会,理解

第六章

所谓诚其意者,毋自欺也。如恶恶臭^①,如好好色^②,此之谓自谦^③,故君子必慎其独也^④!

小人闲居为不善^⑤,无所不至,见君子而后厌然^⑥,揜其不善^⑦,而著其善。人之视己,如见其肺肝然^⑧,则何益矣。此谓诚于中,形于外,故君子必慎其独也。

曾子曰:"十目所视,十手所指,其严乎!"富润屋,德润身,心广体胖^⑨,故君子必诚其意。

右传之六章。释诚意。

第七章

所谓修身在正其心者:身有所忿懥^⑩,则不得其正;有所恐惧,则不得其正;有所好乐,则不得其正;有所忧患,则不得其正。

---

① 恶(wù)恶(è)臭(xiù):厌恶腐臭的气味。臭:气味,较现代单指臭(chòu)味的含义宽泛。
② 好(hào)好(hǎo)色:喜爱美丽的女子。好色:美好的容颜,美色。
③ 谦:同"慊",快也,足也,心安理得的样子。
④ 慎其独:独自一人时也能保持谨慎不苟。"独者,人所不知而己所独知之地也。言欲自修者知为善以去其恶,则当实用其力,而禁止其自欺。"语出《礼记·中庸》:"莫见乎隐,莫显乎微,故君子慎其独也。"
⑤ 闲居:独处。
⑥ 厌然:躲躲闪闪的样子。
⑦ 揜(yǎn):通"掩",遮掩,掩盖。
⑧ 如见肺肝:就像看透肺肝一样。比喻心里想些什么,人们看得清清楚楚,含贬义。
⑨ 润屋:装饰房屋;润身:修养自身。心广体胖:心中坦然,身体舒泰。胖(pán):安泰舒适。
⑩ 身:程颐认为应为"心"。忿懥(zhì):愤怒。

Chapter VI

What is meant by "making the thoughts sincere," is the allowing no self-deception①, as when we hate a bad smell, and as when we love what is beautiful. This is called self-enjoyment. Therefore, the superior man must be watchful over himself when he is alone.

There is no evil to which the man, dwelling retired, will not proceed, but when he sees a superior man, he instantly tries to disguise② himself, concealing③ his evil, and displaying what is good. The other beholds him, as if he saw his heart and reins④; — of what use is his disguise? This is an instance of the saying — "what truly is within will be manifested⑤ without." therefore, the superior man must be watchful over himself when he is alone.

The disciple Tsang said, "What ten eyes behold, what ten hands point to, is to be regarded with reverence⑥!" Riches adorn⑦ a house, and virtue adorns the person. The mind is expanded, and the body is at ease. Therefore, the superior man must make his thoughts sincere.

The above sixth chapter of commentary explains making the thoughts sincere.

Chapter VII

What is meant by, "The cultivation of the person depends on rectifying the mind," may be thus illustrated: — If a man be under

---

① self-deception/'selfdı'sepʃən/ *n*. 自欺
② disguise/dıs'gaız/ *v*. 伪装,掩饰
③ conceal/kən'siːl/ *v*. 隐藏,掩盖,隐瞒
④ reins/reınz/ *n*. 肾脏,感情的源泉,腰
⑤ manifest/'mænıfest/ *v*. 表明,证明,使显现
⑥ reverence/'revərəns/ *n*. 尊敬,敬重
⑦ adorn/ə'dɔːn/ *v*. 装饰,使生色

the influence of passion①, he will be incorrect in his conduct. He will be the same, if he is under the influence of terror, or under the influence of fond regard, or under that of sorrow and distress.

---

① passion/'pæʃn/ n. 激情,热情

心不在焉,视而不见,听而不闻,食而不知其味。

此谓修身在正其心。

右传之七章,释正心修身。

第八章

所谓齐其家在修其身者,人之其所亲爱而辟焉①,之其所贱恶而辟焉,之其所畏敬而辟焉,之其所哀矜而辟焉②,之其所敖惰而辟焉③。故好而知其恶,恶而知其美者,天下鲜矣!

故谚有之曰:"人莫知其子之恶,莫知其苗之硕④。"

此谓身不修不可以齐其家。

右传之八章,释修身齐家。

---

① 之:即"于",对于。辟:偏颇,偏向。

② 哀矜:哀怜,怜悯。

③ 敖惰:傲慢怠惰。敖:通"傲",骄傲。惰:怠慢。

④ 硕:大,苗壮。

When the mind is not present, we look and do not see; we hear and do not understand; we eat and do not know the taste of what we eat.

This is what is meant by saying that the cultivation① of a person depends on the rectifying② of the mind.

The above seventh chapter of commentary explains rectifying the mind and cultivating the person.

Chapter VIII

What is meant by "The regulation of one's family depends on the cultivation of his person," is this: — Men are partial③ where they feel affection and love; partial where they despise④ and dislike; partial where they stand in awe and reverence; partial where they feel sorrow and compassion⑤; partial where they are arrogant⑥ and rude. Thus it is that there are few men in the world who love and at the same time know the bad qualities of the object of their love, or who hate and yet know the excellence of the object of their hatred.

Hence it is said, in the common adage⑦, "A man does not know the wickedness of his son; he does not know the richness of his growing corn."

This is what is meant by saying that if the person be not cultivated, a man cannot regulate his family.

The above eighth chapter of commentary explains cultivating the person and regulating the family.

---

① cultivation/ˌkʌltɪˈveɪʃn/ *n*. 教化,培养

② rectify/ˈrektɪfaɪ/ *v*. 矫正,纠正

③ partial/ˈpɑːʃl/ *adj*. 部分的,偏爱的,偏袒的

④ despise/dɪˈspaɪz/ *v*. 鄙视,看不起

⑤ compassion/kəmˈpæʃn/ *n*. 同情,怜悯

⑥ arrogant/ˈærəgənt/ *adj*. 傲慢的,自大的

⑦ adage/ˈædɪdʒ/ *n*. 格言,古训

第九章

所谓治国必先齐其家者,其家不可教而能教人者,无之。故君子不出家而成教于国:孝者,所以事君也;弟者①,所以事长也;慈者②,所以使众也。

《康诰》曰:"如保赤子③。"心诚求之,虽不中不远矣④。未有学养子而后嫁者也!

一家仁,一国兴仁;一家让,一国兴让;一人贪戾⑤,一国作乱:其机如此⑥。此谓一言偾事⑦,一人定国。

尧、舜帅天下以仁⑧,而民从之;桀、纣帅天下以暴,而民从之;其所令反其所好,而民不从。是故君子有诸己而后求诸人,无诸己而后非诸人。所藏乎身不恕⑨,而能喻诸人者⑩,未之有也。

---

① 弟:通"悌(tì)",敬爱兄长,亦泛指敬重长上。
② 慈:上爱下;父母爱子女。
③ 如保赤子:《尚书·周书·康诰》原文作"若保赤子",周成王告诫康叔的话,意为保护平民百姓如母亲保护婴孩一样。赤子:婴孩。
④ 中(zhòng):达到目标。
⑤ 贪戾:贪婪,暴戾。
⑥ 机:本指弩箭上的发动机关,引申为事物变化之所由。
⑦ 偾事:把事情搞坏。偾(fèn):败,坏。
⑧ 帅:同"率",率领,统帅。
⑨ 恕:即恕道,推己及人,仁爱待物。孔子云:"己所不欲,勿施于人。"这种推己及人、将心比己的品德就是儒学所倡导的恕道。
⑩ 喻:晓谕,告知,开导。

Chapter IX

What is meant by "In order rightly to govern the state, it is necessary first to regulate the family," is this: — It is not possible for one to teach others, while he cannot teach his own family. Therefore, the ruler, without going beyond his family, completes the lessons for the state. There is filial piety: — therewith① the sovereign② should be served. There is fraternal③ submission④: — therewith elders and superiors should be served. There is kindness: — therewith the multitude⑤ should be treated.

In *the Announcement to K'ang*, it is said, "Act as if you were watching over an infant." If (another) is really anxious about it, though she may not hit exactly the wants of her infant, she will not be far from doing so. There never has been a girl who learned to bring up a child that she might afterwards marry.

From the loving example of one family a whole state becomes loving, and from its courtesies⑥ the whole state become courteous, while from the ambition and perverseness of the One man, the whole state may be led to rebellious disorder; — such is the nature of the influence. This verifies the saying, "Affairs may be ruined by a single sentence; a kingdom may be settled by its One man."

Yao and Shun led on the kingdom with benevolence, and the people followed them. Chiech and Chau led on the kingdom with violence, and the people followed them. The orders which these issued were contrary to the practices which they loved, and so the

---

① therewith/ðeə'wɪθ/*adv*. (古用法)于是,随即
② sovereign/'sɒvrɪn/*n*. 皇帝,君主
③ fraternal/frə'tɜːnl/*adj*. 兄弟的,友爱的,兄弟似的
④ submission/səb'mɪʃn/*n*. 服从,恭顺
⑤ multitude/'mʌltɪtjuːd/*n*. 群众,大众
⑥ courtesy/'kɜːtəsɪ/n. 谦恭有礼,有礼貌的举止(或言辞)

people did not follow them. On this account, the ruler must himself be possessed of the good qualities and then he may require them in the people. He must not have the bad qualities in himself, and then he may require that they shall not be in the people. Never has there been a man, who, not having reference to his own character and wishes in dealing with others, was able effectually to instruct them.

故治国在齐其家。

《诗》云^①："桃之夭夭，其叶蓁蓁^②；之子于归，宜其家人^③。"宜其家人，而后可以教国人。

《诗》云^④："宜兄宜弟。"宜兄宜弟，而后可以教国人。

《诗》云^⑤："其仪不忒^⑥，正是四国^⑦。"其为父子兄弟足法，而后民法之也。

此谓治国在齐其家。

　　　右传之九章，释齐家治国。

第十章

所谓平天下在治其国者，上老老而民兴孝^⑧，上长长而民兴弟^⑨，上恤孤而民不倍^⑩，是以君子有絜矩之道也^⑪。

---

① 引自《诗经·周南·桃夭》。
② 夭夭：鲜嫩，美丽。蓁蓁(zhēn)，茂盛的样子。
③ 之子于归：之子：这个女子。于归：指女子出嫁。宜：善。
④ 引自《诗经·小雅·蓼萧》。
⑤ 引自《诗经·曹风·鸤鸠》。
⑥ 仪：仪表，仪容。忒(tè)：差错。
⑦ 正是：做正面榜样。四国：四周的邦国。
⑧ 老老：尊敬老人。
⑨ 长长：尊重长辈。弟：通"悌"。
⑩ 恤：体恤，周济。孤：孤儿，古时候专指幼年丧失父亲的人。倍：通"背"，背弃，背叛。
⑪ 絜(xié)：度量。矩：画直角或方形用的尺子，引申为法度，规则。儒家以絜矩来象征道德上的规范。儒家伦理思想之一，指一言一行要有示范作用。

Thus we see how the government of the state depends on the regulation of the family.

In *the Book of Poetry*，it is said，"That peach tree，so delicate① and elegant! How luxuriant is its foliage②! This girl is going to her husband's house. She will rightly order her household." Let the household be rightly ordered，and then the people of state may be taught.

In *the Book of Poetry*，it is said，"They can discharge③ their duties to their elder brothers. They can discharge their duties to their younger brothers." Let the ruler discharge his duties to his elder and younger brothers，and then he may teach the people of the state.

In *the Book of Poetry*，it is said，"In his deportment there is nothing wrong; he rectifies all the people of the state." Yes，when the ruler as a father，a son，and a brother，is a model，then the people imitate him.

This is what is meant by saying，"the government of his kingdom depends on his regulation of the family."

The above ninth chapter of commentary explains regulating the family and governing the kingdom.

Chapter X

What is meant by "making the whole kingdom peaceful and happy depends on the government of his state," is this — when the sovereign behaves to his aged，as the aged should be behaved to，the people become filial; when the sovereign behaves to his elders，as the elders should be behaved to，the people learn brotherly

---

① delicate/ˈdelɪkət/*adj*. 精美，精致，优雅
② foliage/ˈfəʊlɪɪdʒ/*n*. 植物的叶子(总称)，叶子及梗和枝
③ discharge/dɪsˈtʃɑːdʒ/*v*. 释放，解除，免除

submission; when the sovereign treats compassionately^{①} the young and helpless, the people do the same. Thus the ruler has a principle with which, as with a measuring square, he may regulate his conduct.

---

① compassionately/kəmˈpæʃənɪtlɪ/ *adv*. 同情地,富有同情心地

所恶于上，毋以使下；所恶于下，毋以事上；所恶于前，毋以先后；所恶于后，毋以从前；所恶于右，毋以交于左；所恶于左，毋以交于右；此之谓絜矩之道。

《诗》云："乐只君子，民之父母①。"民之所好好之，民之所恶恶之，此之谓民之父母。

《诗》云："节彼南山，维石岩岩。赫赫师尹，民具尔瞻②。"有国者不可以不慎，辟则为天下僇矣③。

《诗》云："殷之未丧师，克配上帝。仪监于殷，峻命不易④。"道得众则得国，失众则失国。

是故君子先慎乎德。有德此有人⑤，有人此有土，有土此有财，有财此有用。

德者，本也；财者，末也。

---

① 引自《诗经·小雅·南山有台》。乐：快乐，喜悦。只，语助词。
② 引自《诗经·小雅·节南山》。节：高大。岩岩：险峻的样子。师尹：太师尹氏，周代的三公之一。具：通"俱"，全，都。瞻：瞻仰，仰望。
③ 辟：偏私，邪僻。僇（lù）：通"戮"，杀戮；一说，侮辱。
④ 引自《诗经·大雅·文王》。师：民众。配：符合。上帝：天帝；君主，帝王。仪：宜。监：鉴戒。峻：大。不易：不容易保有。
⑤ 此：乃，才。

What a man dislikes in his superior, let him not display in the treatment of his inferior; what he dislikes in inferiors, let him not display in the service of his superiors; what he hates in those who are before him, let him not therewith precede those who are behind him; what he hates in those who are behind him, let him not therewith follow those who are before him; what he hates to receive on the right, let him not bestow① on the left; what he hates to receive on the left, let him not bestow on the right: — this is what is called "The principle with which, as with a measuring square, to regulate one's conduct."

In *the Book of Poetry*, it is said, "How much to be rejoiced in are these princes, the parents of the people!" When a prince loves what the people love, and hates what the people hate, then is he what is called the parent of the people.

In *the Book of Poetry*, it is said, "Lofty② is that southern hill, with its rugged masses of rocks! Greatly distinguished are you, O grand-teacher Yin, the people all look up to you." Rulers of states may not neglect to be careful. If they deviate③ to a mean selfishness, they will be a disgrace in the kingdom.

In *the Book of Poetry*, it is said, "Before the sovereign of the Yin dynasty has lost the hearts of the people, they could appear before God. Take warning from the House of Yin. The great decree is not easily preserved." This shows that, by gaining the people, the kingdom is gained, and by losing the people, the kingdom is lost.

On this account, the ruler will first take pains about his own virtue. Possessing virtue will give him the people. Possessing the

---

① bestow/bɪ'stəu/ v. 赠予,授予
② lofty/'lɔftɪ/ adj. 高的,傲慢的,高超的
③ deviate/'diːvɪeɪt/ v. 背离,偏离

people will give him the territory. Possessing the territory will give him the wealth. Possessing the wealth，he will have resources① for expenditure②.

Virtue is the root；wealth is the result.

---

① resource/rɪˈsɔːs/ n . （常作复数）资源，财力
② expenditure/ɪkˈspendɪtʃə(r)/ n . 花费，开支

外本内末,争民施夺①。

是故财聚则民散,财散则民聚。

是故言悖而出者,亦悖而入②;货悖而入者,亦悖而出。

《康诰》曰:"惟命不于常③!"道善则得之,不善则失之矣。

《楚书》曰④:"楚国无以为宝,惟善以为宝。"

舅犯曰:"亡人无以为宝,仁亲以为宝⑤。"

《秦誓》曰⑥:"若有一介臣,断断兮无他技,其心休休焉,其如有容焉⑦。人之有技,若己有之;人之彦圣⑧,其心好之,不啻若自其口出⑨,实能容之,以能保我子孙黎民,尚亦有利哉。人之有技,媢嫉以恶之⑩;

---

① 争民施夺:争民,与民争利。施夺,施行劫夺。

② 悖:逆。

③ 命:天命。

④ 《楚书》,楚昭王时史书。楚昭王派王孙圉出使晋国。晋国赵简子问楚国珍宝美玉现在怎么样了。王孙圉答曰:楚国从来没有把美玉当作珍宝,只是把善人如观射父这样的大臣看作珍宝。参见《国语·楚语》。汉代刘向的《新序》中亦有类似记载。

⑤ 舅犯,晋文公重耳的舅舅狐偃,字子犯。亡人,流亡的人,指重耳。鲁僖公四年十二月,晋献公因受骊姬的谗言,逼迫太子申生自缢而死。重耳避难逃亡在外。在狄国时,晋献公逝世。秦穆公派人劝重耳归国掌政。重耳将此事告诉子犯,子犯以为不可,对重耳说了这几句话。语见《礼记·檀弓下》。

⑥ 《秦誓》:《尚书·周书》中的一篇。

⑦ 断断:真诚的样子。休休:宽宏大量。有容:能够容人。

⑧ 彦圣:德才兼备。彦,美。圣,明。

⑨ 不啻:不但。

⑩ 媢(mào)疾:妒嫉。

If he make the root his secondary object, and the result his primary, he will only wrangle① with his people, and teach them rapine②.

Hence, the accumulation of wealth is the way to scatter③ the people; and the letting it be scattered among them is the way to collect the people.

And hence, the ruler's words going forth contrary to right will come back to him in the same way, and wealth, gotten by improper ways, will take its departure by the same.

In *the Announcement to K'ang*, it is said, "The decree indeed may not always rest on us;" that is, goodness obtains the decree, and the want of goodness loses it.

In *the Book of Ch'u*, it is said, "The Kingdom of Ch'u does not consider that to be valuable. It values, instead, its good men."

Duke Wan's uncle, Fan said, "Our fugitive④ does not account that to be precious. What he considers precious is the affection due to his parent."

In *the Declaration of the Duke of Ch'in*, it is said, "Let me have not one minister, plain and sincere, not pretending to other abilities, but with a simple and upright mind; and possessed of generosity, regarding the talents of others as if he himself possessed them, and where he finds accomplished and perspicacious⑤ men, loving them in his heart more than his mouth expresses, and really showing himself able to bear them and employ them: — such a minister will be able to preserve my sons and grandsons and black-

---

① wrangle/'ræŋgl/ v . 争论,激辩,吵架

② rapine/'ræpaɪn/ n . 抢夺,掠夺

③ scatter/'skætə(r)/ v . 使散开,驱散

④ fugitive/'fjuːdʒətɪv/ n . 逃亡者,亡命者

⑤ perspicacious/ˌpɜːspɪ'keɪʃəs/ adj . 颖悟的,有洞察力的,聪明的

haired people，and benefits likewise to the kingdom may well be looked for from him. But if it be his character，when he finds men of abilities，to be jealous and hate them.

人之彦圣，而违之俾不通①：实不能容，以不能保我子孙黎民，亦曰殆哉。"

唯仁人放流之，迸诸四夷②，不与同中国③。此谓唯仁人为能爱人，能恶人。

见贤而不能举，举而不能先，命也④；见不善而不能退，退而不能远，过也。

好人之所恶，恶人之所好，是谓拂人之性，灾必逮夫身⑤。

是故君子有大道，必忠信以得之，骄泰以失之⑥。

生财有大道，生之者众，食之者寡，为之者疾⑦，用之者舒⑧，则财恒足矣。

仁者以财发身⑨，不仁者以身发财。

---

① 违：阻抑。俾：使。
② 四夷：古代华夏族对四方少数民族的统称。含有轻蔑之意。孔传："言东夷、西戎、南蛮、北狄，被发左衽之人，无不皆恃赖三君之德。"《后汉书·东夷传》："凡蛮、夷、戎、狄总名四夷者，犹公、侯、伯、子、男皆号诸侯云。"
③ 放流：流放。迸，即"屏"，驱逐。中国：古代华夏族建国于黄河流域一带，以为居天下之中，故称中国。古时"中国"含义不一：或指京师为"中国"，《诗经·大雅·民劳》："惠此中国，以绥四方。"毛传："中国，京师也。"《史记·五帝本纪》："夫而后中国，践天子位焉。"裴骃集解："刘熙曰：'帝王所都为中，故曰中国。'或指华夏族，汉族地区为中国（以其在四夷之中）。《诗经·小雅·六月序》："《小雅》尽废，则四夷交侵，中国微矣。"又《礼记·中庸》："是以声名洋溢乎中国，施及蛮貊。"而华夏族，汉族多建都于黄河南北，因称其地为"中国"，与"中土""中原""中州""中夏""中华"含义相同。初时本指河南省及其附近地区，后来华夏族，汉族活动范围扩大，黄河中下游一带，也被称为"中国"。《晋书·宣帝纪》："孟达于是连吴固蜀，潜图中国。"（"中国"指立国于黄河中下游的魏国），甚至把所统辖的地区，包括不属于黄河流域的地方，也全部称为"中国"。《史书·天官书》："其后秦遂以兵灭六国，并中国。"十九世纪中叶以来，"中国"始专指我国全部领土，不作他用。
④ 命：郑玄认为其为"慢"字之误。慢即轻慢。
⑤ 拂：逆，违背。逮：及、到。夫(fū)：助词。
⑥ 骄泰：骄横放纵。
⑦ 疾：快。
⑧ 舒：舒缓。
⑨ 发身：修身；一说，成名，起家。发，发达，发起。

And, when he finds accomplished and perspicacious men, to oppose them and not allow their advancement, showing himself really not able to bear them: — such a minister will not be able to protect my sons and grandsons and black-haired people; and may not also be pronounced dangerous to the state?

It is only the truly virtuous man who can send away such a man and banish① him, driving him out among the barbarous② tribes around, determined not to dwell along with him in the Middle Kingdom. This is in accordance with the saying, "It is only the truly virtuous man who can love or who can hate others."

To see men of worth and not be able to raise them to office; to raise them to office, but not to do so quickly: this is disrespectful. To see bad men and not be able to remove them; to remove them, but not to do so to a distance: — this is weakness.

To love those whom men hate, and to hate those whom men love; — this is to outrage③ the natural feeling of men. Calamities④ cannot fail to come down on him who does so.

Thus we see that the sovereign has a great course to pursue. He must show entire self-devotion and sincerity to attain it, and by pride and extravagance⑤ he will fail of it.

There is a great course also for the production of wealth. Let the procedures be many and the consumers few. Let there be activity in the production and economy in the expenditure. Then the wealth will always be sufficient.

---

① banish/'bænɪʃ/v. 流放,放逐,开除
② barbarous/'bɑːbərəs/adj. 野蛮的
③ outrage/'autreɪdʒ/v. 震骇或触犯(某人);大大激怒(某人)
④ calamity/kəl'æmətɪ/n. 灾祸,灾难
⑤ extravagance/ɪks'trævɪgəns/n. 奢侈,铺张

The virtuous ruler，by means of his wealth，makes himself more distinguished. The vicious ruler accumulates^① wealth，at the expense of his life.

———————————

① accumulate/əˈkjuːmjuleɪt/ *v*. 积聚，累积

未有上好仁而下不好义者也,未有好义其事不终者也,未有府库财非其财者也①。

孟献子曰②:"畜马乘,不察于鸡豚③;伐冰之家④,不畜牛羊;百乘之家⑤,不畜聚敛之臣。与其有聚敛之臣,宁有盗臣⑥。"此谓国不以利为利,以义为利也。

长国家而务财用者⑦,必自小人矣。彼为善之,小人之使为国家,菑害并至⑧。虽有善者,亦无如之何矣⑨!此谓国不以利为利,以义为利也。

右传之十章,释治国平天下。凡传十章,前四章统论纲领指趣,后六章细论条目工夫,其第五章乃明善之要,第六章乃诚身之本,在初学尤为当务之急,读者不可以其近而忽之也。

---

① 府库:国家收藏财物的地方。
② 孟献子:鲁国大夫,姓仲孙,名蔑。
③ 畜:养。乘(shèng):指用四匹马拉的车。畜马乘是士人初作大夫官的待遇。察:关注。
④ 伐冰之家:指丧祭时能用冰保存遗体的人家,是卿大夫类大官的待遇。
⑤ 百乘之家:拥有一百辆车的人家,指有封地的诸侯王。
⑥ 盗臣:盗窃府库财物的家臣。
⑦ 长(zhǎng)国家:成为国家之长,指君王。
⑧ 菑:古灾字。
⑨ 无如之何:没有办法。

Never has there been a case of the sovereign loving benevolence, and the people not loving righteousness. Never has there been a case where the people have loved righteousness, and the affairs of the sovereign have not been carried to completion. And never has there been a case where the wealth in such a state, collected in the treasuries and arsenals①, did not continue in the sovereign's possession.

The officer Mang Hsien said, "He who keeps horses and a carriage does not look after fowls and pigs. The family which keeps its stores of ice does not rear cattle or sheep. So the house which possesses a hundred chariots should not keep a minister to look out for imposts that he may lay them on the people. That to have such a minister, it were better for that house to have one who should rob it of its revenues②." This is in accordance with the saying: "In a state, pecuniary gain is not to be considered to be prosperity, but its prosperity will be found in righteousness.

When he who presides over a state or a family makes his revenues his chief business, he must be under the influence of some small, mean man. He may consider this man to be good; but when such a person is employed in the administration of a state or family, calamities from Heaven, and injuries from men will befall it together, and though a good man may take his place, he will not be able to remedy the evil. This illustrate again the saying, "In a state, gain is not to be considered prosperity, but its prosperity will be found in righteousness."

The above tenth chapter of commentary explains the government of the state, and the making the kingdom peaceful and happy.

---

① arsenal/ˈɑːsənl/ *n.* 军械库,兵工厂
② revenue/ˈrevənjuː/ *n.* 税收,岁入

There are thus, in all, ten chapters of commentary, the first four of which discuss in a general manner, the scope of the principal topic of the Work; while the other six go particularly into an exhibition of the work required in its subordinate branches. The fifth chapter contains the important subject of comprehending true excellence, and the sixth, what is the foundation of the attainment of true sincerity. Those two chapters demand the especial attention of the learner. Let not the reader despise them because of their simplicity.

【推荐阅读】

一、中文版本及注疏

程颐,程颢.二程遗书.上海：上海古籍出版社,1992 年。

李学勤主编.十三经注疏(标点本)·礼记正义.北京：北京大学出版社,1999 年。

阮元校刻.十三经注疏附校勘记.北京：中华书局,1980 年。

汪受宽,金良年.孝经.大学.中庸译注.上海：上海古籍出版社,2012 年。

王夫之.船山全书(之四)·礼记章句.长沙：岳麓书社,1996 年。

王国轩译注.大学.北京：中华书局,2006 年。

王文锦译注.大学中庸.北京：中华书局,2013 年。

朱熹.四书章句集注.北京：中华书局,1983 年。

朱熹.朱子四书语类.上海：上海古籍出版社,1992 年。

朱熹.大学或问(《朱子全书》第陆册).上海：上海古籍出版社,2002 年。

二、英文译本

Collie，David. 1828. *The Chinese Classical Work Commonly Called The Four Books*. Serampore，Printed at the Mission press.

De Bary，Theodore，et al. 2000. *Sources of Chinese Tradition：From Earliest Times to 1600*. New York：Columbia University Press.

Gardner，Daniel K. 2007. *The Four Books. The Teachings of the Later Confucian Tradition*. Indianapolis：Hackett Publishing.

Legge，James. 1861. *The original Chinese texts of the work of Laou-tsze，the Great learning，the Doctrine of the mean*. Oxford：The Clarendon Press.

Legge，James. 1893. *The Chinese Classics*. Oxford：The Clarendon

Press.

Legge，James. 1960. *The Chinese Classics*. Hong Kong：Hong Kong University Press.

Marshman，J. 1814. *Elements of Chinese Grammar*. Serampore：Printed at the Mission Press.

Morrison，Robert. 1812. *Horae Sinicae：Translations from the Popular Literature of the Chinese*. London：printed for Black and Parry.

Lin，Yutang. 1938. *The Wisdom of Confucius*. New York：Modern Library.

第三单元 《诗经》

【导言】

　　《诗经》,先秦称为《诗》,亦称《诗三百》,中国最早的诗歌总集,收集了周朝初年(公元前十一世纪)至春秋中期(公元前六世纪)的诗歌305首。《诗经》所收录的诗歌按照音乐类型分为《风》《雅》《颂》三类,均可吟唱。其中,"风"(亦称"国风")收诗160首,多为周代各地的民间歌谣,是《诗经》中最富思想意义和艺术价值的篇章;"雅"分为《小雅》和《大雅》,《小雅》74首,多为西周贵族宴会用的乐歌,也有部分民间歌谣,《大雅》31首,为诸侯朝会时的乐歌;"颂"40首,为王庭和贵族宗庙祭祀的乐歌。《诗经》通过赋、比、兴的艺术表现手法,反映统治者征战田猎、贵族集团奢侈荒淫的生活,以及普通百姓的劳动生活和婚姻爱情等。西汉时被尊为儒家经典,始称《诗经》,为"五经"之一。

　　《诗经》的作者及采编者大多无从考证。《史记》和《汉书》言孔子删诗,《左传》载"古者天子命史采歌谣,以观民风"。关于《诗经》的版本,历史上曾流传过鲁、齐、韩、毛四家。前三家传本均已亡佚,只剩毛诗一家流传至今。《诗经》的主要注本包括:汉代经学大师郑玄作的"笺",唐代孔颖达的《毛诗正义》,宋代朱熹的《诗集传》,清代陈启源的《毛诗稽古编》、马瑞辰的《毛诗传笺通释》、胡承珙的《毛诗后笺》、陈奂的《毛诗传疏》以及近代林光义的《诗经通解》、吴凯生的《诗义会通》、程俊英的《诗经译注》、余冠英的《诗经选》、陈子展的《诗经直解》、高亨的《诗经今注》、金启华的《诗经诠译》、袁愈荌的《诗经诠译》、袁梅的《诗经诠译》等。

　　《诗经》也随着儒家"四书五经"开始其西方的译介。1626年,比利时人金尼阁(Nicolas Trigault)用拉丁语翻译了包括《诗经》在内的《五经》,在杭州镌板印行。此为已知最早的《诗经》西文译本。威廉·琼斯(William Jones)于十八世纪80年代用拉丁文翻译了《诗经》中的《卫风·淇奥》《周南·桃夭》和《节南山》三首诗,后译成英语,此为《诗经》英译之滥觞。1871年,理雅各在香港出版了《诗经》散体英文译本。1876年,他用韵体重译《诗经》在伦敦特鲁布纳(Trübner)出版公司出版,该译本于 1967 年在纽约重印。继理雅各之后,1891 年伦敦出版了阿连璧(C.F.R. Allen)和詹宁斯(William Jennings)的韵体《诗经》英译本。1937 年,英国汉学家阿瑟·韦利(Arthur Waley)译本在伦敦出版。1950 年,瑞典汉学家高本汉(Bernhard Karlgren)的《诗经》英文全译本由瑞典斯德哥尔摩远东古籍博物馆出版,在中西《诗经》学界引起强烈反响。高本汉译本对《诗经》的文字、音韵及训诂三方面进行了深入探讨,译文严谨准确,为后世所称道。1954 年,庞德的《诗经》全译本由哈佛大学出版社出版,书名为《孔子诗集》。1993 年,许渊冲的《诗经》英文译本由湖南出版社出版,此为中国学者自己翻译的首个《诗经》英文全译本。1995 年,汪榕培、任秀桦合作翻译的《诗经》由辽宁教育出版社出版。

氓①

氓之蚩蚩②，抱布贸丝③。

匪来贸丝④，来即我谋⑤。

送子涉淇⑥，至于顿丘⑦。

匪我愆期⑧，子无良媒。

将子无怒⑨，秋以为期。

乘彼垝垣⑩，以望复关⑪。

不见复关，泣涕涟涟。

既见复关，载笑载言⑫。

尔卜尔筮⑬，体无咎言⑭。

以尔车来，以我贿迁⑮。

---

① 出自《国风·卫风》，汉语原文根据阮元校刻《十三经注疏》之《毛诗正义》校改。
② 氓（méng）：古代称百姓。《说文》云："氓，民也。"蚩（chī）蚩：通"嗤嗤"，笑嘻嘻。一说憨厚、老实的样子。
③ 布：布匹。一说，货币。贸：交换，买。
④ 匪：通"非"，不是。
⑤ 即：接近。谋：谋划，指商谈婚事。
⑥ 子：中国古代对男子的美称。涉：渡。淇：水名，又名"淇河"，在今河南淇县。
⑦ 顿丘：地名，今河南清丰县。
⑧ 愆（qiān）：超过，延误。
⑨ 将（qiāng）：愿，请。
⑩ 乘（chéng）：登上。垝（guǐ）垣（yuán）：毁坏了的墙壁。
⑪ 复关：地名。朱熹《诗集传》云："复关，男子之所居也。不敢显言其人，故托言之耳。"
⑫ 载：语助词，则，就。
⑬ 卜：卜卦。用火灼龟甲，看甲上的裂纹来判断吉凶。筮（shì）：用蓍（shī）草排比推算来占卦。
⑭ 体：卦体，用龟蓍占卜所显示的卦象。咎言：不吉利的话。
⑮ 贿：财物，此处指嫁妆。迁：搬走。

Meng

Translated by Bernhard Karlgren①

A jesting②（jolly③）man of the people，you carried cloth to barter④ it for silk；

But it was not that you came to buy silk，you came to lay plans for approaching me；

I followed you wading⑤ the K'i，I came as far as Tun-k'iu；

And it was not that I procrastinated⑥，you had no good go-between；

I prayed you not to be angry，and we made autumn the appointed time.

I ascended⑦ that dilapidated⑧ wall，in order to look for you coming back to the barrier⑨；

When I did not see you come back to the barrier，my tears were dropping in a continuous flow；

When I saw you come back to the barrier，then I laughed，then I talked；

---

① 本译文选自：Karlgren，Bernhard. 1974. *The Book of Odes：Chinese Text，Transcription and Translation*. Stockholm：The Museum of Far Eastern Antiquities，pp. 38－41。

② jesting/'dʒestɪŋ/*adj*. 爱开玩笑的，打趣的，说着玩的

③ jolly/'dʒɔlɪ/*adj*. 兴高采烈的，快活的，有趣的

④ barter/'bɑːtə/*v*. 物物交换，交换，以（货物、财产等）交换其他货物等（不使用货币）

⑤ wade/weɪd/*v*. 跋涉，涉水

⑥ procrastinate/prəʊ'kræstɪneɪt/*v*. 拖延，耽搁

⑦ ascend/ə'send/*v*. 登上

⑧ dilapidated/dɪ'læpɪdeɪtɪd/*adj*.（家具、建筑物等）残破的，破烂的，失修的

⑨ barrier/'bærɪə/*n*. 栅栏，壁垒，关卡

You consulted① the tortoise-shell oracle② and the milfoil-stalks③ oracle, their pronouncements④ had no inauspicious⑤ words;

You came with your carriage and carried me away with my (goods;) dowry⑥.

---

① consult/kənˈsʌlt/v. 向……请教,查阅
② oracle/ˈɔrəkl/n. 神谕,预言
③ milfoil-stalk/ˈmɪlfɔɪl stɔːk/n. milfoil:蓍草;stalk:茎,梗,柄
④ pronouncement/prəˈnaunsmənt/n. 判断,看法,(权威性)表述;声明,公告
⑤ inauspicious/ˌɪnɔːˈspɪʃəs/adj. 不吉的,不祥的,不利的
⑥ dowry/ˈdauərɪ/n. 嫁妆,嫁奁,妆奁

桑之未落,其叶沃若①。

于嗟鸠兮②!无食桑葚③。

于嗟女兮!无与士耽④。

士之耽兮,犹可说也⑤。

女之耽兮,不可说也。

桑之落矣,其黄而陨。⑥

自我徂尔⑦,三岁食贫⑧。

淇水汤汤⑨,渐车帷裳⑩。

女也不爽,士贰其行⑪。

士也罔极⑫,二三其德。

---

① 沃若:润泽柔嫩貌。
② 于嗟(jiē):叹词,表示赞叹或悲叹。于:同"吁",叹词。鸠:鸟名,即斑鸠,此喻男子,鸟是古代生殖崇拜的象征物。
③ 桑葚:桑树的果实。食桑葚过多会醉,此处比喻不要沉醉在爱情中。
④ 士:指男子。耽(dān):沉溺欢乐,此谓迷恋之意。
⑤ 说:通"脱",摆脱,丢开。
⑥ 陨(yǔn):落下。用叶黄落下比喻女子色衰。
⑦ 徂(cú):往,到。尔:你家。徂尔:嫁到你家。
⑧ 三岁:多年,并非实指。食贫:食物缺乏。
⑨ 汤汤(shāng):水势很大的样子。
⑩ 渐(jiān):沾湿,浸湿。帷裳:车上的布幔。
⑪ 爽:差错,过失。贰:通"忒",表示差错;一说,不专一。
⑫ 罔极:无常,不可测。罔:无。极:中,准则。

When the mulberry① tree has not yet shed②(its leaves), how glossy③ are the leaves!

Oh you dove, do not eat the fruits of the mulberry!

Oh you girl, do not take pleasure with a gentleman!

That a gentleman takes pleasure can still be (explained) excused;

But that a girl takes pleasure, cannot be excused.

When the mulberry tree sheds its leaves, they are yellow and drop;

Since I went to you, for three years I have eaten poverty④;

(And now) the waters of the K'i are voluminous⑤, they wet the curtains⑥ of my carriage;

(I), the woman, have not deviated⑦(in my allegiance⑧), but (you,) the man, have (doubled) shown duplicity⑨ in your behaviour;

(You,) the man (have had no limit) have been reckless⑩; you have been very variable⑪ in your conduct⑫.

---

① mulberry/'mʌlbrɪ/ n. 桑树,桑椹
② shed/ʃed/ v. 脱落,剥落,蜕下
③ glossy/ɡlɔsɪ/ adj. 有光泽的,光滑的
④ poverty/'pɔvətɪ/ n. 贫乏,缺乏
⑤ voluminous/və'lu:mɪnəs/ adj. 大量的,体积大的
⑥ curtain/'kɜːtn/ n. 幕,帘,帷
⑦ deviate/'diːvɪeɪt/ v. 偏离(路线、标准等),背离
⑧ allegiance/ə'liːdʒəns/ n. 忠贞,效忠
⑨ duplicity/djuː'plɪsətɪ/ n. 口是心非,表里不一,不诚实
⑩ reckless/'reklɪs/ adj. 不考虑后果的,不顾危险的,鲁莽的,由冲动引起的
⑪ variable/'veərɪəbl/ adj. 变化的,可变的,易变的
⑫ conduct/'kɔndʌkt/ n. (人的)行为(尤指道德方面),品德,品行

三岁为妇①,靡室劳矣②。

夙兴夜寐③,靡有朝矣。

言既遂矣④,至于暴矣⑤。

兄弟不知,咥其笑矣⑥。

静言思之,躬自悼矣⑦。

及尔偕老,老使我怨。

淇则有岸,隰则有泮⑧。

总角之宴,言笑晏晏⑨,

信誓旦旦⑩,不思其反⑪。

反是不思⑫,亦已焉哉⑬!

---

① 三岁:虚数,此处指她结婚初期而言。
② 靡:无,没有,表否定。室:居所,夫妇所居为室,一门之内为家。室劳:家务劳动。此句指氓结婚后再无家务之劳,全由妻子承担了。
③ 夙兴夜寐:早起晚睡。夙:早。兴:起床。寐:睡。
④ 言:语首助词,无义。既:已经。遂:安,指生活安定,称心如意。
⑤ 暴:凶暴。指氓以凶暴的态度对等妻子。
⑥ 咥(xì):笑,讥笑。
⑦ 躬自:自己,亲自。悼:悲痛,哀伤。
⑧ 隰(xí):低湿的地。泮(pàn):通"畔",岸,边。
⑨ 总角:孩子童年时,把头发扎起成两角状。总:扎。晏晏:温和融洽。
⑩ 信誓:真挚的誓言。旦旦:诚恳的样子。
⑪ 不思:想不到。反:反复,变心。
⑫ 反是:违反了这誓言。是:这,指誓言。不思:不再顾及。指氓把誓言丢在脑后。
⑬ 亦已焉哉:那就此算了吧。已:止。已焉:到此为止。

For three years I was your wife, I（had no toil① from the household＝）never felt toiled by the household;

Early I rose and late I went to sleep, I（had no morning）never had the leisure② of a morning;

My words have been（achieved）fulfilled, but I have（come to）met with maltreatment③;

My brothers take no cognizance④, jeering⑤ is their laughter;

Silently I brood⑥ over it, I feel grief⑦ for myself.

Together with you I was to grow old;（ageing）as we passed the years, you caused me to have resentment⑧;

The K'i, at least it has its bands, the swamp⑨, at least it has its shores;

During the pleasant time of the（tied horns）girlhood-hairtufts⑩, we chatted and laughed pleasantly;

We were sworn to good faith（painfully）earnestly; I did not think that it would be reversed⑪;

To reverse this was something I could not imagine; and yet now it is all over.

---

① toil/tɔɪl/ n . 长时间或辛苦工作
② leisure/ˈleʒə/ n . 空暇,闲暇
③ maltreatment/ˌmælˈtriːtmənt/ n . 虐待,粗暴对待
④ cognizance/ˈkɔɡnɪzəns/ n . 知觉,获知,认识
⑤ jeer/dʒɪə/ v . 嘲笑,嘲弄
⑥ brood/bruːd/ v . （忧闷地）沉思
⑦ grief/griːf/ n . 忧伤,悲伤
⑧ resentment/rɪˈzentmənt/ n . 怨恨,愤恨
⑨ swamp/swɔmp/ n . 沼泽
⑩ tuft/tʌft/ n . 一束毛发、一簇羽毛或一丛草等
⑪ reverse/rɪˈvɜːs/ v . 反转,倒转

【推荐阅读】

一、中文版本及注疏

陈子展.诗经直解.上海:复旦大学出版社,1983年。

程俊英.诗经译注.上海:上海古籍出版社,2004年。

程俊英,蒋见元.诗经注析.北京:中华书局,1999年。

(清)方玉润.诗经原始(上下).北京:中华书局,1986年。

高亨.诗经今注.上海:上海古籍出版社,1980年。

金启华.诗经全译.南京:江苏古籍出版社,1984年。

(唐)孔颖达.毛诗正义——十三经注疏(标点本).北京:北京大学出版
　　社,1999年。

(清)姚际恒.诗经通论.北京:中华书局,1958年。

余冠英.诗经选.北京:人民文学出版社,1982年。

袁愈荌,唐莫尧.诗经全译.贵阳:贵州人民出版社,1981年。

朱熹集注,赵长征点校.诗集传.北京:中华书局,2011年。

二、英文译本

Allen, Clement F. R. 1891. *The Book of Chinese Poetry*. London.

Jennings, William. 1891. *The Shi King: The Old Poetry Classic of the Chinese*. London.

Karlgren, Bernhard. 1950. *The Book of Odes: Chinese Text, Transcription and Translation*. Stockholm: The Museum of Far Eastern Antiquites.

Legge, James. 1876. *The She King; or, The Book of Ancient Poetry, Translated in English Verse, with Essays and Notes*. London: Trübner & Co.

Legge, James. 1931. *The Book of Poetry-Chinese Texts with English Translations*. London.

Pound, Ezra. 1976. *Shih-Ching: The Classic Anthology Defined by*

Confucius. New York：Harvard University Press.

Waley，Arthur. 1949. T*he Book of Songs*. Boston and New York：Houghton Miffin Company.

汪榕培,任秀桦.诗经英译.辽宁：辽宁教育出版社,1995 年。

许渊冲.诗经：汉英对照.北京：中国对外翻译出版公司,2009 年。

第四单元 《论语》

【导言】

《论语》是孔子及其弟子的语录结集，是儒家重要经典著作之一，由孔子弟子及再传弟子在春秋时期编纂，战国初期成书。西汉时有《鲁论语》(20 篇)、《齐论语》(22 篇)和《古论语》(21 篇)。西汉末安昌侯张禹本《鲁论语》参考《齐论语》编订，称《张侯论》。东汉末，郑玄据此本参照《齐论语》《古论语》作注，成为传世之《论语》(20 篇)。唐文宗时，《论语》被列入经书。南宋时，朱熹将《论语》与《大学》《中庸》《孟子》合称"四书"，列入官方科举取仕必读书。

孔子(公元前 551 年—公元前 479 年)，名丘，字仲尼，春秋末期鲁国昌平乡陬邑(今山东曲阜市东南)人，中国古代著名思想家、教育家和儒家学派创始人。相传，孔子有弟子三千，贤徒七十二人。他曾整理修订《诗》《书》《礼》《乐》，序《周易》，撰《春秋》，所开创的儒家学说对中国文化产生了广泛而深远的影响。

《论语》共 20 篇，内容涉及政治主张、教育原则、伦理观念、品德修养诸方面，其语言"简而易晓，含蓄有致，为语录的典范"(王力)。《论语》的注疏汉代时即有多家，以后各代更多，通行的注本有三国魏何晏的《论语集解》、宋代邢峻的《论语正义》、朱熹的《论语集注》、清代刘宝楠的《论语正义》、今人杨伯峻的《论语译注》等。

《论语》在西方世界亦广为流传。最早把儒家学说介绍给西方的是明清时期来华传教士利玛窦。1593 年，他首次把《论语》翻译成拉丁文，称其为"中国知识"，与当时著名的"欧洲知识"相对应，随后被译成意大利文、法文、德文、俄文等，引发了西方各国学者的广泛关注。1691年，蓝登·泰勒以柏应理的《中国的哲学家孔子》和法国人彼埃尔·萨夫亥的《孔子的道德中国的哲学》两译本为蓝本，将《论语》译成英语，此译本被数次印刷，成为当时西方了解孔子和中国的主要渠道之一。至 20 世纪 60 年代，孔子学说走出学术圈，在西方大众文化中形成一股"东方热"，儒学成为一门世界的哲学，孔夫子成为东方文化的代言人。《论语》的英文全译本和节译本大约有 60 种左右。影响较大的英译者包括，理雅各（James Legge）(1861)、苏慧廉（William Edward Soothill)(1910)、赖发洛（Leonard A. Lyall)(1909)、翟林奈（Lionel Giles)(1907)、阿瑟·韦利（Arthur Waley)(1938)、庞德（Ezra Pound) (1969)、托玛斯·柯立瑞（Thomas Cleary)(1992)、白牧之和白妙子 (E. Bruce Brooks，A. Tacko Brooks)夫妇(1998)、大卫·欣顿 (David Hintin)(1998)等。华人译者主要有：辜鸿铭（Ku Hung-Ming)(1898)、林语堂（Lin Yutang)(1938)；刘殿爵（D. C. Lau) (1992)、黄继忠（Chichung Huang)(1997)、李祥甫（David H. Li) (1999)、李天辰(1991)、许渊冲(2005)等。

论语(节选)

学而第一①

子曰②:"学而时习之③,不亦说乎④? 有朋自远方来⑤,不亦乐乎⑥? 人不知而不愠⑦,不亦君子乎⑧?"

有子曰⑨:"其为人也孝弟⑩,而好犯上者鲜矣⑪;不好犯上,而好作乱者,未之有也⑫。君子务本⑬,本立而道生⑭。孝弟也者,其为仁之本与⑮。"

子曰:"巧言令色⑯,鲜矣仁。"

---

① 学而:篇名。《论语》本无篇名,后人选取每篇第一句的两个字作为篇名。

② 子:古人对老师的尊称。《论语》中指孔子。

③ 时:在适当的时候。

④ 说(yuè):同"悦",愉快、高兴。

⑤ 朋:古代的朋和友是有区别的,同(师)门为朋,同志为友。

⑥ 乐:高兴。悦在内心,乐则见于外。

⑦ 人不知:别人不了解自己。愠(yùn):恼怒,怨恨。

⑧ 君子:指道德高尚的人。

⑨ 有子:孔子的学生,姓有,名若,比孔子小13岁,一说小33岁。《论语》中记载的孔子学生,一般都称字,只有曾参和有若称"子"。许多人据此推断《论语》著述者为曾参和有若的学生。

⑩ 孝弟(tì):孝,善事父母;弟,同"悌",敬爱兄长。

⑪ 犯上:冒犯或违抗尊长。

⑫ 未之有也:此为"未有之也"的倒装句型。

⑬ 务:专心、致力于。本:根本。

⑭ 道:指孔子提倡的仁道,即以仁为核心的整个道德思想体系及其在实际生活的体现;简言之就是儒家提倡的治国做人的基本原则。

⑮ 其:大概。为仁之本,即以孝悌作为仁的根本。与:同"欤",感叹词。

⑯ 巧言令色:朱熹注曰:"好其言,善其色,致饰于外,务以说人。"巧、令均含美好之意,巧言令色意为装出和颜悦色的样子。

The Analects of Confucius (Excerpts)

Translated by William Jennings①

Book I　On Learning：Miscellaneous② Sayings

"To learn," said the Master, "and then to practice opportunely③ what one has learnt does not this bring with it a sense of satisfaction? To have associates④ in study coming to one from distant parts does not this also mean pleasure in store⑤? And are not those who, while not comprehending all that is said, still remain not unpleased to hear, men of the superior order?"

A saying of the Scholar Yu："It is rarely the case that those who act the part of true men in regard to their duty to parents and elder brothers are at the same time willing to turn currishly⑥ upon their superiors⑦; it has never yet been the case that such as desire not to commit that offence have been men willing to promote anarchy⑧ or disorder. Men of superior mind busy themselves first in getting at the root of things; and when they have succeeded in this the right course is open to them. Well, are not filial piety⑨ and friendly subordination⑩ among brothers a root of that right feeling which is owing generally from man to man?"

---

① 译文选自：Wilson，Epiphanius. 1900. *The Wisdom of Confucius*. New York & Boston：Books，Inc.，pp. 8 - 15。
② miscellaneous/ˌmɪsəˈleɪnɪəs/*adj*. 各种各样的，不同种类的
③ opportunely/ˈɒpətjuːnlɪ/*adv*. 恰好地，适时地，及时地
④ associate/əˈsəʊʃɪət/*n*. 伙伴，朋友，同事，合伙人
⑤ in store 必将来到或发生，等候
⑥ currishly/ˈkɜːrɪʃlɪ/*adv*. 易怒地，脾气坏地
⑦ superior/suːˈpɪərɪə/*n*. 长者，占优势的人，上级
⑧ anarchy/ˈænəkɪ/*n*. 混乱，无秩序，无政府状态
⑨ filial piety/ˈfɪlɪəlˈpaɪətɪ/孝顺，孝心
⑩ subordination/səˌbɔːdɪˈneɪʃn/*n*. 服从，附属，从属关系

The Master observed, "Rarely do we meet with the right feeling due from one man to another where there is fine speech and studied mien[①]."

---

① mien/miːn/ n. 风采, 样子, 态度, 神态

曾子曰①："吾日三省吾身②——为人谋而不忠乎③？与朋友交而不信乎④？传不习乎⑤？"

子曰："道千乘之国⑥，敬事而信⑦，节用而爱人，使民以时⑧。"

子曰："弟子入则孝⑨，出则弟⑩。谨而信⑪，泛爱众，而亲仁⑫。行有余力⑬，则以学文⑭。"

子夏曰⑮："贤贤易色⑯，事父母能竭其力，事君能致其身⑰，与朋友交言而有信。虽曰未学，吾必谓之学矣。"

---

① 曾子：名参（shēn），字子舆，鲁国武城人，孔子的学生。

② 省（xǐng）：检查、察看，自我反省。

③ 忠：此处指对人应当尽心竭力。

④ 信：诚实。

⑤ 传：老师传授给的知识。习：复习、温习。

⑥ 道：治理。乘（shèng）：四匹马拉的战车。千乘之国：拥有一千辆战车的国家，春秋时，指中等诸侯国。

⑦ 敬：认真对待。

⑧ 使民：役使百姓。以时：按照农时耕作与收获。

⑨ 弟子：年纪幼小的人。入：进到父亲住处。

⑩ 出：外出拜师学习。

⑪ 谨：寡言少语。

⑫ 仁：有仁德之人。

⑬ 行：实践。

⑭ 文：主要有《诗》《书》《礼》《乐》等古代文献。

⑮ 子夏：姓卜，名商，字子夏，孔子的学生。

⑯ 贤贤：尊重贤者。

⑰ 致：献纳。

The Scholar Tsang once said of himself: "On three points I examine myself daily, viz.①, whether, in looking after other people's interests, I have not been acting whole-heartedly; whether, in my intercourse② with friends, I have not been true; and whether, after teaching, I have not myself been practicing what I have taught."

The Master once observed that to rule well one of the larger states meant strict attention to its affairs and conscientiousness③ on the part of the ruler; careful husbanding④ of its resources⑤, with at the same time a tender⑥ care for the interests of all classes; and the employing of the masses⑦ in the public service⑧ at suitable seasons.

"Let young people," said he, "show filial piety at home, respectfulness towards their elders when away from home; let them be circumspect⑨, be truthful; their love going out freely towards all, cultivating good-will to men. And if, in such a walk⑩, there be time or energy left for other things, let them employ⑪ it in the acquisition of literary or artistic accomplishments⑫."

The disciple Tsz-hia said, "The appreciation⑬ of worth in men

---

① viz/vɪz/源自拉丁文 videlicet/vɪ'deliset/,通常读作 namely,即,就是
② intercourse/'ɪntəkɔːs/n. 交往,交流
③ conscientiousness/ˌkɒnʃɪ'enʃəsnɪs/n. 按良心办事,认真,尽责
④ husband/'hʌzbənd/v. 节约地使用,节俭地管理
⑤ resource/rɪ'sɔːs/n. [通常作复数]资源
⑥ tender/'tendə/adj. 温柔的,体贴的
⑦ mass/mæs/n. [通常作复数]群众,劳动者阶层(尤指政治领导人或思想家所指的劳动群众)
⑧ public service 公用事业,公益服务
⑨ circumspect/'sɜːkəmspekt/adj. [通常作表语]小心,慎重,细心
⑩ in a walk 轻而易举地
⑪ employ/ɪm'plɔɪ/v. 利用(时间、注意力等)
⑫ accomplishment/ə'kʌmplɪʃmənt/n. 才艺,技艺,教养(尤指在社交方面),社交礼仪
⑬ appreciation/əˌpriːʃɪ'eɪʃn/n. 赏识,鉴别,感激

of worth, thus diverting① the mind from lascivious② desires ministering③ to parents while one is the most capable of so doing serving one's ruler when one is able to devote himself entirely to that object being sincere in one's language in intercourse with friends; this I certainly must call evidence of learning, though others may say there has been 'no learning.'"

---

① divert/daɪˈvɜːt/ v. 转移某人的注意力，使分心，转向，转移
② lascivious/ləˈsɪvɪəs/ adj. 好色的，猥亵的，挑动情欲的
③ minister/ˈmɪnɪstə/ v. 辅助或伺候某人，为某人或某事物服务

子曰:"君子不重则不威①,学则不固②。主忠信③。无友不如己者④。过则勿惮改⑤。"

曾子曰:"慎终追远⑥,民德归厚矣⑦。"

子禽问于子贡曰⑧:"夫子至于是邦也⑨,必闻其政,求之与?抑与之与⑩?"

子贡曰:"夫子温、良、恭、俭、让以得之⑪,夫子之求之也,其诸异乎人之求之与⑫?"

子曰:"父在,观其志;父没,观其行⑬;三年无改于父之道⑭,可谓孝矣。"

有子曰:"礼之用⑮,和为贵⑯。先王之道⑰,斯为美,小大由之⑱。

---

① 重:庄重、自重。

② 学则不固:人见闻少,学了就可以不固陋。

③ 主:意动用法,以……为首选。

④ 无:通"毋","不要"的意思。友:结交朋友。

⑤ 过:犯错。惮(dàn):害怕、畏惧。

⑥ 终:老死曰终,这里指父母的去世。追远:祖先虽久远,也须按时祭祀,表示怀念。

⑦ 归:趋向,归属。

⑧ 子禽:姓陈名亢,字子禽,有人说是孔子的学生,有人说不是。子贡:姓端木,名赐,字子贡,卫国人,孔子的学生。

⑨ 夫子:古代对男子的尊称。《论语》中孔子的学生用以专称孔子。是:这。邦:国家。

⑩ 抑:或是。与:给予。

⑪ 温、良、恭、俭、让:温顺、善良、恭敬、俭朴、谦让。

⑫ 其诸:表示不能肯定的语气。

⑬ 行:行为举止。

⑭ 三年:要经过一个较长的时间,不一定仅指三年。道:为人处世的准则。

⑮ 礼:在春秋时代,"礼"泛指典章制度和道德规范。

⑯ 和:调和、谐调。

⑰ 先王:指尧、舜、禹、汤、文、武、周公等古代帝王。道:治世的方法。

⑱ 由:顺随。

Sayings of the Master: "If the great man be not grave①, he will not be revered②, neither can his learning be solid③. Give prominent④ place to loyalty and sincerity⑤. Have no associates in study who are not advanced⑥ somewhat like yourself. When you have erred⑦, be not afraid to correct yourself."

A saying of the Scholar Tsang: "The virtue of the people is renewed⑧ and enriched when attention is seen to be paid to the departed⑨, and the remembrance⑩ of distant ancestors kept and cherished⑪."

Tsz-k'in put this query⑫ to his fellow disciple Tsz-kung, said he, "When our Master comes to this or that state, he learns without fail how it is being governed. Does he investigate⑬ matters? Or are the facts given him?"

Tsz-kung answered, "Our Master is a man of pleasant manners, and of probity⑭, courteous⑮, moderate⑯, and unassuming⑰; it is by his being such that he arrives at the facts. Is not his way of arriving at things different from that of others?"

---

① grave/ɡreɪv/*adj.*（指人）严肃的，一本正经的
② revere/rɪ'vɪə/*v.* 崇敬，尊敬，敬畏
③ solid/'sɒlɪd/*adj.* 牢靠的，有信誉的，可靠的
④ prominent/'prɒmɪnənt/*adj.* 卓越的，显著的，突出的
⑤ sincerity/sɪn'serɪtɪ/*n.* 诚挚，真挚
⑥ advanced/əd'vɑːnst/*adj.* 水平高于其余的，在前的，高级的
⑦ err/ɜː/*v.* 犯错误，出错
⑧ renew/rɪ'njuː/*v.* 使更新，使恢复，使复原，重新开始
⑨ departed/dɪ'pɑːtɪd/*adj.* [委婉表达，前加冠词 the]逝者，故去的人
⑩ remembrance/rɪ'membrəns/*n.* 记忆，追忆
⑪ cherish/'tʃerɪʃ/*v.* 怀有（某种感情或想法），怀念，珍爱
⑫ query/'kwɪərɪ/*n.* 疑问，问题
⑬ investigate/ɪn'vestɪɡeɪt/*v.* 调查，调查研究
⑭ probity/'prəʊbətɪ/*n.* 正直，诚实，刚正不阿
⑮ courteous/'kɜːtɪəs/*adj.* 彬彬有礼的，客气的
⑯ moderate/'mɒdərət/*adj.* 见解（通常指政治方面）不极端的，不偏激的，温和的，有节制的
⑰ unassuming/ˌʌnə'sjuːmɪŋ/*adj.* 谦逊的，不装腔作势的

A saying of the Master: "He who, after three years' observation① of the will of his father when alive, or of his past conduct if dead, does not deviate② from that father's ways, is entitled to be called 'a dutiful son.'"

Sayings of the Scholar Yu: "For the practice of the Rules of Propriety③, one excellent way is to be natural. This naturalness became a great grace in the practice of kings of former times; let everyone, small or great, follow their example.

① observation/ˌɒbzəˈveɪʃn/ n. 执行,遵守

② deviate/ˈdiːvɪeɪt/ v. 偏离(路线、标准等),背离

③ propriety/prəˈpraɪətɪ/ n. 合乎社交或道德规范的举止,行为规范,礼节;得体,合宜

有所不行。知和而和，不以礼节之^①，亦不可行也。"

有子曰："信近于义^②，言可复也^③。恭近于礼，远耻辱也。因不失其亲，亦可宗也^④。"

子曰："君子食无求饱，居无求安。敏于事而慎于言^⑤，就有道而正焉^⑥，可谓好学也已。"

子贡曰："贫而无谄^⑦，富而无骄，何如？"

子曰："可也，未若贫而乐，富而好礼者也。"

子贡曰："《诗》云^⑧：'如切如磋，如琢如磨'^⑨。其斯之谓与？"

子曰："赐也^⑩，始可与言《诗》已矣。告诸往而知来者^⑪。"

子曰："不患人之不己知^⑫，患不知人也。"

---

① 节：节制，约束。
② 信：诚信。
③ 复：回答。言可复，指可实践自己的诺言。
④ 宗：宗主，这里指可靠。
⑤ 敏：敏捷、敏锐。
⑥ 就：靠近、看齐。正：匡正、端正。
⑦ 谄(chǎn)：巴结、奉承。
⑧ 《诗》：即《诗经》，中国最早的一部诗歌总集。
⑨ 如切二句：为《诗经·卫风·淇奥》中诗句，有精益求精之意。
⑩ 赐：子贡名。
⑪ 诸：之于。往：过去的事情；来：未来的事情。
⑫ 患：忧虑，怕。不己知：即不知己，倒装句。

"It is not, however, always practicable①; and it is not so in the case of a person who does things naturally, knowing that he should act so, and yet who neglects to regulate his acts according to the Rules."

"When truth and right are hand in hand, a statement will bear repetition. When respectfulness and propriety go hand in hand, disgrace② and shame are kept afar-off. Remove all occasion for alienating③ those to whom you are bound by close ties, and you have them still to resort to④."

A saying of the Master: "The man of greater mind who, when he is eating, craves⑤ not to eat to the full; who has a home, but craves not for comforts in it; who is active and earnest in his work and careful in his words; who makes towards men of high principle, and so maintains his own rectitude⑥-that man may be styled a devoted student."

Tsz-kung asked, "What say you, sir, of the poor who do not cringe⑦ and fawn⑧; and what of the rich who are without pride and haughtiness⑨?"

"They are passable⑩," the Master replied, "yet they are scarcely in the same category as the poor who are happy, and the rich who love propriety."

"In the 'Book of the Odes,'" Tsz-kung went on to say, "we

① practicable/'præktɪkəbl/*adj*. 可以实施的,行得通的
② disgrace/dɪs'ɡreɪs/*n*. 出丑,丢脸,令人感到羞耻的事物或人
③ alienate/'eɪlɪəneɪt/*v*. 使疏远,离间
④ resort to 求助于(某物,常指不好的),诉诸,用
⑤ crave/kreɪv/*v*. 渴望,热望,恳求
⑥ rectitude/'rektɪtjuːd/*n*. 正直,正确,公正
⑦ cringe/krɪndʒ/*v*. 卑躬屈膝,畏缩
⑧ fawn/fɔːn/*v*. (指狗)(摇尾、用爪子抓或用舌舔等)表示亲热;奉承,讨好
⑨ haughtiness/'hɔːtɪnɪs/*n*. 傲慢,不逊
⑩ passable/'pɑːsəbl/*adj*. 还好的,尚可的,过得去的

read of one：

Polished, as by the knife and file,

The graving-tool, the smoothing-stone.

Does that coincide with your remark?"

"Ah! Such as you," replied the Master, "may well commence a discussion on the Odes. If one tells you how a thing goes, you know what ought to come."

"It does not greatly concern me," said the Master, "that men do not know me; my great concern is, my not knowing them."

为政第二

子曰："为政以德^①，譬如北辰^②，居其所而众星共之^③。"

子曰："《诗》三百^④，一言以蔽之^⑤，曰：'思无邪'^⑥。"

子曰："道之以政^⑦，齐之以刑^⑧，民免而无耻^⑨；道之以德，齐之以礼，有耻且格^⑩。"

子曰："吾十有五而志于学^⑪，三十而立^⑫，四十而不惑^⑬，五十而知天命^⑭，六十而耳顺^⑮，七十而从心所欲，不逾矩。"

---

① 为政以德：指统治者应以道德进行统治，即"德治"。
② 北辰：北极星。
③ 所：处所，位置。共：同"拱"，环绕。
④ 《诗》：指《诗经》，共 305 篇。
⑤ 蔽：概括。
⑥ 思无邪：出自《诗经·鲁颂》；思：思想；无邪：纯正。
⑦ 道：引导。
⑧ 齐：整齐，约束。
⑨ 免：避免。耻：羞耻之心。
⑩ 格：纠正，匡正。一说：亲近，归服。
⑪ 有：同"又"。
⑫ 立：建树，成就。
⑬ 不惑：不被外界事物所迷惑。
⑭ 天命：天道运行变化的规律，指不能为人力所支配的事情。
⑮ 耳顺：听到逆耳之言也能正确对待。

Book II   Good Government — Filial Piety — The Superior Man

Sayings of the Master: "Let a ruler base his government upon virtuous principles, and he will be like the pole-star①, which remains steadfast② in its place, while all the host③ of stars turn towards it.

"The 'Book of Odes' contains three hundred pieces, but one expression in it may be taken as covering the purport④ of all, viz., Unswerving⑤ mindfulness⑥.

"To govern simply by statute⑦, and to reduce all to order by means of pains and penalties⑧, is to render⑨ the people evasive⑩, and devoid⑪ of any sense of shame. To govern upon principles of virtue, and to reduce them to order by the Rules of Propriety, would not only create in them the sense of shame, but would moreover reach⑫ them in all their errors.

"When I attained⑬ the age of fifteen, I became bent upon⑭ study. At thirty, I was a confirmed⑮ student. At forty, nought⑯ could move me from my course. At fifty, I comprehended the will

---

① pole-star 北极星
② steadfast/'stedfɑːst/ *adj.* 坚定的,不动摇的,固定不动的
③ host/həʊst/ *n.* 大群,众多,许多
④ purport/'pɜːpət/ *n.* 要旨,大意,意图
⑤ unswerving/ʌn'swɜːvɪŋ/ *adj.* 不歪的,坚定的,不偏离的
⑥ mindfulness/'maɪndflnɪs/ *n.* 留意,留心
⑦ statute/'stætʃuːt/ *n.* 成文法,法规,法令
⑧ penalty/'penltɪ/ *n.* 刑罚,处罚,惩罚
⑨ render/'rendə/ *v.* 使(某人或某事物)处于某种状况
⑩ evasive/ɪ'veɪsɪv/ *adj.* 逃避的,规避的,推托的
⑪ devoid/dɪ'vɔɪd/ *adj.* 没有或毫无某事物
⑫ reach/riːtʃ/ *v.* 影响,对…起作用
⑬ attain/ə'teɪn/ *v.* [文雅语]达到
⑭ bent upon 决心要,专心于,下决心
⑮ confirmed/kən'fɜːmd/ *adj.* 被证实的,根深蒂固的,坚定的
⑯ nought/nɔːt/ *n.* 零,无,无物

and decrees① of Heaven. At sixty, my ears were attuned② to them. At seventy, I could follow my heart's desires, without overstepping③ the lines of rectitude."

---

① decree/dɪˈkriː/ *n*. 法令,判决,天意
② attune/əˈtjuːn/ *v*. 使合调,使相合
③ overstep/ˌəʊvəˈstep/ *v*. 超越(正常或容许的范围)

　　孟懿子问孝①。子曰："无违②。"樊迟御③,子告之曰:"孟孙问孝于我,我对曰,无违。"樊迟曰:"何谓也?"子曰:"生,事之以礼;死,葬之以礼,祭之以礼。"

　　孟武伯问孝④。子曰:"父母唯其疾之忧。"

　　子游问孝⑤。子曰:"今之孝者,是谓能养⑥。至于犬马,皆能有养;不敬,何以别乎?"

　　子夏问孝。子曰:"色难⑦。有事,弟子服其劳⑧;有酒食,先生馔⑨,曾是以为孝乎?"

　　子曰:"吾与回言终日⑩,不违⑪,如愚。退而省其私⑫,亦足以发⑬,回也不愚。"

　　子曰:"视其所以⑭,观其所由⑮,察其所安⑯。人焉廋哉⑰? 人焉廋哉?"

---

① 孟懿子:鲁国大夫,姓仲孙,名何忌,"懿"是谥号。
② 无违:不要违背礼。
③ 樊迟御:姓樊名须,字子迟,孔子的弟子,比孔子小 46 岁,曾与冉求一起帮助季康子进行革新。
④ 孟武伯:孟懿子之子,名彘,武为其谥号。
⑤ 子游:姓言名偃,字子游,吴人,孔子弟子,比孔子小 45 岁。
⑥ 养(yàng):养活。
⑦ 色,脸色和顺愉悦;难,不容易。
⑧ 弟子:学生和晚辈。服其劳:担负其辛劳,即服侍。
⑨ 先生:长者或父母。馔(zhuàn):饮食、吃喝。
⑩ 回:姓颜名回,字子渊,鲁国人,孔子的门生,比孔子小 30 岁。
⑪ 不违:不提相反的意见与问题。
⑫ 退而省其私:考察颜回私下里与其他学生讨论学问的言行。
⑬ 发:发挥,阐发。
⑭ 所以:所做的事情。
⑮ 所由:所走过的道路。
⑯ 所安:所安的心境。
⑰ 廋(sōu):隐藏、藏匿。

To a question of Mang-I, as to what filial piety consisted in, the Master replied, "In not being perverse①." Afterwards, when Fan Ch'I was driving him, the Master informed him of this question and answer, and Fan Ch'I asked, "What was your meaning?" The Master replied, "I meant that the Rules of Propriety should always be adhered to in regard to those who brought us into the world: in ministering to them while living, in burying them when dead, and afterwards in the offering to them of sacrificial② gifts."

To a query of Mang Wu respecting filial piety, the Master replied, "Parents ought to bear③ but one trouble that of their own sickness."

To a like question put by Tsz-yu, his reply was this: "The filial piety of the present day simply means the being able to support one's parents which extends even to the case of dogs and horses, all of which may have something to give in the way of support. If there be no reverential④ feeling in the matter, what is there to distinguish between the cases?"

To a like question of Tsz-hia, he replied: "The manner is the difficulty. If, in the case of work to be done, the younger folks simply take upon themselves the toil of it; or if, in the matter of meat and drink, they simply set these before their elders is this to be taken as filial piety?"

Once the Master remarked, "I have conversed with Hwui the whole day long, and he has controverted⑤ nothing that I have said, as if he were without wits. But when his back was turned, and I

---

① perverse/pə'vɜːs/adj. (指人)固执错误的,(指行为)任性的,(指感情)不近情理的
② sacrificial/ˌsækrɪ'fɪʃl/adj. 供奉的,献祭的
③ bear/beə/v. 忍受,忍耐,承受
④ reverential/ˌrevə'renʃl/adj. 出于尊敬的,恭敬的
⑤ controvert/ˌkɒntrə'vɜːt/v. 争论,反驳

looked attentively at his conduct apart from me, I found it satisfactory in all its issues. No, indeed! Hwui is not without his wits."

Other observations of the Master: "If you observe what things people (usually) take in hand, watch their motives①, and note particularly what it is that gives them satisfaction, shall they be able to conceal from you what they are? Conceal themselves, indeed!"

---

① motive/ˈməutɪv/ *n*. 动机，原因

子曰:"温故而知新①,可以为师矣。"

子曰:"君子不器②。"

子贡问君子。子曰:"先行其言,而后从之。"

子曰:"君子周而不比③,小人比而不周。"

子曰:"学而不思则罔④,思而不学则殆⑤。"

子曰:"攻乎异端⑥,斯害也己⑦。"

子曰:"由⑧!诲女知之乎!知之为知之,不知为不知,是知也。"

子张学干禄⑨。子曰:"多闻阙疑⑩,慎言其余,则寡尤⑪;多见阙殆,慎行其余,则寡悔。言寡尤,行寡悔,禄在其中矣。"

哀公问曰⑫:"何为则民服?"

---

① 故:过去所学的知识。新:刚刚学到的知识。

② 器:器皿、器具。孔子的意思是说作为一个君子,应博学广识,而不仅仅是掌握一种专门的知识,如同器具一样只有某一方面的用途。

③ 周:忠信。引申为亲密。比(bǐ):勾结。朱熹集注:"比,偏党也。"

④ 罔:迷惑、糊涂。

⑤ 殆:疑惑、危险。

⑥ 攻:攻击;一说,致力于学习或研究。异端:不正确的言论。古代儒家称其他学说、学派为异端。朱熹集注:"异端,非圣人之道,而别为一端,如杨墨是也。"

⑦ 也已:语气词。

⑧ 由:姓仲名由,字子路,孔子的学生。

⑨ 子张:姓颛孙名师,字子张,孔子的学生,比孔子小 48 岁。干禄:求取官职。

⑩ 阙:缺,意为放置一旁。疑:怀疑。

⑪ 寡尤:寡,少。尤,过错。

⑫ 哀公:姓姬名蒋,谥号哀,鲁国国君,公元前 494—前 468 年在位。

"Be versed in① ancient lore②, and familiarize yourself with the modern; then may you become teachers.

"The great man is not a mere receptacle③."

In reply to Tsz-kung respecting the great man: "What he first says, as a result of his experience, he afterwards follows up."

"The great man is catholic-minded④, and not one-sided⑤. The common man is the reverse."

"Learning, without thought, is a snare⑥; thought, without learning, is a danger."

"Where the mind is set much upon heterodox⑦ principles there truly and indeed is harm."

To the disciple of Tsz-lu the Master said, "Shall I give you a lesson about knowledge? When you know a thing, maintain that you know it; and when you do not, acknowledge your ingnorance. This is characteristic of knowledge."

Tsz-chang was studying with an eye to⑧ official income. The Master addressed him thus: "Of the many things you hear hold aloof⑨ from those that are doubtful, and speak guardedly with reference to the rest; your mistakes will then be few. Also, of the many courses you see adopted, hold aloof from those that are risky, and carefully follow the others; you will then seldom have occasion for regret. Thus, being seldom mistaken in your utterances, and

---

① be versed in 精通
② lore/lɔ:/ n. 学问，学识
③ receptacle/rɪ'septəkl/ n. 接收器，容器
④ catholic/'kæθəlɪk/ adj. 包罗万象的，广泛的，普遍的
⑤ one-sided/ˌwʌn'saɪdɪd/ adj. 有偏见的，偏袒的，倒向一边的
⑥ snare/sneə/ n. 陷阱，罗网，圈套
⑦ heterodox/'hetərədɒks/ adj. 非正统的，异端的
⑧ with an eye to 着眼于，对……有企图，考虑到
⑨ aloof/ə'lu:f/ adj. 疏远的，冷淡的

having few occasions for regret in the line you take, you are on the high road to your preferment[①]. "

To a question put to him by Duke Ngai as to what should be done in order to render the people submissive to authority, Confucius replied,

---

① preferment/prɪˈfɜːmənt/ *n*. 晋升,升任

孔子对曰:"举直错诸枉①,则民服;举枉错诸直,则民不服。"

季康子问②:"使民敬、忠以劝③,如之何?"

子曰:"临之以庄④,则敬;孝慈,则忠;举善而教不能,则劝。"

或谓孔子曰:"子奚不为政?"

子曰:"《书》云⑤:'孝乎惟孝,友于兄弟,施于有政⑥。'是亦为政,奚其为为政?"

子曰:"人而无信,不知其可也。大车无輗⑦,小车无軏⑧,其何以行之哉?"

---

① 举:选拔;直:正直公平;错:通"措",放置;枉:不正直。

② 季康子:姓季孙名肥,谥号康,鲁哀公时任正卿,是当时政治上最有权势的人。

③ 劝:勉励。

④ 临:对待。

⑤ 《书》:《尚书》的简称,最早的关于中国上古时期的典章文献的汇编。传说为孔子所辑,后被列为儒家经典著作之一。

⑥ 施:推行。

⑦ 輗(ní):古代牛车车辕前面横木上的木销子。

⑧ 軏(yuè):古代小车车辕前面横木上的木销子。

"Promote the straightforward, and reject those whose courses are crooked①, and the thing will be effected. Promote the crooked and reject the straightforward, and the effect will be the reverse."

When Ki K'ang asked of him how the people could be induced② to show respect, loyalty, and willingness to be led, the Master answered, "Let there be grave dignity③ in him who has the oversight④ of them, and they will show him respect; let him be seen to be good to his own parents, and kindly in disposition⑤, and they will be loyal to him; let him promote those who have ability, and see to the instruction of those who have it not, and they will be willing to be led."

Some one, speaking to Confucius, inquired, "Why, sir, are you not an administrator of government?"

The Master rejoined⑥, "What says the 'Book of the Annals,' with reference to filial duty? — 'Make it a point to be dutiful to your parents and amicable⑦ with your brethren⑧; the same duties extend to an administrator.' If these, then, also make an administrator, how am I to take your words about being an administrator?"

On one occasion the Master remarked, "I know not what men are good for, on whose word no reliance can be placed. How should your carriages, large or little, get along⑨ without your whipple-trees⑩ or swing-trees⑪?"

---

① crooked/ˈkrʊkɪd/ *adj.* 弯曲的,歪斜的
② induce/ɪnˈdjuːs/ *v.* 劝诱,导致,促使
③ dignity/ˈdɪɡnətɪ/ *n.* 尊严,高贵
④ oversight/ˈəuvəsaɪt/ *n.* 疏忽,失察
⑤ disposition/ˌdɪspəˈzɪʃn/ *n.* 性情,处理,处置
⑥ rejoin/ˌriːˈdʒɔɪn/ *v.* 回答,反驳
⑦ amicable/ˈæmɪkəbl/ *adj.* 友好的,无敌意的
⑧ brethren/ˈbreðrən/ *n.* 弟兄,同胞
⑨ get along 继续前进,走,进展
⑩ whipple-tree/ˈwɪplˌtriː/ *n.* =whiffletree, swingletree 车前横木,单驾横木
⑪ swing-tree/swɪŋtriː/ *n.* =swingletree, whiffletree 马车前部两端系曳绳之横木

　　子张问:"十世可知也^①?"

　　子曰:"殷因于夏礼^②,所损益^③,可知也;周因于殷礼,所损益,可知也;其或继周者,虽百世,可知也。"

　　子曰:"非其鬼而祭之^④,谄也。见义不为,无勇也。"

---

① 世:古时称三十年为一世。
② 因:因袭,沿用。
③ 损益:减少和增加。
④ 鬼:这里泛指鬼神。

Tsz-chang asked if it were possible to forecast the state of the country ten generations hence. The Master replied in this manner: "The Yin dynasty adopted the rules and manners of the Hia line of kings, and it is possible to tell whether it retrograded① or advanced. The Chow line has followed the Yin, adopting its ways, and whether there has been deterioration② or improvement may also be determined. Some other line may take up in turn those of Chow; and supposing even this process to go on for a hundred generations, the result may be known."

Other saying of the Master: "It is but flattery③ to make sacrificial offerings④ to departed spirits not belonging to one's own family. It is moral cowardice⑤ to leave undone what one perceives to be right to do."

---

① retrograde/'retrəgreɪd/ v. 倒退,逆行,退步
② deterioration/dɪˌtɪərɪə'reɪʃn/ n. 恶化,变坏,堕落,退化
③ flattery/'flætərɪ/ n. 谄媚,阿谀奉承,巴结
④ offering/'ɔfrɪŋ/ n. 供奉
⑤ cowardice/'kaʊədɪs/ n. 胆小,懦弱,卑怯

【推荐阅读】

一、中文版本及注疏

程树德.论语集释.北京：中华书局,2006 年。

杜道生.论语新注新译.北京：中华书局,2011 年。

何晏.论语集解.北京：中华书局,2006 年。

何根祥.论语通读.上海：上海人民出版社,2011 年。

钱穆.论语新解.北京：九州出版社,2011 年。

孙立权等.论语注译.长春：吉林出版集团,2011 年。

杨伯峻.论语译注.北京：中华书局,2006 年。

朱熹.论语集注.北京：北京图书馆出版社,2001 年。

二、英文译本

Ames，Roger. 1999. *The Analects of Confucius：A Philosophical Translation*. New York：Ballantine Books.

Brooks，E. Bruce，and A. Tacko Brooks. 1998. *The Original Analects：Sayings of Confucius and His Successor*（0479 - 0249）. New York：Columbia University Press.

Chichung Huang. 1997. *The Analects of Confucius*. New York：Oxford University Press.

David，Li. 1999. *The Analects of Confucius，A New-Millennium Translation*. Mariland：Premier Publishing Company.

Dawson，Raymond. 1993. *The Analects*. Oxford：Oxford University Press.

Giles，Lionel. 1907. *The Sayings of Confucius：A New Translation of the Greater Part of the Confucius Analects*. London：John Murray.

Hintin，David. 1998. *The Analects*. Washington，D. C.：Counterpoint.

Ku，Hung-ming. 1898. *The Discourse and Sayings of Confucius*. Shanghai：Kelly and Walsh，Ltd.

Lau，D. C. *The Analects*. 1979. Harmondsworth：Penguin.

Legge，James. 1861. *The Analects*. Vol. 1 of *The Chinese Classics*. Reprint，Hong Kong：University of Hong Kong Press，1960.

Lin，Yutang. 1938. *The Wisdom of Confucius*. New York：The Modern Library.

Pound，Ezra. 1951. *Confucius：The Great Digest*，*The Unwobbling Pivot*，*The Analects*. New York：New Directions.

Slingerland，Edward. 2003. *Confucius Analects：With Selections from Traditional Commentaries*. Indianapolis：Hackett.

Soothill，William. 1937. *The Analects of Confucius*. Oxford：Oxford University Press.

Waley，Authur. 1938. *The Analects of Confucius*. London：George Allen & Unwin.

Watson，Burton. 2007. *The Analects of Confucius*. New York：Columbia University Press.

李天辰译.论语汉英对照读本.济南：山东大学出版社,1991 年.

许渊冲译.汉英对照论语.北京：高等教育出版社,2005 年.

第五单元 《孟子》

【导言】

《孟子》,儒家"四书"之一,为孟子的言论汇编,由孟子及其弟子编撰,约战国中期成书。南宋时,朱熹将其与《大学》《中庸》《论语》合在一起称"四书"。今有七篇,十四卷传世,约三万五千余字,包括《梁惠王》(上下)、《公孙丑》(上下)、《滕文公》(上下)、《离娄》(上下)、《万章》(上下)、《告子》(上下)、《尽心》(上下),为"四书"中篇幅最长者。

孟子(约公元前 372—公元前 289 年),名轲,字子舆,战国中期邹国(今山东省邹城)人,中国历史上伟大的思想家、政治家、教育家,儒家学派代表人物之一,后人尊为"亚圣",与孔子并称"孔孟"。《史记·孟子荀卿列传》言孟子"受业子思之门人",主张人性本善,提倡行仁政、施德治,提出"民贵君轻"的民本思想。

东汉赵岐的《孟子章句》是现存最早的《孟子》注。宋神宗时,《孟子》被正式列为经书。宋代朱熹《四书章句集注》有《孟子集注》十四卷,为宋人注释《孟子》的代表作。宋代赵械的《癸巳孟子说》也是理学家解说《孟子》义理的名著。清代焦循撰《孟子正义》三十卷,以赵歧注为基础,集历代注疏之大成,为历代《孟子》注疏最详备者。清代的《孟子》研究著述还有戴震的《孟子字义疏证》、康有为的《孟子微》、崔述的《孟子事实考》等。近人钱穆的《先秦诸子系年考辨》,对孟子及其弟子的事实论考颇详,补充了孟子事迹不详的阙略,是了解孟子其人及其学派的必读材料。杨伯峻依据朱熹的《孟子集注》和焦循的《孟子正义》所著《孟子译注》为现代较有影响的注本。

《孟子》的西译始于十六世纪下半叶。但其英译却起步较晚。最早的英译本为 1828 年高大卫(David Colie)的《中国经典:通称四书》(*The Chinese Classical Work Commonly Called the Four Books*)中的《孟子》。1861—1872 年,英国传教士汉学家理雅各(James Legge)的《中国经典》(*The Chinese Classics*)分五卷相继在香港出版,《孟子》英译本收录在 1861 年出版的第二卷中,后多次再版,成为一百多年来《孟子》的经典英文译本之一。进入二十世纪,《孟子》英文译本层出不穷,主要译者有翟林奈(Lionel Giles，1942)、魏鲁男(James R. Ware，1960)、道伯森(W. A. Dobson，1963)、亨顿(David Hinton，1998)等。中国译者有蔡元定、蔡沉父子(1965)、刘殿爵(D. C. Lau，1970)、赵甄陶(1993)、何祚康(1999)等。

告子章句(上)①

(一)

告子曰②:"性犹杞柳也③,义犹桮桊也④;以人性为仁义,犹以杞柳为桮桊。"

孟子曰:"子能顺杞柳之性而以为桮桊乎?将戕贼杞柳而后以为桮桊也⑤?如将戕贼杞柳而以为桮桊,则亦将戕贼人以为仁义与⑥?率天下之人而祸仁义者,必子之言夫!"

(二)

告子曰:"性犹湍水也⑦,决诸东方则东流⑧,决诸西方则西流。人性之无分于善不善也,犹水之无分于东西也。"

孟子曰:"水信无分于东西⑨,无分于上下乎?人性之善也,犹水之就下也。人无有不善,水无有不下。今夫水,搏而跃之⑩,可使过颡⑪;激而行之,可使在山⑫。是岂水之性哉?其势则然也。人之可使为不善,其性亦犹是也。"

---

① 选自《孟子》第六篇,全篇共 20 章,集中讨论人性问题,是孟子"性善论"思想较为完整的体现。本部分亦讨论仁义道德与个人修养的问题,对精神与物质、感性与理性、人性与动物性等问题也有所涉及。

② 告子:生平不详,孟子的学生,为深入研究人性之理,反复求教于孟子。

③ 杞(qǐ)柳:杨柳科植物,落叶丛生灌木,枝条柔韧,去皮晒干后可编制箱筐等器物。

④ 桮桊(bēi quān):桮,同"杯",盘、盎、盆、盏等器物的通称。桊,用树条编成的饮器。

⑤ 戕(qiāng)贼:伤害。

⑥ 人:人的本性。

⑦ 湍(tuān):急流的水。《说文》云:"湍,急濑也。"朱熹《集注》云:"波流漾回之貌也。"

⑧ 决:打开缺口排水。

⑨ 信:诚,真,的确。

⑩ 搏而跃之:水受拍打而飞溅起来。搏:拍击。

⑪ 颡(sǎng):额头。

⑫ 激而行之:堵住通道让水倒行。激:堵住水流使之水位提高。可使在山:能使它流上山岗。

Mencius (Excerpts)

Translated by James Legge①

Chapter I

The philosopher Kaou said, "Man's nature is like the *ke* willow, and righteousness② is like a cup or a bowl. The fashioning benevolence③ and righteousness out of man's nature is like the making cups and bowls from the *ke* willow."

Mencius replied, "Can you, leaving untouched the nature of the willow, make with it cups and bowls? You must do violence and injury to the willow, before you can make cups and bowls with it. If you must do violence and injury to the willow in order to make cups and bowls with it, on your principles you must in the same way do violence and injury to humanity in order to fashion④ from it benevolence and righteousness! Your words, alas! would certainly lead all men on to reckon benevolence and righteousness to be calamities⑤."

Chapter II

The philosopher Kaou said, "Man's nature is like water whirling round *in a corner*. Open a passage for it to the east, and it will flow to the east; open a passage for it to the west, and it will flow to the west. Man's nature is indifferent⑥ to good and evil, just as the water is indifferent to the east and west."

---

① 译文选自: Legge, James. 1895. *The Works of Mencius*. Oxford: Clarendon Press, pp. 394 – 414。

② righteousness/ˈraɪtʃəsnəs/ *n*. 正当,正义,正直

③ benevolence/bəˈnevələns/ *n*. 善意,慈悲,善行

④ fashion/ˈfæʃn/ *vt*. 形成,塑造

⑤ calamity/kəˈlæmətɪ/ *n*. 灾难

⑥ indifferent/ɪnˈdɪfrənt/ *adj*. 不感兴趣

Mencius replied, "Water indeed will flow indifferently to the east or west, but will it flow indifferently up or down? The tendency of man's nature to good is like the tendency of water to flow downwards. There are none but have this tendency to good, just as all water flows downwards.

Now by striking water and causing it to leap up, you may make it go over your forehead, and, by damaging and leading it, you may force it up a hill; — but are such movements according to the nature of water? It is the force applied which causes them. When men are made to do what is not good, their nature is dealt with in this way."

（三）

告子曰："生之谓性①。"

孟子曰："生之谓性也，犹白之谓白与？"

曰："然。"

"白羽之白也，犹白雪之白；白雪之白，犹白玉之白与？"

曰："然。"

"然则犬之性犹牛之性；牛之性犹人之性与？"

（四）

告子曰："食色，性也②。仁，内也，非外也③；义，外也，非内也。"

孟子曰："何以谓仁内义外也？"

曰："彼长而我长之④，非有长于我也。犹彼白而我白之，从其白于外也，故谓之外也。"

曰："异于白马之白也，无以异于白人之白也。不识长马之长也，无以异于长人之长与？且谓长者义乎？长之者义乎？"

曰："吾弟则爱之，秦人之弟则不爱也，是以我为悦者也⑤，故谓之内。长楚人之长，亦长吾之长，是以长为悦者也⑥，故谓之外也。"

曰："耆秦人之炙⑦，无以异于耆吾炙，夫物则亦有然者也，然则耆炙亦有外与？"

---

① 生之谓性：天生的东西叫做本性。《荀子·正名》云："生之所以然者谓之性。"生：天生的。
② 食色，性也：饮食男女，这是本性。食：食欲。色：性欲。《礼记礼云篇》云"饮食男女，人之大欲存焉。"
③ 内：生自内心。外：由外因引起的。
④ 长：第一个"长"意为（比我）年长。第二个长意为尊敬。
⑤ 是以我为悦者：这是由我自己内心决定的。
⑥ 是以长为悦者：这是由年长这个外在因素决定的。
⑦ 耆(shì)：同"嗜"，喜欢。炙：烤熟的肉。

Chapter III

The philosopher Kaou said, "Life is what is to be understood by nature."

Mencius asked him, "Do you say that by nature you mean life, just as you say that white is white?"

"Yes, I do," was the reply.

Mencius added, "Is the whiteness of a white feather like that of white snow, and the whiteness of white snow like that of a white gem?"

Kaou again said "Yes."

"Very well," pursued① Mencius. "Is the nature of a dog like the nature of an ox, and the nature of an ox like the nature of a man?"

Chapter IV

The philosopher Kaou said, "To enjoy food and delight in colors is nature. Benevolence is internal and not external; righteousness is external and not internal."

Mencius asked him, "What is the ground of your saying that benevolence is internal and righteousness external?"

He replied, "There is a man older than I, and I give honor to his age. It is not that there is first in me a principle of such reverence② to age. It is just as when there is a white man, and I consider him white; — according as③ he is so externally to me. On this account, I pronounce④ of righteousness that it is external."

Mencius said, "There is no difference between our pronouncing of a white horse to be white and our pronouncing a white man to be white. But is there no difference between the regard with which we

---

① pursue/pəˈsjuː/ v. 追问

② reverence/ˈrevərəns/ n. 尊敬

③ according as: conj. 依照，根据，随…而定，取决于

④ pronounce/prəˈnaʊns/ vt. 宣称，断言

acknowledge the age of an old horse and that with which we acknowledge the age of an old man? And what is it which is called righteousness? — the fact of a man's being old? or the fact of our giving honor to his age?"

Kaou said, "There is my younger brother; — I love him. But the younger brother of a man of Ts'in I do not love; that is, the feeling is determined by myself, and therefore I say that benevolence is internal. On the other hand, I give honor to an old man of Ts'oo, and I also give honor to an old man of my own people; that is, the feeling is determined by the age, and therefore I say that righteousness is external."

Mencius answered him, "Our enjoyment of meat roasted by a man of Ts'in does not differ from our enjoyment of meat roasted by ourselves. Thus, what you insist on takes place also in the case of such things, and will you say likewise that our enjoyment of a roast is external?"

（五）

孟季子问公都子曰①:"何以谓义内也?"

曰:"行吾敬②,故谓之内也。"

"乡人长于伯兄一岁③,则谁敬?"

曰:"敬兄。"

"酌则谁先④?"

曰:"先酌乡人⑤。"

"所敬在此,所长在彼,果在外,非由内也。"

公都子不能答,以告孟子。

孟子曰:"敬叔父乎,敬弟乎? 彼将曰,'敬叔父。'曰,'弟为尸⑥,则谁敬?' 彼将曰:'敬弟。'子曰,'恶在其敬叔父也?' 彼将曰:"在位故也⑦。'子亦曰,'在位故也。庸敬在兄⑧,斯须之敬在乡人⑨。'"

季子闻之,曰:"敬叔父则敬,敬弟则敬,果在外,非由内也。"

公都子曰:"冬日则饮汤⑩,夏日则饮水,然则饮食亦在外也?"

① 孟季子:人名,其人不详。或谓此处之孟季子乃《公孙丑下》篇中孟仲之弟。赵歧注直称"季子"而无"孟",故前人疑原文中本无"孟",季子乃别为一人,或即《告子下》中之季任。

② 行吾敬:表达我的敬意。行:表达,施行。

③ 乡人:本乡人。伯兄:大哥。

④ 酌则谁先:假如在一起喝酒,该先给谁斟酒?

⑤ 酌:给……斟酒。

⑥ 尸:古代祭祀时不用牌位或者神主,更无画像,而用男女儿童为受祭代理人,称为"尸"。尸,主也。朱熹云:"尸,祭祀所主以象神,虽子弟为之,然敬之当如祖考也。"

⑦ 在位故也:处在受恭敬之位的缘故。

⑧ 庸:平常,平时。

⑨ 斯须:这会儿。朱熹《集注》云:"暂时也。"

⑩ 汤:热水。

Chapter V

The disciple Mǎng Ke asked Kung-too, saying, "On what ground is it said that righteousness is internal?"

Kung-too replied, "We therein act out① our feeling of respect, and therefore it is said to be internal."

The other objected, "Suppose the case of a villager older than your elder brother by one year, to which of them would you show the greater respect?"

"To my brother," was the reply.

"But for which of them would you first pour out wine at a feast?"

"For the villager." Mǎng Ke argued, "Now your feeling of reverence rests on the one, and now the honor due to age is rendered to the other; — this is certainly determined by what is without, and does not proceed from② within."

Kung-too was unable to reply, and told the conversation to Mencius. Mencius said, "You should ask him, 'which do you respect most, — your uncle, or your younger brother?' He will answer, 'My uncle.' Ask him again, 'If your younger brother be personating③ a dead ancestor, to which do you show the greater respect, — to him or to your uncle?' He will say, 'To my younger brother.' You can go on, 'But where is the respect due, as you said, to your uncle?' He will reply to this, 'I show the respect to my younger brother, because of the position which he occupies,' and you can likewise say, 'So my respect to the villager is because of the position which he occupies. Ordinarily, my respect is rendered

---

① act out: 将……付诸行动

② proceed from: *vt.* 从……出发,出自,由……产生

③ personate/ˈpɜːsəneɪt/ *vt.* 饰演,冒充

to my elder brother; for a brief season, on occasion, it is rendered to the villager. '"

Mǎng Ke heard this and observed, "When respect is due to my uncle, I respect him, and when respect is due to my younger brother, I respect him; — the thing is certainly determined by what is without, and does not proceed from within."

Kung-too replied, "In winter we drink things hot, in summer we drink things cold; and so, on your principle, eating and drinking also depend on what is external?"

（六）

公都子曰："告子曰：'性无善无不善也。'或曰：'性可以为善，可以为不善；是故文、武兴，则民好善；幽、厉兴，则民好暴①。'或曰：'有性善，有性不善。是故以尧为君而有象，以瞽瞍为父而有舜，以纣为兄之子且以为君，而有微子启、王子比干②。'今曰'性善'，然则彼皆非与？"

孟子曰："乃若其情，则可以为善矣③，乃所谓善也。若夫为不善，非才之罪也④。侧隐之心，人皆有之；羞恶之心，人皆有之⑤；恭敬之心，人皆有之；是非之心，人皆有之。侧隐之心，仁也；羞恶之心，义也；恭敬之心，礼也；是非之心，智也。仁义礼智，非由外铄我也，我固有之也，弗思耳矣⑥。故曰：'求则得之，舍则失之⑦。'或相倍蓰而无算者⑧，不能尽其才者也。《诗》曰：'天生蒸民，有物有则⑨。民之秉彝，好是懿德⑩。'孔子曰：'为此诗者，其知道乎！故有物必有则；民之秉彝也，故好是懿德。'"

---

① 文、武：即周文王、周武王，周代的两个圣王。幽、厉：指周幽王、周厉王，周代两个暴君。
② 微子启：商纣王的庶兄，名启，曾屡次劝谏商纣。周灭商后，称臣于周，后被封于宋，为宋国始祖。王子比干：纣王叔父，因屡次劝谏商纣王，被纣王剖心而死。
③ 乃若：朱熹《集注》云："发语辞。"焦循《正义》引程瑶田《通艺录》云："乃若者，转语也。"情：质性。戴震云："情犹素也，实也。"
④ 才：天性。《说文》云："才，草木之初也。"草木之初曰才，人初生之性亦可曰才。朱熹《集注》云："犹材质，人之能也。"
⑤ 侧隐：同情心。羞恶：羞耻心。
⑥ 铄（shuò）：授予，赠给。弗思：不去思考。
⑦ 求：探求。舍：放弃。
⑧ 或相倍蓰（xǐ）而无算者：有人（同别人比）相差一倍、五倍甚至无数倍。无算：无法计算。
⑨ 有物有则：每一样事物都有它的规律。则：法则，规律。
⑩ 《诗》：指《诗经·大雅·烝民》，是一首赞美周宣王的诗歌。生：生养。蒸民：众民。蒸：《诗》作烝，毛传释为"众"。物：事物。秉：保持，郑笺云："执也。"彝：常。懿（yì）德：美德。

Chapter VI

The disciple Kung-too said, "The philosopher Kaou says, 'Man's nature is neither good nor bad.'" "Some say, 'Man's nature may be made to practice good, and it may be made to practice evil,' and accordingly, under Wan and Woo, the people loved what was good, while under Yew and Le, they loved what was cruel." "Some say, 'The nature of some is good, and the nature of others is bad.' Hence it was that under such a sovereign as Yaou there yet appeared Seang; that with such a father as Koo-sow there yet appeared Shun; and that with Chow for their sovereign, and the son of their elder brother besides, there were found K'e, the viscount① of Wei, and the prince Pe-kan'. And now you say, 'The nature is good.' Then are all those wrong?"

Mencius said, "From the feelings proper to② it, it is constituted for the practice of what is good. This is what I mean in saying that the nature is good. If men do what is not good, the blame cannot be imputed③ to their natural powers. The feeling of commiseration④ belongs to all men; so does that of shame and dislike; and that of reverence and respect; and that of approving and disapproving. The feeling of commiseration implies the principle of benevolence; that of shame and dislike, the principle of righteousness; that of reverence and respect, the principle of propriety⑤; and that of approving and disapproving, the principle of knowledge. Benevolence, righteousness, propriety, and knowledge are not

---

① viscount/'vaɪkaʊnt/ n. 子爵
② proper to 恰当的
③ impute/ɪm'pjuːt/ v. 归罪于,归因于
④ commiseration/kəˌmɪzə'reɪʃn/ n. 怜悯,同情
⑤ propriety/prə'praɪətɪ/ n. 适当,正当,得体

infused into us from without. We are certainly furnished with[①] them. And a different view is simply from want of reflection. Hence it is said：'Seek and you will find them. Neglect and you will lose them.' Men differ from one another in regard to them; — some as much again as others, some five times as much, and some to an incalculable amount：— it is because they cannot carry out fully their natural powers. It is said in the *Book of Poetry*：

'Heaven, in producing mankind,

Gave them their various faculties and relations with their specific laws.

These are the invariable rules of nature for all to hold,

And all love this admirable virtue.'

Confucius said, 'The maker of this ode knew indeed the principle of our nature!' We may thus see that every faculty and relation must have its law, and since there are invariable rules for all to hold, they consequently love this admirable virtue."

---

① be furnished with 备有,配有

（十）

孟子曰："鱼，我所欲也，熊掌，亦我所欲也；二者不可得兼，舍鱼而取熊掌者也。生，亦我所欲也，义，亦我所欲也；二者不可得兼，舍生而取义者也。生亦我所欲，所欲有甚于生者，故不为苟得也①；死亦我所恶，所恶有甚于死者，故患有所不辟也。如使人之所欲莫甚于生，则凡可以得生者，何不用也？使人之所恶莫甚于死者，则凡可以辟患者，何不为也？由是则生而有不用也，由是则可以辟患而有不为也，是故所欲有甚于生者，所恶有甚于死者。非独贤者有是心也，人皆有之，贤者能勿丧耳②。一箪食，一豆羹③，得之则生，弗得则死，呼尔而与之，行道之人弗受④；蹴尔而与之⑤，乞人不屑也。万钟则不辨礼义而受之⑥。万钟于我何加焉？为宫室之美、妻妾之奉、所识穷乏者得我欤⑦？乡为身死而不受⑧，今为宫室之美为之；乡为身死而不受，今为妻妾之奉为之；乡为身死而不受，今为所识穷乏者得我而为之，是亦不可以已乎！此之谓失其本心。"

---

① 苟：随便。

② 非独：不只是。丧：丧失。

③ 箪：盛饭的竹器。豆：古代一种盛食物的器皿，形似高脚盘。

④ 呼尔：大声叫喊，呵斥，吆喝。赵歧注云"咄啐之貌也。"行道之人：路上的行人。

⑤ 蹴（cù）：踢，踩踏。朱熹《集注》云："践踏也。"

⑥ 钟：古代量器，六石四斗为一钟。

⑦ 得：通"德"，此处作动词，感激。

⑧ 乡：通"向"，以往。

Chapter X

Mencius said, "I like fish and I also like bear's paws. If I cannot have the two together, I will let the fish go, and take the bear's paw. So, I like life, and I also like righteousness. If I cannot keep the two together, I will let life go and choose righteousness.

"I like life indeed, but there is that which I like more than life, and therefore, I will not seek to possess it by any improper ways. I dislike death indeed, but there is that which I dislike more than death, and therefore there are occasions when I will not avoid danger.

"If among the things which man likes there were nothing which he liked more than life, why should he not use every means by which he could preserve it? If among the things which man dislikes there were nothing which he disliked more than death, why should he not do everything by which he could avoid danger?

"There are cases when men by a certain course might preserve life, and they do not employ it; when by certain things they might avoid danger, and they will not do them.

"Therefore, men have that which they like more than life, and that which they dislike more than death. They are not men of distinguished talents and virtue only who have this mental nature. All men have it; what belongs to such men is simply that they do not lose it.

"Here are a small basket of rice and a platter① of soup, and the case is one in which the getting them will preserve life, and the want of them will be death; — if they are offered with an insulting voice even a tramper will not receive them, or if you first tread upon them, even a beggar will not stoop to take them.

———————————

① platter/plætə/ *n.* 大盘子

"And yet a man will accept of ten thousand *chung*, without any consideration of propriety or righteousness. What can the ten thousand *chung* add to him? When he takes them, is it not that he may obtain beautiful mansions, that he may secure the services of wives and concubines①, or that the poor and needy of his acquaintance may be helped by him?

"In the former case the offered bounty② was not received, though it would have saved from death, and now the emolument③ is taken for the sake of beautiful mansions. The bounty that would have preserved from death was not received, and the emolument is taken to get the service of wives and concubines. The bounty that would have saved from death was not received, and the emolument is taken that one's poor and needy acquaintance may be helped by him. Was it then not possible likewise to decline this? This is a case of what is called 'Losing the proper nature of one's mind.'"

---

① concubine/ˈkɔŋkjubaɪn/ *n*. 妾,妃子

② bounty/ˈbaʊntɪ/ *n*. 慷慨,慷慨的赠予物

③ emolument/ɪˈmɒljumənt/ *n*. 薪资,报酬,〈古〉优势

（十一）

孟子曰："仁，人心也；义，人路也。舍其路而弗由^①，放其心而不知求^②，哀哉！人有鸡犬放，则知求之；有放心而不知求。学问之道无他，求其放心而已矣。"

（十二）

孟子曰："今有无名之指，屈而不信^③，非疾痛害事也^④，如有能信之者，则不远秦、楚之路，为指之不若人也^⑤。指不若人，则知恶之；心不若人，则不知恶，此之谓不知类也^⑥。"

（十三）

孟子曰："拱把之桐梓^⑦，人苟欲生之，皆知所以养之者。至于身，而不知所以养之者，岂爱身不若桐梓哉？弗思甚也。"

（十四）

孟子曰："人之于身也，兼所爱。兼所爱，则兼所养也。无尺寸之肤不爱焉，则无尺寸之肤不养也。所以考其善不善者，岂有他哉？于己取之而已矣。体有贵贱，有小大。无以小害大，无以贱害贵^⑧。养其小者为小人，养其大者为大人。今有场师^⑨，舍其梧槚^⑩，养其樲棘^⑪，则为贱场师焉。

---

① 由：经过，通过。
② 放：放弃，丧失。求：寻求。
③ 信：通"伸"。无名之指，屈而不信：无名指弯曲而不能伸直。
④ 害事：妨碍做事。
⑤ 不若人：不及别人。
⑥ 不知类：不知轻重。朱熹《集注》云："言不知轻重之等也。"
⑦ 拱把：赵歧注云："拱，合两手也；把，以一手把之也。"言树尚细小。
⑧ 无以小害大，无以贱害贵：朱熹集注云："贱而小者，口腹也；贵而大者，心志也。"
⑨ 场师：古代的园艺师。
⑩ 梧槚(jiǎ)：果木名，梧桐树和山楸树，两者皆良木，所以并称，比喻良才。
⑪ 樲(èr)棘：果木名，即酸枣和荆棘，两者皆无用之木，所以并称，比喻贱才。

Chapter XI

Mencius said, "Benevolence is man's mind, and righteousness is man's path.

"How lamentable① is it to neglect the path and not pursue it, to lose this mind and not know to seek it again!

"When men's fowls and dogs are lost, they know to seek for them again, but they lose their mind, and do not know to seek for it.

"The great end of learning is nothing else but to seek for the lost mind."

Chapter XII

Mencius said, "Here is a man whose fourth finger is bent and cannot be stretched out straight. It is not painful, nor does it incommode② his business, and yet if there be any one who can make it straight, he will not think the way from Ts'in to Ts'oo far to go to him; — because his finger is not like the finger of other people.

"When a man's finger is not like those of other people, he knows to feel dissatisfied, but if his mind be not like that of other people, he does not know to feel dissatisfaction. This is called — 'Ignorance of the relative importance of things.'"

Chapter XIII

Mencius said, "Anybody who wishes to cultivate the *t'ung* or the *tsze*, which may be grasped with both hands, perhaps with one, knows by what means to nourish③ them. In the case of their own persons, men do not know by what means to nourish them. Is it to be supposed that their regard of their own persons is inferior to their

---

① lamentable/ˈlæməntəbl/*adj*. 可悲的,哀伤的,可怜的

② incommode/ˌɪnkəˈməʊd/*vt*.(使)感不便,添麻烦,打扰

③ nourish/ˈnʌrɪʃ/*v*. 滋养,给营养

regard for a *t'ung* or a *tsze*? Their want of reflection is extreme."

Chapter XIV

Mencius said, "There is no part of himself which a man does not love, and as he loves all, so he must nourish all. There is not an inch of skin which he does not love, and so there is not an inch of skin which he will not nourish. For examining whether his way of nourishing be good or not, what other rule is there but this, that he determine by reflecting on himself where it should be applied?

"Some parts of the body are noble, and some ignoble①; some great, and some small. The great must not be injured for the small, nor the noble for the ignoble. He who nourishes the little belonging to him is a little man, and he who nourishes the great is a great man.

"Here is a plantation keeper, who neglects his *woo* and *kea*, and cultivates his sour wild date trees; — he is a poor plantation keeper.

---

① ignoble/ɪgˈnəubl/ *adj*. 平民的,卑贱的,卑鄙的,不光彩的

养其一指而失其肩背,而不知也,则为狼疾人也①。饮食之人,则人贱之矣,为其养小以失大也。饮食之人无有失也,则口腹岂适为尺寸之肤哉②?"

---

① 狼疾:即"狼藉",糊涂。
② 适:通"啻"(chì),但,只。

"He who nourishes one of his fingers，neglecting his shoulders or his back，without knowing that he is doing so，is a man who resembles① a hurried wolf. A man who only eats and drinks is counted mean② by others；— because he nourishes what is little to the neglect of what is great. If a man，fond of his eating and drinking，were not to neglect what is of more importance，how should his mouth and belly be considered as no more than an inch of skin?"

---

① resemble/rɪ'zembl/ v. 与……相似，像
② mean/miːn/ adj. 卑鄙的，卑贱的

【推荐阅读】

一、中文版本及注疏

戴震(撰),何文光(整理).孟子字义疏证.北京:中华书局,1982 年。

金良年.孟子译注.上海:上海古籍出版社,2004 年。

焦循(撰),沈文倬(点校).孟子正义.北京:中华书局,1987 年。

万丽华、蓝旭译注.中华经典藏书·孟子.北京:中华书局,2006 年。

王治心.孟子研究.上海:群学社,1928 年。

杨伯峻.孟子导读.成都:巴蜀书社,1987 年。

杨伯峻.孟子译注.北京:中华书局,1984 年。

杨大膺.孟子学说研究.北京:中华书局,1937 年。

赵岐(注),孙奭(疏),黄侃(句读).孟子注疏.上海:上海古籍出版社,
    1990 年。

赵岐(注),孙奭(疏).孟子注疏解经.北京:中华书局,1980 年。

二、英文译本

Bloom,Irene. 2009. *Mencius*, *edited and with an introduction by
    Philip J. Ivanhoe*. New York:Columbia University Press.

Collie,David. 1828. *The Chinese Classical Work Commonly Called
    The Four Books*. Malacca:The Mission Press.

Lau,D.C. 1970. *Mencius*. London/New York/Victoria/Toronto/
    Auckland:Penguin Group.

Legge,James. 1895. *The Works of Mencius*. Oxford:Clarendon
    Press.

赵甄陶,张文庭,周定之英译.大中华文库汉英对照·孟子(*Mencius*).
    长沙:湖南人民出版社,1999 版。

第六单元 《史记》

【导言】

《史记》原名《太史公书》，是中国历史上第一部纪传体通史，由西汉著名史学家司马迁撰写完成。全书包括十二本纪（"以序帝王"）、十表（"以系时事"）、八书（"以详制度"）、三十世家（"以记侯国"）、七十列传（"以志人物"），共一百三十篇，五十二万余字，记载了上至黄帝时代，下至汉武帝元狩元年（公元前 122 年）共 3000 多年的历史，被列为"二十四史"之首，与《汉书》《后汉书》《三国志》合称"前四史"。《史记》"究天人之际，通古今之变，成一家之言"，不仅是一部优秀的历史著作，在中国文学史上亦占有重要地位，被鲁迅誉为"史家之绝唱，无韵之《离骚》"。

司马迁（前 145 或前 135—前 87 年）字子长，左冯翊夏阳（今陕西韩城西南）人，西汉史学家和文学家。十岁开始习学古文书传，曾师从董仲舒和孔安国。二十岁出京师长安遍游江淮流域和中原。返京后担任郎中，为汉武帝的侍卫和扈从，曾多次随驾西巡，并奉命出使巴蜀。元封三年（前 108 年）任太史令，继承父业，著述历史，于汉武帝太初元年（公元前 104 年）开始编写《史记》。天汉二年（前 99 年），因其为投降匈奴的李陵辩护触怒汉武帝，被处以宫刑。后获赦出狱，任中书令，"隐忍苟活"，继续著书，完成了《史记》这部历史巨著。

魏晋时期，《史记》以传抄形式广为流传，南朝宋裴骃著《史记集解》与唐代司马贞的《史记索隐》和张守节的《史记正义》，为现存最早最有影响的"《史记》三家注"。北宋开始把三家注散列于正文之下，合为一编。现存最早的本子有南宋黄善夫刻本，经商务印书馆影印，收入百衲本《二十四史》。此后较有影响者有明嘉靖、万历年间南北监刻的《二十一史》，毛氏汲古阁刻的《十七史》和清乾隆年间武英殿刻的《二十四史》。其中武英殿本最为通行，有各种翻刻或影印本。清同治年间，金陵书局刊行《史记集解索隐正义合刻本》一百三十卷，经张文虎根据钱泰吉校本和他自己所见各种旧刻古本、时本加以考订，择善而从，校刊精审，是清朝后期的善本。

　　《史记》英文节译始于十九世纪末。利昂·罗斯尼（Lion de Rosny）和赫伯特·艾伦（H. J. Allen）曾尝试翻译《史记》。1894年，艾伦翻译了《史记》中的《五帝的起源》在《皇家亚洲文会会刊》发表。此后，一些学者陆续节译《史记》中的部分内容。《史记》的主要译者有华兹生（Burton Watson）、倪豪士（William H. Nienhauser, Jr.），以及杨宪益和戴乃迭（Gladys B. Tayler）夫妇。1951年，华兹生的硕士论文即是《史记》卷124的译文。华兹生1956年开始翻译《史记》，于1961、1969、1993年出版了三个译本，共翻译了《史记》中的80卷，为已经出版的《史记》英文译本中最为完整者。倪豪士于二十世纪80年代末开始着手《史记》英译，他相继与郑再发、罗伯特·雷诺兹（Robert Reynolds）、陈照明、吕宗力等合作，翻译出版了《史记·汉以前的本纪》(1995)、《史记·汉以前的列传》(1995)、《史记·汉本纪》(2002)、《史记·汉以前的世家（上）》(2006)、《史记·汉代的列传（上）》(2008)五卷。

项羽本纪(节选)①

　　沛公军霸上②,未得与项羽相见。沛公左司马曹无伤使人言于项羽曰:"沛公欲王关中③,使子婴为相④,珍宝尽有之。"项羽大怒,曰:"旦日飨士卒⑤,为击破沛公军!"当是时,项羽兵四十万,在新丰鸿门⑥,沛公兵十万,在霸上。范增说项羽曰⑦:"沛公居山东时⑧,贪于财货,好美姬⑨。今入关,财物无所取,妇女无所幸,此其志不在小。吾令人望其气⑩,皆为龙虎,成五采⑪,此天子气也。急击勿失。"

　　楚左尹项伯者⑫,项羽季父也⑬,素善留侯张良。张良是时从沛公⑭,项伯乃夜驰之沛公军⑮,私见张良,具告以事⑯,欲呼张良与俱去⑰,曰:"毋从俱死也。"张良曰:"臣为韩王送沛公⑱,沛公今事有急,亡去不义⑲,不可不语。"

---

① 本节汉语原文根据中华书局 1999 年版《史记》(简体字本)校改。
② 军:驻军。霸上:地名,即霸水之西的白鹿原,在今陕西西安东。
③ 欲王:想要在关中称王。
④ 子婴:一说秦二世之兄,一说为秦二世之侄,一说为秦始皇之弟,二世之叔。二世三年(前207 年)八月,赵高杀胡亥,另立子婴为三世。子婴与其二子合力杀掉赵高,灭其族,为帝46 日后刘邦入关,子婴遂降刘邦。
⑤ 旦日:明天。飨(xiǎng):用酒食慰劳。
⑥ 新丰:地名,故城在今陕西临潼东北。鸿门:在新丰东十七里,旧大道北下阪口名也,今名项王营。
⑦ 说(shuì):说服,劝说。
⑧ 山东:崤(xiáo)山的东边,泛指旧时的东方六国之地。
⑨ 好美姬:喜爱美女。
⑩ 望其气:望,观看。气:云气,云的形状、色彩。望气是古代方士观察云气以预知人和事吉凶福祸的迷信方法。
⑪ 龙虎、五采:指云气的纹样,这是天子之气。
⑫ 左尹:楚国最高长官令尹的副职。
⑬ 季父:叔父,父亲的幼弟。
⑭ 从:跟随。
⑮ 夜驰:连夜骑马。
⑯ 具告以事:把事情详细地告诉了他。
⑰ 与俱去:和他一起离开。
⑱ 为韩王送沛公:指韩公子成,张良先人五世相韩,他曾请项梁立成为韩王,自为司徒。刘邦西进,韩成留守阳翟,故有此说。送,这里意为"跟从"。
⑲ 亡去:逃走。

The Basic Annals of Hsiang Yu (Excerpt)

Translated by Burton Watson[1]

The governor of P'ei was camped at Pa-shang and had not yet had an opportunity to meet with Hsiang Yu. Ts'ao Wu-shang, marshal[2] of the left to the governor of P'ei sent a messenger to report to Hsiang Yu, saying, "The governor of P'ei is planning to become king of the area within the Pass, employ Tzu-ying as his prime minister, and keep possession of all the precious articles and treasures of the capital." Hsiang Yu was in a rage. "Tomorrow," he announced, "I shall feast my soldiers and then we will attack and crush[3] the governor of P'ei."

At this time Hsiang Yu had a force of 400,000 men encamped at Hung-men in Hsin-feng. The governor of P'ei with a force of 100,000, was at Pa-shang. Fan Tseng counseled[4] Hsiang Yu, saying, "When the governor of P'ei was living east of the mountains he was greedy for possessions and delighted in beautiful girls. But now that he has entered the Pass he has not taken a single thing, nor has he dallied[5] with any of the wives or maidens. This proves that his mind is not set upon minor joys. I have sent men to observe the sky over the place where he is encamped, and they all found it full of shapes like dragons and tigers and colored with five colors. These are the signs of a Son of Heaven. You must attack him at once and

---

① 译文选自 Watson, B, tr. 1961. *Records of the Grand Historian of China*. New York & London: Columbia University Press, pp. 49 – 55。

② marshal/'mɑːʃl/ *n*. (陆军)元帅,最高指挥官,王室最高军务官

③ crush/krʌʃ/ *v*. 压碎;镇压,制服

④ counsel/'kaʊnsl/ *v*. 劝告,忠告;协商,讨论

⑤ dally/'dælɪ/ *v*. 嬉戏,调情

not lose this chance!"

Hsiang Po, the Ch'u commander of the left, was an uncle of Hsiang Yu and for a long time had been good friends with Chang Liang, the marquis① of Liu. Chang Liang was at this time serving under the governor of P'ei. That night Hsiang Po galloped② on horse to the camp of the governor of P'ei and visited Chang Liang in secret, telling him of Hsiang Yu's plans and begging Chang Liang to come away with him. "Do not throw your life away along with all the others!" he urged.

"I have been sent by the king of Han to accompany the governor of P'ei." Chang Liang replied. "Now when he is faced with these difficulties, it would not be right for me to run away and leave him. I must report to him what you have told me."

---

① marquis/'mɑːkwɪs/ n. 侯爵
② gallop/'gæləp/ v. 疾驰，飞奔

　　良乃入，具告沛公。沛公大惊，曰："为之奈何①?"张良曰："谁为大王此计者?"曰："鲰生说我曰②'距关③，毋内诸侯④，秦地可尽王也'，故听之。"良曰："料大王士卒足以当项王乎?"沛公默然，曰："固不如也，且为之奈何?"张良曰："请往谓项伯，言沛公不敢背项王也。"沛公曰："君安与项伯有故?"张良曰："秦时与臣游⑤，项伯杀人，臣活之。今事有急，故幸来告良。"沛公曰："孰与君少长⑥?"良曰："长于臣。"沛公曰："君为我呼入⑦，吾得兄事之。"张良出，要项伯⑧。项伯即入见沛公。沛公奉卮酒为寿⑨，约为婚姻⑩，曰："吾入关，秋毫不敢有所近⑪，籍吏民⑫，封府库⑬，而待将军。所以遣将守关者，备他盗之出入与非常也⑭。日夜望将军至，岂敢反乎! 愿伯具言臣之不敢倍德也⑮。"项伯许诺。谓沛公曰："旦日不可不蚤自来谢项王⑯。"沛公曰："诺。"于是项伯复夜去⑰，至军中，具以沛公言报项王。因言曰⑱："沛公不先破关中，公岂敢入乎? 今人有大功而击之，不义也，不如因善遇之。"项王许诺。

---

① 为之奈何：这件事怎么办?

② 鲰(zōu)生：见识短浅的小子。鲰：小杂鱼，此以喻浅妄无知。说(shuì)：劝。

③ 距：通"拒"，守住；关：函谷关。

④ 毋内诸侯：不要放诸侯进来。内，通"纳"。

⑤ 游：交往。

⑥ 孰与君少长：他和你年龄谁大谁小。

⑦ 君为我呼入：你替我请他进来。

⑧ 要：通"邀"，邀请。

⑨ 奉：恭敬地用手捧着。卮(zhī)：古代盛酒的器皿。

⑩ 约为婚姻：和项伯约定结为儿女亲家。

⑪ 秋毫：鸟兽在秋天新长的细毛，比喻微小的事物。

⑫ 籍吏民：将官民的户口登记在册。籍：登记。

⑬ 封府库：封闭了仓库。

⑭ 非常：意外的变故。

⑮ 倍德：背叛恩德。倍：通"背"，违背，背叛。

⑯ 蚤：通"早"。谢：谢罪，赔礼。

⑰ 复夜去：连夜离去。

⑱ 因言：趁机。

Chang Liang then went and reported the situation in full to the governor of P'ei. "What shall we do?" exclaimed the governor in great consternation①.

"Who was it who thought up this plan of action for you?" asked Chang Liang.

"Some fool advised me that if I guarded the Pass and did not let the other leaders enter, I could rule the entire region of Ch'in, and so I followed his plan," he replied.

"Do you believe that you have enough soldiers to stand up against Hsiang Yu?" Chang Liang asked.

The governor was silent for a while, and then said, "No, certainly not. But what should we do now?"

"You must let me go and explain to Hsiang Po," said Chang Liang, "and tell him that you would not dare to be disloyal to Hsiang Yu."

"How do you happen to be friends with Hsiang Po?" asked the governor.

"We knew each other in the time of Ch'in," replied Chang Liang, "and once when Hsiang Po killed a man I saved his life. Now that we are in trouble, he has for that reason been good enough to come and report to me."

"Is he older or younger than you?" asked the governor.

"He is older than me," replied Chang Liang.

"Call him in for me," said the governor, "and I will treat② him as I would an elder brother."

Chang Liang went out and urged Hsiang Po to enter. Hsiang Po came in to see the governor of P'ei who offered him a cup of wine

---

① consternation/ˌkɒnstəˈneɪʃn/ n. 惊愕，惊骇
② treat/triːt/ v. 请客，招待，对待

and drank to his long life, swearing an oath of friendship. "Since I entered the Pass," he said, "I have not dared to lay a finger on a single thing. I have preserved the registers[①] of the officials and people and sealed up the storehouses, awaiting the arrival of General Hsiang Yu. The reason I sent officers to guard the Pass was to prevent thieves from getting in and to prepare for any emergency. Day and night I have looked forward to the arrival of the general. How would I dare be disloyal to him? I beg you to report to him in full and tell him that I would not think of turning my back upon his kindness!"

Hsiang Po agreed to do so, adding, "You must come early tomorrow and apologize in person to General Hsiang." "I shall," promised the governor, and with this Hsiang Po went back out into the night.

When he reached his own camp, he reported to Hsiang Yu all that the governor had said. "If the governor of P'ei had not first conquered the land within the Pass how would you have dared to enter?" he said. "When a man has done you a great service it would not be right to attack him. It is better to treat him as a friend." Hsiang Yu agreed to this.

---

① register/'redʒɪstə/ n. 记录，登记，注册

　　沛公旦日从百余骑来见项王①,至鸿门,谢曰:"臣与将军勠力而攻秦②,将军战河北③,臣战河南,然不自意能先入关破秦④,得复见将军于此。今者有小人之言,令将军与臣有郤⑤。"项王曰:"此沛公左司马曹无伤言之;不然,籍何以至此。"项王即日因留沛公与饮。项王、项伯东向坐⑥,亚父南向坐⑦。亚父者,范增也。沛公北向坐,张良西向侍。范增数目项王⑧,举所佩玉玦以示之者三⑨,项王默然不应。范增起,出召项庄⑩,谓曰:"君王为人不忍⑪。若入前为寿⑫,寿毕,请以剑舞,因击沛公于坐,杀之。不者⑬,若属皆且为所虏⑭。"庄则入为寿。寿毕,曰:"君王与沛公饮,军中无以为乐⑮,请以剑舞。"项王曰:"诺。"项庄拔剑起舞,项伯亦拔剑起舞,常以身翼蔽沛公⑯,庄不得击。于是张良至军门,见樊哙⑰。樊哙曰:"今日之事何如?"良曰:"甚急。今者项庄拔剑舞,其意常在沛公也。"哙曰:"此迫矣⑱,臣请入,与之同命⑲。"

---

① 从:带领随从。
② 勠力:合力。
③ 河北:黄河以北。
④ 不自意:自己没有料到。
⑤ 郤(xì):同"隙"。
⑥ 东向坐:朝东坐。战国秦汉时期除升殿升堂仍南向之外,其他场合多以东向为尊,其次为南向、北向,最下为西向。于此可见项羽之倨傲。
⑦ 亚父:项羽对范增的敬称,言对其侍奉的礼数仅次于父。
⑧ 数(shuò)目:多次使眼色。
⑨ 玦(jué):有缺口的玉环。范增举玦示意项羽下决心杀掉刘邦。
⑩ 项庄:项羽的堂兄弟。
⑪ 不忍:不狠心。
⑫ 若:尔,你。寿:敬酒。
⑬ 不者:不这样。不,通"否"。
⑭ 若属:尔等,你们。且:将。
⑮ 无以为乐(lè):什么可以用来作为娱乐的。
⑯ 翼蔽:像鸟儿张开翅膀那样用身体掩护。
⑰ 樊哙(kuài):吕后的妹夫,刘邦的开国功臣,沛人,原以屠狗为业,因战功封舞阳侯。
⑱ 迫:危急。
⑲ 同命:(与刘邦)同生死。

The next day the governor of P'ei accompanied by a hundred some horsemen, came to visit Hsiang Yu. When he reached Hsiang Yu's camp at Hung-men, he made his apologies, saying, "You and I have joined forces to attack Ch'in, you fighting north of the Yellow River, I fighting south. Quite beyond my expectation it happened that I was able to enter the Pass first, conquer Ch'in, and meet with you again here. Now it seems that some worthless person has been spreading talk① and trying to cause dissension② between us."

"It is your own marshal of the left, Ts'ao Wu-shang, who has been doing the talking," replied Hsiang Yu. "If it were not for him, how would I ever have doubted you?"

On the same day Hsiang Yu invited the governor of P'ei to remain and drink with him. Hsiang Yu and Hsiang Po as hosts sat facing east. Fan Tseng (whose other name was Ya-fu) took the place of honor facing south, while the governor of P'ei sat facing north with Chang Liang, as his attendant, facing west. Fan Tseng from time to time eyed Hsiang Yu and three times lifted up the jade pendant③ in the form of a broken ring which he wore and showed it to Yu, hinting that he should "break once and for all④ with the governor, but Hsiang Yu sat silent and did not respond. Fan Tseng then rose and left the tent and, summoning Hsiang Yu's cousin, Hsiang Chuang, said to him, "Our lord is too kind-heated a man. Go back in and ask to propose a toast, and when the toast is finished, request to be allowed to perform a sword dance. Then attack the governor of P'ei and kill him where he sits. If you don't, you and all of us will end up as his prisoners!"

---

① talk/tɔːk/ *n.* 传闻,谣言
② dissension/dɪˈsenʃn/ *n.* 意见不合,倾轧,纠纷
③ pendant/ˈpendənt/ *n.* 垂饰,挂件
④ once and for all 一劳永逸地,永远地

Hsiang Chuang entered and proposed a toast. When the toast was finished, he said, "Our lord and the governor of P'ei are pleased to drink together but I fear that, this being an army camp, we have nothing to offer by way of entertainment. I beg therefore to be allowed to present a sword dance." "Proceed," said Hsiang Yu, whereupon Hsiang Chuang drew his sword and began to dance. But Hsiang Po also rose and danced, constantly shielding and protecting the governor of P'ei with his own body so that Hsiang Chuang could not attack him.

With this, Chang Liang left and went to the gate of the camp to see Fan K'uai. "How are things proceeding today?" asked Fan K'uai.

"The situation is very grave," replied Chang Liang. "Now Hsiang Chuang has drawn his sword and is dancing, always with his eyes set on the governor of P'ei!"

"This is serious indeed!" said Fan K'uai. "I beg you to let me go in and share the fate of the rest!"

　　哙即带剑拥盾入军门①。交戟之卫士欲止不内②，樊哙侧其盾以撞，卫士仆地，哙遂入，披帷西向立③，瞋目视项王④，头发上指，目眦尽裂⑤。项王按剑而跽曰⑥："客何为者⑦？"张良曰："沛公之参乘樊哙者也⑧。"项王曰："壮士，赐之卮酒。"则与斗卮酒⑨。哙拜谢，起，立而饮之。项王曰："赐之彘肩⑩。"则与一生彘肩。樊哙覆其盾于地，加彘肩上，拔剑切而啖之⑪。项王曰："壮士，能复饮乎？"樊哙曰："臣死且不避，卮酒安足辞！夫秦王有虎狼之心，杀人如不能举，刑人如不恐胜⑫，天下皆叛之。怀王与诸将约曰'先破秦入咸阳者王之⑬。'今沛公先破秦入咸阳，毫毛不敢有所近，封闭宫室，还军霸上⑭，以待大王来。故遣将守关者，备他盗出入与非常也。劳苦而功高如此，未有封侯之赏，而听细说⑮，欲诛有功之人。此亡秦之续耳⑯，窃为大王不取也。"项王未有以应，曰："坐。"樊哙从良坐⑰。坐须臾，沛公起如厕，因招樊哙出。

---

① 拥盾：持盾于身前。拥：前持。
② 交戟之卫士：卫士将戟交叉举起，以示禁止入内。
③ 披帷西向立：揭开门帘，在西面对着项羽站立。
④ 瞋(chēn)目：瞪大眼睛。
⑤ 目眦(zì)：眼眶。
⑥ 跽(jì)：古人席地跪坐，臀部离开小腿，身子挺直，叫做跽。
⑦ 何为：为何，干什么的。
⑧ 参乘(shèng)：古代在王侯右侧充当警卫的人。
⑨ 斗卮酒：大酒杯。
⑩ 彘(zhì)肩：猪的前腿。
⑪ 啖(dàn)：大口吃。
⑫ 杀人如不能举，刑人如不恐胜：杀人唯恐不能尽，用刑唯恐不够。举：完全。胜：尽。
⑬ 王之：封作王。
⑭ 还：退回。
⑮ 细说：小人的谗言。
⑯ 此亡秦之续耳：这是灭亡了的秦朝的继续。
⑰ 从良坐：挨着张良坐下。

Fan K'uai buckled① on his sword, grasped his shield, and entered the gate of the camp. The sentries② standing with crossed spears tried to stop him from entering but, tipping his shield to either side, he knocked the men to the ground. Entering the camp, he went and pulled back the curtain of the tent and stood facing west, glaring fixedly at Hsiang Yu. His hair stood on end and his eyes blazed with fire.

Hsiang Yu put his hand on his sword and raised himself up on one knee. "Who is our guest?" he asked.

"Fan K'uai, the carriage attendant of the governor of P'ei." announced Chang Liang.

"He is a stouthearted③ fellow," said Hsiang Yu. "Give him a cup of wine!" A large cup of wine was passed to Fan K'uai, who knelt and accepted it, and then rose again and drank it standing up. "Give him a shoulder of pork," ordered Hsiang Yu, and he was given a piece of parboiled④ pork shoulder. Fan K'uai placed his shield upside down on the ground, put the pork shoulder on top of it, drew his sword, and began to cut and eat the meat.

"You are a brave man," said Hsiang Yu. "Can you drink some more?"

"I would not hesitate if you offered me death! Why should I refuse a cup of wine?" he replied. "The king of Ch'in had the heart of a tiger and a wolf. He killed men as though he thought he could never finish, he punished men as though he were afraid he would never get around to them all, and the whole world revolted⑤ against

---

① buckle/'bʌkl/ v. 扣住,扣紧
② sentry/'sentrɪ/ n. 哨兵
③ stouthearted/ˌstaut'hɑːtɪd/ adj. 勇敢的,无畏的
④ parboil/'pɑːbɔɪl/ v. 把……煮成半熟
⑤ revolt/rɪ'vəult/ v. 反叛,叛乱,反抗

him. King Huai of Ch'u made a promise with all the leaders that whoever defeated Ch'in first and entered the capital of Hsien-yang should become its king. Now the governor of P'ei has defeated Ch'in and entered Hsien-yang ahead of all others. He has not dared to lay a finger on the slightest thing, but has closed up and sealed the palace rooms and returned to Pa-shang to encamp and await your arrival. The reason he sent officers to guard the Pass was to prevent thieves from getting in and to prepare for an emergency. After suffering great hardship and winning such merit①, he has not been rewarded by the grant of a fief② and title. Instead you have listened to some worthless talk and are about to punish a man of merit. This is no more than a repetition of the fated Ch'in. If I may be so bold, I advise you not to go through with③ it!"

Hsiang Yu, having no answer to this, said "Sit down!" Fan K'uai took a seat next to Chang Liang. After they had been seated for a while, the governor of P'ei got up and went to the toilet, summoning Fan K'uai to go with him.

---

① merit/ˈmerɪt/ *n*. 功绩
② fief/fiːf/ *n*. 封地
③ go through with 完成，把……进行到底

　　沛公已出,项王使都尉陈平召沛公①。沛公曰:"今者出,未辞也,为之奈何?"樊哙曰:"大行不顾细谨②,大礼不辞小让③。如今人方为刀俎④,我为鱼肉,何辞为?"于是遂去。乃令张良留谢。良问曰:"大王来何操⑤?"曰:"我持白璧一双,欲献项王,玉斗一双⑥,欲与亚父,会其怒⑦,不敢献。公为我献之。"张良曰:"谨诺。"当是时,项王军在鸿门下,沛公军在霸上,相去四十里。沛公则置车骑⑧,脱身独骑,与樊哙、夏侯婴、靳强、纪信等四人持剑盾步走,从郦山下⑨,道芷阳间行⑩。沛公谓张良曰:"从此道至吾军,不过二十里耳。度我至军中,公乃入。"沛公已去,间至军中⑪。张良入谢,曰:"沛公不胜桮杓⑫,不能辞。谨使臣良奉白璧一双,再拜献大王足下⑬,玉斗一双,再拜奉大将军足下。"项王曰:"沛公安在⑭?"良曰:"闻大王有意督过之⑮,脱身独去,已至军矣。"项王则受璧,置之坐上。亚父受玉斗,置之地,拔剑撞而破之,曰:"唉!竖子不足与谋⑯。夺项王天下者,必沛公也,吾属今为之虏矣。"沛公至军,立诛杀曹无伤。

① 使:派。陈平:阳武(今河南兰考境内)人,原为项羽部下,后投刘邦为谋士。召:叫。
② 大行:大事。细谨:小节。
③ 小让:细小的礼让。
④ 刀俎(zǔ):菜刀和砧板。
⑤ 何操:带了什么。
⑥ 玉斗:玉制酒器。
⑦ 会:碰上。
⑧ 置车骑:丢弃来时随从的百余骑车马。这是为了不惊动里面的项羽、范增。置:抛弃,留下。
⑨ 郦山:在今陕西临潼东南,地处当时的鸿门西南,霸上之东北。
⑩ 道芷阳间行:取道经芷阳的小路。芷阳:秦县名,在郦山西侧,故城在今陕西长安东。间行:抄小路走。
⑪ 间:估计。
⑫ 不胜桮(bēi)杓(sháo):禁受不起酒力。桮:通"杯";杓:通"勺"。
⑬ 再拜献:郑重奉上之意。再拜:拜两次。
⑭ 安在:在哪里。
⑮ 督过:责备,怪罪。过:动词,责其过失。
⑯ 竖子:小子。此处骂项庄,实指项羽。

When they had been outside for a while, Hsiang Yu sent Colonel Ch'en P'ing to call the governor back in.

"When I left just now," said the governor, "I failed to say good-by. What should I do?"

"Great deeds do not wait on petty caution; great courtesy does not need little niceties①," replied Fan K'uai. "This fellow is about to get out his carving knife and platter and make mincemeat of② us! Why should you say good-by to him?"

With this, the governor of P'ei left, ordering Chang Liang to stay behind and make some excuse for him, "What did you bring as gifts?" asked Chang Liang.

"I have a pair of white jade discs which I intended to give to Hsiang Yu," replied the governor, "and a pair of jade wine dippers for Fan Tseng, but when I found that they were angry I did not dare to present them. You must present them for me." "I will do my best," said Chang Liang.

At this time Hsiang Yu's camp was at Hung-men, and the governor of P'ei's camp at Pa-shang some forty *li* away. The governor of P'ei left his carriages and horsemen where they were and slipped away from the camp on horseback, accompanied by only four men, Fan K'uai, Lord T'eng, Chin Ch'iang, and Chi Hsin, who bore swords and shields and hastened on foot. Following the foot of Mount Li, they returned by a secret way through Chih-yang.

When the governor left the camp he told Chang Liang, "By the road I will take it is no more than twenty *li* back to our camp. When you think I have had time to reach the camp, then go back

---

① nicety/'naɪsətɪ/ *n.* [常用复数]微细差异,微妙的差别,细节

② make mincemeat of 把……剁烂; mincemeat/'mɪnsˌmiːt/ *n.* 肉馅,剁碎的肉

and joining the party." After the governor of P'ei had left and enough time had elapsed him to reach camp, Chang Liang went in and made apologies. "The governor of P'ei was regrettably rather far gone in his cups and was unable to say good-by. He has respectfully requested me on his behalf to present this pair of white jade discs to Your Lordship with his humblest salutation, and to General Fan Tseng this pair of jade wine dippers."

"Where is the governor of P'ei?" asked Hsiang Yu.

"He perceived that Your Lordship was likely to reprove him for his shortcomings," replied Chang Liang, "and so he slipped away alone and returned to his camp.'"

Hsiang Yu accepted the jade discs and placed them beside him on his mat, but Fan Tseng put the dippers on the ground, drew his sword and smashed them to pieces. "Ah!" he said, "it does not do to lay plans with an idiot! It is the governor of P'ei who will snatch the world out of our hands, and on that day all of us will become his prisoners."

When the governor of P'ei got back to his camp he immediately had Ts'ao Wu-shang seized and executed.

【推荐阅读】

一、中文版本及注疏

韩兆琦译注.中华经典藏书·史记.北京：中华书局,2007 年。

司马迁.史记(明嘉靖南监本).西安：三秦出版,2001 年。

司马迁.史记(南宋建安黄善夫本).台湾：艺文印书馆,1949 年。

司马迁.史记(全十册).北京：中华书局,1959 年。

司马迁.史记(全十册修订版).北京：中华书局,2014 年。

许嘉璐主编.二十四史全译·史记.上海：汉语大词典出版社,
　　2004 年。

王冉冉.《史记》讲读.上海：华东师范大学出版社,2005 年。

二、英文译本

Dawson，Raymond. 1994. *Sima Qian：Historical Records，Translated with an Introduction and Notes*. New York：Oxford University Press.

Dawson，Raymond. 2007. *The First Emperor：Selections from the Historical Records*. New York：Oxford University Press.

Dolby，W. & Scott J.，1974. *Sima Qian：Warlords，Translated with Twelve Stories from His Historical Records*. Edinburgh：Southside.

Nienhauser，W. H. Jr. (ed.)，Tsai-fa Cheng，et. al. trans. 1994. *The Grand Scribe's Records，Volume I：The Basic Annals of Pre-Han China by Ssu-ma Ch'ien*. Bloomington & Indianapolis：Indiana University Press.

Watson，B，tr. 1961. *Records of the Grand Historian of China*. New York & London：Columbia University Press. Rev.：*Recoreds of the Grand Historian：Han Dynasty I & II*. Hong Kong & New York：Columbia University Press.

Watson, B, tr. 1969. *Records of the Historian*. New York & London: Columbia University Press.

Watson, B, tr. 1993. *Records of the Grand Historian: Qin Dynasty*. Hong Kong & New York: The Chinese University of Hong Kong, Columbia University Press.

Yang, Xianyi & Gladys Yang, tr. 2008. *Selections from Records of the Historian*. Beijing: Foreign Languages Press.

Yang, Hsien-yi & Gladys Yang, tr. 1974. *Records of the Historians*. Hong Kong: Commercial Press.

第七单元　《老子》

【导言】

《老子》，又名《道德经》《道德真经》，先秦道家典籍，为道家学派的开山之作，被奉为道教"第一经典"，其说博大精深，是"中国文化取之不尽，用之不竭的源泉"。通行版《老子》共八十一章，约五千字，分上下两篇，前37章为《道篇》，后44章为《德篇》，长沙马王堆汉墓出土的帛书《老子》则《德经》在前，《道经》在后。

据《史记》载，作者老子姓李，名耳，字聃，楚国苦县（今河南鹿邑）人，曾任周守藏史。相传老子西出函谷关时，关令尹喜求其著述，老子述《道德经》，"言道德之意五千言而去"，后"莫知其所终"。

自韩非《解老》《喻老》开始，中国历代《老子》注者不绝。先秦以降，有关《老子》的注疏多达数百种。朱谦之先生将其分为两大系统：一是以河上公《老子道德经河上公章句》为代表的"民间系统"，如严遵本、景龙碑本、遂州碑本和敦煌本等，其"文句简古"，"多古字，亦杂俗俚"；二是以王弼《老子注》为代表的"文人系统"，如傅奕、苏辙、陆希声、吴澄诸本，其"文笔晓畅"，"多善属文，而参错己见，与古《老子》相远"。1973年长沙马王堆汉墓出土的帛书《老子》甲、乙本，为迄今所见最古传本，其虽非最好传本，但均可作其他传本之参校。

作为东方智慧的结晶，《老子》亦倍受西方的青睐与推崇。自18世纪开始，《老子》在世界各地被广泛译介。据统计，《老子》在世界主要语种、国家均有译本，其发行量及普及程度仅次于《圣经》，其中尤以英文译本最多。1868年，湛约翰（John Chalmers）的《"老哲学家"老子关于玄学、政治及道德的思考》(*Speculations on Metaphysics，Polity，and Morality of "The Old Philosopher，" Lao-Tsze*)在英国伦敦出版，此为《道德经》首个英文译本。至1899年金斯密（T. W. Kingsmill）译本发表，短短30年间，共有12个英文译本问世，其中以巴尔福（Frederic Henry Balfour）(1884)、理雅各（James Legge）(1891)、保罗·卡鲁斯（Paul Carus）(1896)等的译本影响最大。进入二十世纪，《道德经》英文译本更是大量涌现。其中，亚瑟·韦利（Arthur Waley）(1934)、初大告(Chu Ta-kao)(1937)、吴经熊(John C. H. Wu)(1939),柏宾(Witter Bynner)(1944),林语堂(1948)、阿奇·巴姆(Archie J. Bahm)(1958)、陈荣捷(Chan Wing-tsit)(1963)、冯家福(Feng Gia-fu)和英格里希(Jane English)(1972)、林振述(Paul J. Lin)(1977)、史蒂芬·米切尔(Stephen Mitchel)(1988)、陈张婉莘(Chen Ellen Marie)(1989)等译本影响甚大。湖南长沙马王堆汉墓帛书及湖北荆门郭店楚简出土以后,又掀起了一场《老子》英译热潮。其最重要者有刘殿爵(D.C. Lau)(1982)、韩禄伯(Robert G. Henricks)(1989)、梅维恒(Victor H. Mair)(1990)等译本。

《道德经》(节选)①

第一章

道可道②,非常道。

名可名③,非常名。

无名,天地之始;

有名,万物之母。

故常无欲,以观其妙,

常有欲,以观其徼④。

此两者同出而异名。

同谓之玄⑤,

玄之又玄,众妙之门。

---

① 本单元汉语原文依据理雅各的汉语底本,参校任继愈著《老子绎读》。

② 第一个"道"为名词,指宇宙的本源和实质。第二个"道"为动词,指言说。

③ 第一个"名"为名词,称"道"之名。第二个"名"为动词,称谓。

④ 徼(jiào):边际,端倪。

⑤ 玄:深奥,玄妙。

The Tao Teh King (Exerpt)

Translated by James Legge[1]

CHAPTER I

The Tao that can be trodden[2] is not the enduring and unchanging Tao. The name that can be named is not the enduring and unchanging name.

(Conceived of as) having no name, it is the Originator[3] of heaven and earth; (conceived of as) having a name, it is the Mother of all things.

Always without desire we must be found,

If its deep mystery we would sound[4];

But if desire always within us be,

Its outer fringe[5] is all that we shall see.

Under these two aspects, it is really the same; but as development takes place, it receives the different names. Together we call them the Mystery[6]. Where the Mystery is the deepest is the gate of all that is subtle[7] and wonderful.

---

① 英语译文选自 Legge, James. 1891. *The Texts of Taoism*. London: Trubner & Co.。
② trodden/'trɔdn/ *v.* tread 的过去分词。tread: 踩, 行走, 踏
③ originator/ə'rɪdʒəneɪtə/ *n.* 起源, 发起人, 创办人, 创作者
④ sound/saund/ *v.* 试探, 询问, 调查
⑤ fringe/frɪndʒ/ *n.* 边缘, 边界
⑥ mystery/'mɪstərɪ/ *n.* 谜, 神秘的事物, 难以理解的事物
⑦ subtle/'sʌtl/ *adj.* 微妙的, 不可思议的, 难捉摸的

第三章

不尚贤，

使民不争；

不贵难得之货，

使民不为盗；

不见可欲①，

使民心不乱。

是以圣人之治，

虚其心，

实其腹，

弱其志，

强其骨。

常使民无知无欲。

使夫知者不敢为也。

为无为，

则无不治。

---

① 见（xiàn）：通"现"，出现，显露。意为显示、炫耀。

CHAPTER III

Not to value and employ men of superior ability is the way to keep the people from rivalry[①] among themselves; not to prize articles which are difficult to procure[②] is the way to keep them from becoming thieves; not to show them what is likely to excite their desires is the way to keep their minds from disorder.

Therefore the sage, in the exercise of his government, empties their minds, fills their bellies[③], weakens their wills, and strengthens their bones.

He constantly (tries to) keep them without knowledge and without desire, and where there are those who have knowledge, to keep them from presuming to[④] act (on it). When there is this abstinence[⑤] from action, good order is universal.

---

① rivalry/ˈraɪvlrɪ/ n. 竞争,对抗,对立
② procure/prəˈkjʊə/ v. 获得,取得
③ belly/ˈbelɪ/ n. 肚,腹,腹部,胃
④ presume (to) 竟敢,胆敢
⑤ abstinence/ˈæbstɪnəns/ n. 节制,禁绝

第八章

上善若水。
水善利万物而不争，
处众人之所恶，
故几于道①。

居善地②，
心善渊③，
与善仁④，
言善信，
政善治，
事善能，
动善时。

夫唯不争，
故无尤⑤。

---

① 几（jī）：接近。
② 地：低下。
③ 渊：深。
④ 与：指和别人相交相接。
⑤ 尤：怨恨、归咎。

CHAPTER VIII

The highest excellence is like (that of) water. The excellence of water appears in its benefiting all things, and in its occupying, without striving (to the contrary), the low place which all men dislike. Hence (its way) is near to (that of) the Tao.

The excellence of a residence① is in (the suitability of) the place; that of the mind is in abysmal② stillness; that of associations is in their being with the virtuous; that of government is in its securing good order; that of (the conduct of) affairs is in its ability; and that of (the initiation③ of) any movement is in its timeliness.

And when (one with the highest excellence) does not wrangle④ (about his low position), no one finds fault with⑤ him.

---

① residence/'rezɪdəns/ *n*. 居住, 驻扎
② abysmal/ə'bɪzməl/ *adj*. 深不可测的, 无底的
③ initiation/ɪˌnɪʃɪ'eɪʃən/ *n*. 发起, 创始
④ wrangle/'ræŋɡl/ 争吵, 争辩
⑤ find fault with 找碴儿, 挑错, 抱怨, 挑剔

第二十五章

有物混成，

先天地生①。

寂兮寥兮②，

独立而不改，

周行而不殆③，

可以为天下母。

吾不知其名，

字之曰道，

强为之名曰大。

大曰逝④，逝曰远，远曰反⑤。

故道大，天大，地大，王亦大⑥。

域中有四大⑦，

而王居其一焉。

人法地⑧，

地法天，

天法道，

道法自然。

---

① 有物混成，先天地生：河上公注云："谓道无形，混沌而成为万物，乃在天地之前。"混成：混然而成。"混然不可得而知，而万物由之以成，故曰混成也。不知其谁之子，故曰先天地生。"

② 寂：静，无声。寥(liáo)：空虚，无形。

③ 周行：环运行。殆：通"怠"，停息。

④ 逝：指道的进行，周流不息。王弼注云："逝，行也。"

⑤ 反：返回原点，返回原状。

⑥ 王亦大：王弼注云："天地之性人为贵，而王是人之主也，虽不识大，亦复为大，与之匹，故曰王亦大也。"

⑦ 域中：宇宙间，空间之中。

⑧ 法：效法，取法。

CHAPTER XXV

There was something undefined① and complete，coming into existence before Heaven and Earth. How still it was and formless，standing alone，and undergoing no change，reaching everywhere and in no danger（of being exhausted）！It may be regarded as the Mother of all things.

I do not know its name，and I give it the designation② of the Tao（the Way or Course）. Making an effort（further）to give it a name I call it The Great.

Great，it passes on（in constant③ flow）. Passing on，it becomes remote. Having become remote，it returns. Therefore the Tao is great；Heaven is great；Earth is great；and the（sage）king is also great. In the universe there are four that are great，and the（sage）king is one of them.

Man takes his law④ from the Earth；the Earth takes its law from Heaven；Heaven takes its law from the Tao. The law of the Tao is its being what it is.

---

① undefined/ˌʌndɪ'faɪnd/ *adj*. 未下定义的，模糊的，不明确规定的
② designation/ˌdezɪg'neɪʃən/ *n*. 称呼，名称
③ constant/'kɔnstənt/ *adj*. 不变的，持续的
④ law/lɔː/ *n*. 规律，法则

第四十二章

道生一^①,

一生二,

二生三,

三生万物。

万物负阴而抱阳,

冲气以为和^②。

人之所恶^③,

唯孤、寡、不穀^④,

而王公以为称。

故物或损之而益^⑤,

或益之而损。

人之所教,

我亦教之。

强梁者不得其死^⑥,

吾将以为教父^⑦。

---

① 一：此处的"一"不是指数目,而是指浑然一体的混沌原始状态。"二""三"也不是数目,而是指混沌状态的逐步分化。

② 冲：交冲,激荡。《说文》云：冲,涌摇也。

③ 恶(wù)：憎恶,厌恶。

④ 不穀(gǔ)：不善,古代王侯自称的谦词。穀：善。

⑤ 损：减损。益：增益。

⑥ 强梁者：强横霸道的人。河上公注云："强梁者,谓不信玄妙,背叛道德,不从经教,尚势任力也。不得其死者,为天命所绝,兵刃所伐,王法所杀,不得以寿命死也。"

⑦ 教父：教人的开始。父：通"甫",开始。河上公注云："老子以强梁之人为教戒之始也。"

CHAPTER XLII

The Tao produced One; One produced Two; Two produced Three; Three produced All things. All things leave behind them the Obscurity[①](out of which they have come), and go forward to embrace the Brightness (into which they have emerged), while they are harmonised by the Breath of Vacancy.

What men dislike is to be orphans, to have little virtue, to be as carriages without naves[②]; and yet these are the designations which kings and princes use for themselves. So it is that some things are increased by being diminished[③], and others are diminished by being increased.

What other men (thus) teach, I also teach. The violent and strong do not die their natural death. I will make this the basis of my teaching.

---

① obscurity/əbˈskjuərɪtɪ/ n . 阴暗,偏僻,朦胧
② nave/neɪv/ n . 车轮毂(此处理雅各将"毂"作"毂")。
③ diminish/dɪˈmɪnɪʃ/ v . 减少,缩减

第五十一章

道生之，

德畜之①，

物形之，

势成之②。

是以万物莫不尊道而贵德。

道之尊，

德之贵，

夫莫之命而常自然。

故道生之，德畜之；

长之育之，

亭之毒之③，

养之覆之④。

生而不有，

为而不恃⑤，

长而不宰，

是谓玄德。

———————

① 畜：养育，繁殖。

② 势：帛书甲乙本均作"器"，指具体的器物。

③ 亭：通"成"，结果实。毒：通"熟"，成熟。河上公本为"孰"。

④ 覆：覆盖，保护，维护。

⑤ 恃：依仗。

CHAPTER LI

All things are produced by the Tao, and nourished① by its outflowing operation②. They receive their forms according to the nature of each, and are completed according to the circumstances of their condition. Therefore all things without exception honour the Tao, and exalt③ its outflowing operation.

This honouring of the Tao and exalting of its operation is not the result of any ordination④, but always a spontaneous tribute⑤.

Thus it is that the Tao produces (all things), nourishes them, brings them to their full growth, nurses them, completes them, matures them, maintains them, and overspreads⑥ them.

It produces them and makes no claim to the possession of them; it carries them through their processes and does not vaunt⑦ its ability in doing so; it brings them to maturity and exercises⑧ no control over them; — this is called its mysterious operation.

---

① nourish/'nʌrɪʃ/ v. 滋养
② operation/ˌɒpə'reɪʃən/ n. 作用,效力
③ exalt/ɪg'zɔːlt/ v. 提升,赞扬,提高
④ ordination/ˌɔːdɪ'neɪʃən/ n. 命令,委任
⑤ tribute/'trɪbjuːt/ n. 表示敬意或称赞的行动、言语或礼物
⑥ overspread/'əʊvə'spred/ v. 覆盖
⑦ vaunt/vɔːnt/ v. 吹嘘,夸耀,宣扬
⑧ exercise/'eksəsaɪz/ v. 使用,运用

第七十六章

人之生也柔弱，

其死也坚强。

万物草木之生也柔脆，

其死也枯槁^①。

故坚强者死之徒^②，

柔弱者生之徒。

是以兵强则灭^③，

木强则折^④。

强大处下，

柔弱处上。

---

① 槁（gǎo）：干枯。
② 徒：类型。
③ 兵强则灭：王弼本为"兵强则不胜"，河上公注云："强大之兵轻战乐杀，毒流怨结，众弱为一强，故不胜。"
④ 折：王弼本作"兵"，河上公本作"共"，任继愈《老子绎读》作"折"。根据韦利译文，亦作"折"。

CHAPTER LXXVI

Man at his birth is supple① and weak；at his death，firm and strong.（So it is with）all things. Trees and plants，in their early growth，are soft and brittle②；at their death，dry and withered③.

Thus it is that firmness and strength are the concomitants④ of death；softness and weakness，the concomitants of life.

Hence he who（relies on）the strength of his forces does not conquer；and a tree which is strong will fill the outstretched arms，（and thereby invites the feller⑤.）

Therefore the place of what is firm and strong is below，and that of what is soft and weak is above.

---

① supple/'sʌpl/ *adj*. 柔软的，易弯曲的
② brittle/'brɪtl/ *adj*. 脆的，易碎的，易损坏的
③ withered/'wɪðəd/ *adj*. 枯萎的，凋谢的
④ concomitant/kən'kɔmɪtənt/ *n*. 相伴物，附随物
⑤ feller/'felə/ *n*. 伐木工人

第八十章

小国寡民。

使有什伯之器而不用①；

使民重死而不远徙②。

虽有舟舆，无所乘之；

虽有甲兵③，无所陈之。

使民复结绳而用之④。

甘其食，美其服，

安其居，乐其俗⑤。

邻国相望，

鸡犬之声相闻，

民至老死，

不相往来。

---

① 什伯（bǎi）之器：俞越等旧注为兵器。任继愈、陈鼓应、严灵峰等认为旧注失之牵强，应指各种各样的器具。《一切经音义》云："什，众也，杂也，会数之名也，资生之物谓之什物。"《史记·五帝本记·索隐》云："什器：什，数也。盖人家常用之器非一，故以十为数；犹今云什物也。"

② 重死：畏死，不轻易冒生命危险。重：看重，重视。

③ 甲：盔甲。兵：武器。

④ 结绳：上古没有文字，用结绳来记事或传递信息。

⑤ 甘：用作动词，意为"以……为甘"，"美""安""乐"用法相同。

CHAPTER LXXX

In a little state with a small population, I would so order it, that, though there were individuals with the abilities of ten or a hundred men, there should be no employment of them; I would make the people, while looking on death as a grievous① thing, yet not remove elsewhere (to avoid it).

Though they had boats and carriages, they should have no occasion to ride in them; though they had buff② coats and sharp weapons, they should have no occasion to don③ or use them.

I would make the people return to the use of knotted cords (instead of the written characters).

They should think their (coarse④) food sweet; their (plain) clothes beautiful; their (poor) dwellings places of rest; and their common (simple) ways sources of enjoyment.

There should be a neighbouring state within sight, and the voices of the fowls⑤ and dogs should be heard all the way from it to us, but I would make the people to old age, even to death, not have any intercourse⑥ with it.

---

① grievous/ˈgriːvəs/ adj. 使人悲痛的，令人伤心的
② buff/bʌf/ n. 浅黄色皮革，用这种皮革制成的军用制服
③ don/dɔn/ v. 披上，穿上
④ coarse/kɔːs/ adj. 粗糙的，下等的
⑤ fowl/faul/ n. 家禽（鸡、鸭、鹅，尤指长成的鸡）
⑥ intercourse/ˈɪntə(ː)kɔːs/ n. 交往，交流

【推荐阅读】

一、中文版本及注疏①

陈鼓应.老子注译及评介.北京：中华书局,1984 年版。

王卡点校.老子道德经河上公章句.北京：中华书局,1993 年版。

任继愈.老子绎读.北京：北京图书馆出版社,2006 年版。

王弼注,楼宇烈校释.老子道德经注校释,北京：中华书局,2008 年版。

严灵峰.老子达解.台北：华正书局有限公司,民国九十七年第二版。

朱谦之.老子校释.北京：中华书局,1984 年版。

二、英文译本②

Addiss，Stephen & Stanley Lombardo. 1993. *Lao Tzu. Tao Te Ching*. Indianapolis：Hackett Publishing Company.

Bahm，Archie J. 1958. *Tao The King：By Lao Tzu , Interpreted as Nature and Intelligence*. New York：F. Ungar.

Bynner，Witter. 1944. *The Way of Life According to Laotzu*. New York：Perigree.

Carus，Paul. 1898. Lao-tze's *Tao-the-king：Chinese and English with Introduction*. Chicago：Open Court Publications.

Carus，Paul & D. T. Suzuki. 1913. *The Canon of Reason and Virtue：Lao Tzu's Tao The King*. Chicago：Open Court Publications.

Chalmers，John. 1868. *The Speculation on Metaphysics，Polity and Morality of "The Old Philosopher ," Lao-tsze*. London：Trubner.

Chan，Wing-tsit. 1963. *The Way of Lao Tzu：Tao-te ching*.

---

① 有关中国历代《老子》注疏,详见陈鼓应《老子注译及评介》第 365—408 页,"历代老子注书评介"及该书附录三"参考书目"。

② 更多《道德经》英文译本目录,请参见 Kohn, Livia & Michael LaFargue, 1998. *Lao-tzu and the Tao-te-ching*, State University of New York Press. pp. 299 – 301。

Indianapolis: Bobbs-Merrill.

Henricks, Robert. 1989. *Lao-Tzu: Te-Tao ching*. New York: Ballantine.

LaFargue, Michael. 1992. *The Tao of the Tao-te-ching*. Albany: State University of New York Press.

Lau, D. C. 1963. *Lao-tzu: Tao Te Ching*. New York: Penguin Books.

Lau, D. C. 1982. *Chinese Classics: Tao Te Ching*. Hong Kong: Hong Kong University Press.

Legge, James. 1891. *The Texts of Taoism*. London: Trubner & Co.

Lin, Yutang. 1942. *The Wisdom of Laotse*. New York: Random House.

Mair, Victor H. 1990. *Tao Te Ching: The Classic Book of Integrity and the Way*. New York: Bantam.

Mitchell, Stephen. 1988. *Tao Te Ching: A New English Version*. New York: Harper & Row.

Waley, Arthur. 1934. *The Way and Its Power: A Study of the Tao Te Ching and Its Place in Chinese Thought*. London: Allen and Unwin.

Wu, Charles Q. *Thus Spoke Laozi: A New Translation With Commentaries of Daodejing*, Beijing: Foreign Language Teaching and Research Press, 2016.

第八单元 《庄子》

【导言】

《庄子》,亦称《南华经》《南华真经》,道家道教经典之一,大致成书于先秦时期。今本《庄子》多源于晋代郭象注本,共三十三篇,其中内篇七,外篇十五,杂篇十一。一般认为,内篇为庄子本人所著,外篇、杂篇中多伪作。《史记·老子韩非列传》言"其学无所不窥,然其要本归于老子之言",但亦对老子思想进行发挥,并形成其鲜明的哲学及艺术特色。

关于庄子其人,历史记载甚少,后世对其了解主要源于《史记》及《庄子》。庄子,名周,战国时宋国蒙人,生卒年不详,大约生活在战国中期,与梁惠王、齐宣王同时,曾任漆园吏,唐玄宗时,加封为南华真人。

早在战国时期,荀子对庄子已有所批判,并对其学说加以改造,以为已用。《吕氏春秋》对庄子思想内容多有引用,西汉时,淮南王刘安、司马迁都对庄子有所研究,秦汉辞赋、经学亦对庄子思想加以吸纳,魏晋注《庄子》者甚多,郭象便是其中之一。至隋唐时期,道教地位提高,庄学盛行,现今可考关于庄子的著作多达二十余种,流传下来者有陆德明的《庄子音义》和成玄英的《庄子注疏》。"以儒评庄,引庄入儒"为宋明时期庄学最大特点,其中以王安石、苏轼影响最大。此时期的道教学者所撰写庄子学专著有陈景元的《南华真经章句音义》、陆西星的《南华真经副墨》等。清代重在对庄子进行义理阐释与文章学研究,如林云铭的《庄子因》、宣颖的《南华经解》、刘凤苞的《南华雪心编》等。到了晚清,还出现了一些集众家研究成果之作,如,郭庆藩的《庄子集释》、王先谦的《庄子集解》等。民国时期,一些学者以传统的训诂校勘方法对《庄子》进行深入研究,如,马叙伦的《庄子义证》、刘文典的《庄子补正》、王叔岷的《庄子校释》、闻一多的《庄子内篇校释》等,还有一些学者吸收西方哲学与科学研究成果对《庄子》进行阐释,如苏甲荣的《庄子哲学》、郎擎霄的《庄子学案》、叶国庆的《庄子研究》等。

《庄子》在西方的译介始于十九世纪。1881 年,巴尔福(Fredric Balfour)将《庄子》译成英文。此为《庄子》的首个英文译本。十九世纪,还诞生了两个非常重要的英文译本,译者分别为翟理斯(Herbert

A. Giles)(1889)和理雅各(James Legge)(1891)。进入二十世纪,《庄子》的译本逐渐增多,其中有节译,亦有全译。影响最大的译者有冯友兰(1933)、韦利(Arthur Waley)(1939)、林语堂(1942)、陈荣捷(1963)、魏鲁男(James R. Ware)(1963)、华兹生(Burton Watson)(1964,1968)、冯家富(Gia-fu Feng)(1974)、葛瑞汉(A. C. Graham)(1981)、梅维桓(Victor H. Mair)(1994)及任博克(2009)等。

逍遥游①

北冥有鱼②,其名为鲲③。鲲之大,不知其几千里也。化而为鸟,其名为鹏④。鹏之背,不知其几千里也;怒而飞⑤,其翼若垂天之云⑥。是鸟也,海运则将徙于南冥⑦。南冥者,天池也⑧。

《齐谐》者,志怪者也。《谐》之言曰:"鹏之徙于南冥也,水击三千里⑨,抟扶摇而上者九万里⑩,去以六月息者也⑪。"野马也,尘埃也,生物之以息相吹也⑫。天之苍苍,其正色邪⑬? 其远而无所至极邪? 其视下也,亦若是则已矣。

且夫水之积也不厚,则其负大舟也无力。覆杯水于坳堂之上⑭,则芥为之舟⑮;置杯焉则胶⑯,水浅而舟大也。风之积也不厚,则其负大翼也无力。故九万里,则风斯在下矣,而后乃今培风⑰;背负青天而莫之夭阏者⑱,而后乃今将图南。

---

① 本单元汉语原文参校陈鼓应.《庄子今注今译》(最新修订版).北京:商务印书馆,2007年版。
② 北冥:北海。冥,通"溟",指海。
③ 鲲(kūn):古代传说中的大鱼名。
④ 鹏:即古"凤"字,大鸟名。
⑤ 怒:同"努",奋力,振奋,奋起。
⑥ 垂:通"陲",边陲,边际。
⑦ 海运:海动,海水翻腾。
⑧ 天池:天然大池。
⑨ 水击:通"水激",拍水,击水,指鹏鸟飞起时双翼拍打水面。
⑩ 抟:拍打,一作"抟"。扶摇:海中飓风。
⑪ 去以六月息:乘着六月风而去。息:风。一说,一去六个月才停歇。此"息"意为"停"。
⑫ 野马:状如奔马的浮动的雾气。尘埃:指空中游尘。生物:空中活动之物。息:风。
⑬ 苍苍:深蓝色。正色:本色。
⑭ 覆:倾倒。坳(ào)堂:室内低洼处。
⑮ 芥:小草。
⑯ 胶:粘着,犹言搁浅。
⑰ 而后乃今培风:这之后方才借助风力。培:通"凭"。
⑱ 夭阏(è):亦作"夭遏",遏止、阻碍。

Transcendental Bliss

Translated by Herbert A. Giles[1]

In the northern ocean there is a fish, called the Leviathan[2], many thousand *li* in size. This leviathan changes into a bird, called the Rukh[3], whose back is many thousand *li* in breadth. With a mighty effort it rises, and its wings obscure[4] the sky like clouds.

At the equinox[5], this bird prepares to start for the Southern Ocean, the Celestial[6] Lake. And in the *Record of Marvels*[7] we read that when the rukh flies southwards, the water is smitten[8] for a space of three thousand *li* around, while the bird itself mounts upon a typhoon to a height of ninety thousand *li*, for a flight of six months' duration.

Just so are the motes[9] in a sunbeam[10], blown aloft[11] by God. For whether the blue of the sky is its real colour, or only the result of distance without end, the effect to the bird looking down would be just the same as to the motes.

If there is not sufficient depth, water will not float large ships.

---

① 本单元英语译文选自：Giles, Herbert A., tr. 1888. *Chuang Tzu: Mystic, Moralist, and Social Reformer*. London: Bernard Quaritch。transcendental/trænsen'dentl/*adj*. 超自然的,超验的;bliss: *n*. 极乐,洪福

② Leviathan/lɪ'vaɪəθən/*n*.《圣经》中象征邪恶的海中怪兽

③ Rukh/rʌk/*n*. 又名 Roc,(阿拉伯、波斯传说中的)大怪鸟,大鹏

④ obscure/əb'skjuə(r)/*v*. 遮蔽,使模糊

⑤ equinox/'iːkwɪnɒks/*n*. 昼夜平分时,春分或秋分

⑥ celestial/sɪ'lestɪəl/*adj*. 天的,天空的,天国的

⑦ marvel/'mɑːvl/*n*. 奇异的事物

⑧ smite/smaɪt/*v*. (smote, smitten)打,重击

⑨ mote/məut/*n*. 尘埃,微粒

⑩ sunbeam/'sʌnbiːm/*n*. 阳光光束,日光

⑪ aloft/ə'lɒft/*adv*. 在空中,在高处

Upset① a cupful into a small hole, and a mustard-seed② will be your boat. Try to float the cup, and it will stick③, from the disproportion④ between water and vessel⑤.

So with air. If there is not a sufficient depth, it cannot support large birds. And for this bird a depth of ninety thousand *li* is necessary; and then, with nothing save⑥ the clear sky above, and no obstacle in the way, it starts upon its journey to the south.

---

① upset/ˌʌpˈset/ *v*. 打翻,倾覆
② mustard/ˈmʌstəd/ *n*. 芥菜,芥末
③ stick/stɪk/ *v*. 粘住
④ disproportion/ˌdɪsprəˈpɔːʃn/ *n*. 不相称,不成比例
⑤ vessel/ˈvesl/ *n*. 船(尤指大船),舰
⑥ save /seɪv/ *prep*. 除了……以外

蜩与学鸠笑之曰①："我决起而飞,抢榆枋②,时则不至,而控于地而已矣③,奚以之九万里而南为④?"适莽苍者⑤,三飡而反⑥,腹犹果然⑦;适百里者,宿舂粮⑧;适千里者,三月聚粮。之二虫又何知!

小知不及大知,小年不及大年⑨。奚以知其然也?朝菌不知晦朔⑩,蟪蛄不知春秋⑪,此小年也。楚之南有冥灵者⑫,以五百岁为春,五百岁为秋;上古有大椿者⑬,以八千岁为春,八千岁为秋,此大年也。而彭祖乃今以久特闻⑭,众人匹之,不亦悲乎!

汤之问棘也是已⑮。穷发之北有冥海者⑯,天池也。有鱼焉,其广数千里,未有知其修者,其名为鲲。有鸟焉,其名为鹏,背若太山⑰,翼若垂天之云,搏扶摇羊角而上者九万里⑱,绝云气,负青天,然后图南,且适南冥也⑲。斥鴳笑之曰⑳:"彼且奚适也?我腾跃而上,不过数仞而下㉑,翱翔蓬蒿之间,此亦飞之至也。而彼且奚适也?"此小大之辩也。

---

① 蜩(tiáo):蝉。学鸠:即鸒鸠,小鸠。学:通"鸒"。
② 决(xuè)起:迅疾而起,即上文怒而飞。抢(qiāng):撞,碰到。榆枋:榆树与枋树。
③ 控:投,跌落。
④ 奚以……为:哪里用得着……呢?
⑤ 适:去,往。莽苍:(原野)景色迷茫,也指原野。
⑥ 飡(cān):同"餐"。反:返回。
⑦ 果然:饱足的样子。
⑧ 宿舂粮:舂一宿之粮。
⑨ 知:通"智"。年:年寿。
⑩ 朝菌:某些朝生暮死的菌类植物,借喻极短的生命。晦朔:农历一个月。晦:阴历每月的最后一天;朔:阴历每月初一。
⑪ 蟪蛄:蝉的一种,体短,吻长,黄绿色,有黑色条纹,翅膀有黑斑,雄的腹部有发音器,夏末自早至暮鸣声不息。
⑫ 冥灵:神话中的树木名。陈鼓应注云:"冥灵:溟海灵龟。"
⑬ 大椿:古寓言中的木名,以一万六千岁为一年。
⑭ 彭祖:中国传说人物,姓籛,名铿,颛顼玄孙。殷王任为大夫,他托病不问政事。自夏代至殷末,活七百六十七岁(一说八百余岁),旧时视为长寿的象征。特闻:独闻于世。
⑮ 汤:商汤,商朝第一代国君。棘:夏革,商朝大夫,商汤之师。汤之问棘的故事见于《列子·汤问篇》。
⑯ 穷发:不毛之地。发:指草木。
⑰ 太山:即泰山。
⑱ 羊角:形似羊角的旋风。
⑲ 陈鼓应先生认为"且适南冥也"五字当系后人据成《疏》"图度南海"误入正文,当删。
⑳ 斥鴳(yàn):指池泽中小雀鸟。斥:池塘,小泽。鴳,亦作鷃,即雀。
㉑ 仞:古代长度单位。周制八尺,汉制七尺。《说文》云:"仞,伸臂一寻八尺也"。

A cicada① laughed, and said to a young dove, "Now, when I fly with all my might, 'tis as much as I can do to get from tree to tree. And sometimes I do not reach, but fall to the ground midway. What then can be the use of going up ninety thousand *li* in order to start for the south?"

He who goes to Mang-ts'ang (A short distance into the country), taking three meals with him, comes back with his stomach as full as when he started. But he who travels a hundred *li* must grind② flour enough for a night's halt③. And he who travels a thousand *li* must supply himself with provisions④ for three months. Those two little creatures, -what should they know? Small knowledge has not the compass⑤ of great knowledge any more than a short year has the length of a long year.

How can we tell that this is so? The mushroom⑥ of a morning knows not the alternation⑦ of day and night. The chrysalis⑧ knows not the alternation of spring and autumn. Theirs are short years.

But in the State of Ch'u there is a tortoise whose spring and autumn are each of five hundred years' duration. And in former days there was a large tree which had a spring and autumn each of eight thousand years' duration. Yet, P'eng Tsu (The Methusaleh of China. His age has not been agreed upon by Chinese writers, but the lowest computation gives him a life of eight hundred years.) is

---

① cicada/sɪˈkɑːdə/ *n.* 蝉
② grind/ɡraɪnd/ *v.* (ground, ground)磨,研磨
③ halt/hɔːlt/ *n.* 暂停,停顿
④ provision/prəˈvɪʒn/ *n.* (usu. *pl.*)食物
⑤ compass/ˈkʌmpəs/ *n.* 境界,范围
⑥ mushroom/ˈmʌʃrum/ *n.* 食用伞菌,蘑菇
⑦ alternation/ˌɔːltəˈneɪʃn/ *n.* 交替,更迭
⑧ chrysalis/ˈkrɪsəlɪs/ *n.* 蛹,(尤指)蝶蛹

still, alas①, an object of envy to all.

It was on this very subject that the Emperor T'ang (B.C. 1766) spoke to Chi, as follows: "At the barren② north there is a great sea, the Celestial Lake. In it there is a fish, several thousand *li* in breadth, and I know not how many in length. It is called the Leviathan. There is also a bird, called the Rukh, with a back like Mount T'ai, and wings like clouds across the sky. Upon a typhoon it soars③ up to a height of ninety thousand *li*, beyond the clouds and atmosphere④, with only the clear sky above it. And then it directs its flight towards the south pole.

A quail⑤ laughed, and said: "Pray⑥, what may that creature be going to do? I rise but a few yards in the air, and settle⑦ again after flying around among the reeds. That is the most I can manage. Now, whereever can this creature be going to?" (The repetition of this story, coupled with its quotation from the *Record of Marvels*, is considered to give an air of authenticity to Chuang Tzu's illustration, which the reader might otherwise suppose to be of his own invention.) Such, indeed, is the difference between small and great.

---

① alas/əˈlɑːs/*int*. 哎呀,唉
② barren/ˈbærən/*adj*. 贫瘠的,不毛的,荒芜的
③ soar/sɔː(r)/*v*. 高飞,翱翔
④ atmosphere/ˈætməsfɪə(r)/*n*. 大气,大气层
⑤ quail/kweɪl/*n*. 鹌鹑
⑥ pray/preɪ/*adv*. (旧式用法)用于礼貌地提问或请求别人做某事,相当于"请""请问"。
⑦ settle/ˈsetl/*v*. 在某处停歇或停留一时

　　故夫知效一官①，行比一乡②，德合一君而征一国者③，其自视也亦若此矣。而宋荣子犹然笑之④。且举世而誉之而不加劝，举世而非之而不加沮⑤，定乎内外之分，辩乎荣辱之境，斯已矣。彼其于世未数数然也⑥。虽然，犹有未树也⑦。夫列子御风而行⑧，泠然善也⑨，旬有五日而后反。彼于致福者⑩，未数数然也。此虽免乎行，犹有所待者也⑪。若夫乘天地之正⑫，而御六气之辩⑬，以游无穷者，彼且恶乎待哉⑭！故曰，至人无己⑮，神人无功⑯，圣人无名⑰。

　　尧让天下于许由⑱，曰："日月出矣，而爝火不息⑲，其于光也，不亦难乎！时雨降矣而犹浸灌，其于泽也⑳，不亦劳乎㉑！夫子立，而天下

① 效：胜任。
② 行：品行。比：适合，投合。陈鼓应注云："比：犹庇。案'比'借为庇，《说文》：'庇，荫也。'"
③ 征：取信。
④ 宋荣子：宋钘（píng），宋国人，战国时期思想家。犹然：喜笑的样子。
⑤ 劝：努力，劝勉。非：责难，批评。沮（jǔ）：沮丧，消极。
⑥ 数数（shuò）然：汲汲然，急促的样子。
⑦ 树：树起或建起，树立。
⑧ 列子御风而行：故事见于《列子·黄帝篇》。列子：即列御寇，春秋时郑国思想家。御：驾驭。
⑨ 泠（líng）然：飘然，轻妙之貌。
⑩ 致：求，得。福：福报。
⑪ 有所待：有所依赖。这里是说列子仍然不能逍遥游，精神不得自主，心灵不得安放。待：依赖。
⑫ 乘天地之正：顺应自然规律。乘：遵循。正：法则，规律。
⑬ 御：顺从。六气：指阴、阳、风、雨、晦、明。辩：通"变"。
⑭ 恶乎待哉：有什么可依待的呢？
⑮ 无己：指没有偏执的我见，即去除自我中心，亦即扬弃为功名束缚的小我，而天臻至与天地精神往来的境界。
⑯ 无功：无意求功于世间。
⑰ 无名：无心汲汲于名位。
⑱ 尧：名放勋，号陶唐氏，上古时代理想中的圣明君王。许由：传说中的高洁隐士，隐于箕山（今河南登封县南），相传尧要让天下给他，他自命高洁而不受。
⑲ 爝（jué）火：小火，火把。息：通"熄"。
⑳ 泽：润泽。
㉑ 劳：徒劳。

治^①，而我犹尸之^②，吾自视缺然^③。请致天下^④。"

---

① 夫子：指许由。立：在位，登位。
② 尸：本指神庙中的神像，引申为徒居名位而无其实，此处谓主其事。
③ 缺然：歉然，自愧的样子。一说，欠缺的样子。
④ 致：与，交给。

Take, for instance, a man who creditably① fills some office, or who is a pattern of virtue in his neighbourhood, or who influences his prince to right government of the State, -his opinion of himself will be much the same as that quail's. The philosopher Yung laughs at such a one. He, if the whole world flattered② him, would not be affected thereby, nor if the whole world blamed him would he lose his faith in himself. For Yung can distinguish between the intrinsic③ and the extrinsic④, between honour and shame, -and such men are rare in their generation. But even he has not established⑤ himself.

There was Lieh Tzu again. He could ride upon the wind, and travel whithersoever⑥ he wished, staying away as long as fifteen days. Among mortals⑦ who attain happiness, such a man is rare. Yet although Lieh Tzu was able to dispense⑧ with walking, he was still dependent upon something. But had he been charioted⑨ upon the eternal⑩ fitness⑪ of Heaven and Earth, driving before him the elements⑫ as his team while roaming⑬ through the realms of For-Ever, -upon what, then, would he have had to depend?

Thus it has been said, "The perfect man ignores *self*; the

---

① creditably/'kredɪtəblɪ/*adv*. 值得称赞地,可钦佩地,有好名声地

② flatter/'flætə(r)/*v*. 恭维,奉承,讨好

③ intrinsic/ɪn'trɪnsɪk/*adj*. 固有的,本质的,内在的

④ extrinsic/ek'strɪnsɪk/*adj*. 外在的,外部的

⑤ establish/ɪ'stæblɪʃ/*v*. 确立稳固地位,设立,建立

⑥ whithersoever/(h)wɪðəsəu'evə/*adv*. 不论在哪里,无论到哪里

⑦ mortal/'mɔːtl/*n*. 凡人

⑧ dispense/dɪ'spens/*v*. 免除,省掉,摆脱

⑨ chariot/'tʃærɪət/*v*. 驾驶(马车)

⑩ eternal/ɪ'tɜːnl/*adj*. 永恒的,不灭的,永远的

⑪ fitness/'fɪtnɪs/*n*. 适合;健康

⑫ element/'elɪmənt/*n*. 元素,[pl.]自然力

⑬ roam/rəum/*v*. 漫步,漫游

divine① man ignores *action*; the true Sage ignores *reputation*②."

The Emperor Yao wished to abdicate③ in favour of Hsü Yu, saying, "If, when the sun and moon are shining, you persist in lighting a torch④, is not that a misapplication⑤ of fire? If, when the rainy season is at its height, you still continue to water the ground, is not this a waste of labour? Now, sir, do you assume the reins⑥ of government, and the empire will be at peace. I am but a dead body, conscious of my own deficiency⑦. I beg you will ascend⑧ the throne⑨."

---

① divine/dɪ'vaɪn/*adj*. 神的,非凡的,神圣的
② reputation/ˌrepju'teɪʃn/*n*. 名气,名声,名誉
③ abdicate/'æbdɪkeɪt/*v*. 让位,辞职,放弃
④ torch/tɔːtʃ/*n*. 火炬,火把
⑤ misapplication/'mɪsˌæplɪ'keɪʃən/*n*. 误用,使用不当
⑥ rein/reɪn/*n*. 缰绳,支配,统治
⑦ deficiency/dɪ'fɪʃnsɪ/*n*. 不足,缺点,缺陷
⑧ ascend/ə'send/*v*. 攀登,登上
⑨ throne/θrəun/*n*. 宝座,王位

　　许由曰：“子治天下，天下既已治也。而我犹代子，吾将为名乎？名者，实之宾也①。吾将为宾乎？鹪鹩巢于深林②，不过一枝；偃鼠饮河③，不过满腹。归休乎君，予无所用天下为！庖人虽不治庖④，尸祝不越樽俎而代之矣⑤。”

　　肩吾问于连叔曰⑥：“吾闻言于接舆⑦，大而无当⑧，往而不反。吾惊怖其言，犹河汉而无极也⑨；大有径庭⑩，不近人情焉⑪。”

　　连叔曰：“其言谓何哉？”

　　曰：“藐姑射之山⑫，有神人居焉，肌肤若冰雪，绰约若处子⑬。不食五谷，吸风饮露；乘云气，御飞龙，而游乎四海之外。其神凝⑭，使物不疵疠而年谷熟⑮。吾以是狂而不信也⑯。”

---

① 宾：次要的、派生的东西。
② 鹪鹩(jiāo liáo)：俗名"巧妇鸟"，一种善于筑巢的小鸟。
③ 偃鼠：鼹鼠，白天隐于土穴中，晚上出来觅食的地鼠。
④ 庖(páo)人：厨师。
⑤ 尸祝：主祭的人。樽，酒器。俎(zǔ)：盛肉的器皿。樽俎：指厨事。成语"越俎代庖"出于此。
⑥ 肩吾、连叔：古时修道之士。历史上是否实有其人，已不可考。庄子笔下的人物，大都经他刻画过，或凭空塑造，或根据一点史实线索加以装扮。
⑦ 接舆：楚国隐士，姓陆名通，字接舆。《论语·微子篇》曾录其言行。此处为庄子笔下的理想人物。
⑧ 当：底，边际。
⑨ 河汉：银河。极：边际。
⑩ 大有径庭：太过度，太离题，言差异很大。清宣颖云："径，门外路也；庭，堂前地也。势相远隔。今言'大有径庭'，则相远之甚也。"
⑪ 不近人情：不附世情，言非世俗所常有。
⑫ 藐：遥远的样子。姑射(gū shè)之山：山名，在山西省临汾县西，即古石孔山，九孔相通。
⑬ 绰(chuò)约：轻盈柔美。处子：处女。
⑭ 神凝：精神内守，凝聚专一。
⑮ 疵疠(cī lì)：恶病，引申为灾害。
⑯ 狂：通"诳"，虚妄之言。

"Ever since you, sire①, have directed the administration②", replied Hsü Yu, "the empire has enjoyed tranquility③. Supposing, therefore, that I were to take your place now, should I gain any reputation thereby? Besides, reputation is but the shadow of reality; and should I trouble myself about the shadow? The tit④, building its nest in the mighty forest, occupies but a single twig⑤. The tapir⑥ slakes⑦ its thirst from the river, but drinks enough only to fill its belly. To you sire, belongs the reputation; the empire has no need for me. If a cook is unable to dress⑧ his funeral sacrifices⑨, the boy who impersonates⑩ the corpse⑪ may not step over the wines and meats and do it for him."

Chien Wu said to Lien Shu, "I heard Chieh Yu utter something unjustifiably⑫ extravagant⑬ and without either rhyme or reason⑭. I was greatly startled at what he said, for it seemed to me boundless⑮ as the Milky Way⑯, though very improbable and removed⑰ from the experiences of mortals."

"What was it?" asked Lien Shu.

---

① sire/'saɪə(r)/n. [古]陛下
② administration/ədˌmɪnɪ'streɪʃn/n. 管理，施政
③ tranquility/træŋ'kwɪlɪtɪ/n. 平静，安宁
④ tit/tɪt/n. 山雀
⑤ twig/twɪg/n. 细枝，嫩枝
⑥ tapir/'teɪpə(r)/n. 貘(产于马来西亚和美洲热带地区)
⑦ slake/sleɪk/v. 解(渴)
⑧ dress/dres/v. 为烹调或食用准备(食物)
⑨ sacrifice/'sækrɪfaɪs/n. 献祭，供奉，祭品
⑩ impersonate/ɪm'pɜːsəneɪt/v. 模仿，扮演
⑪ corpse/kɔːps/n. 尸体
⑫ unjustifiably/ʌn'dʒʌstɪfaɪəblɪ/adv. 无理地
⑬ extravagant/ɪk'strævəgənt/adj. 过度的，过分的，放肆的
⑭ without either rhyme or reason：毫无道理
⑮ boundless/'baundlɪs/adj. 无限的
⑯ Milky Way：银河
⑰ removed/rɪ'muːvd/adj. 远隔的，无关的

"He declared", replied Chien Wu, "that on the Miao-ku-she Mountain there lives a divine man whose flesh[1] is like ice or snow, whose demeanour[2] is that of a virgin[3], who eats no fruit of the earth, but lives on air and dew[4], and who, riding on clouds with flying dragons for his team, roams beyond the limits of mortality. This being is absolutely inert[5]. Yet he wards off[6] corruption[7] from all things, and causes the crops to thrive[8]. Now I call that nonsense, and do not believe it."

---

① flesh/fleʃ/ *n.* （人的）肉体(与精神或灵魂相对)
② demeanour/dɪˈmiːnə(r)/ *n.* 行为,举止,态度
③ virgin/ˈvɜːdʒɪn/ *n.* 处女
④ dew/djuː/ *n.* 露水
⑤ inert/ɪˈnɜːt/ *adj.* 无行动或活动能力的,迟钝的,呆滞的
⑥ ward off 避开,防止
⑦ corruption/kəˈrʌpʃn/ *n.* 腐烂,腐败
⑧ thrive/θraɪv/ *v.* 繁荣,茁壮成长

连叔曰:"然! 瞽者无以与乎文章之观①,聋者无以与乎钟鼓之声。岂唯形骸有聋盲哉? 夫知亦有之。是其言也,犹时女也②。之人也,之德也,将旁礴万物以为一③,世蕲乎乱④,孰弊弊焉以天下为事⑤! 之人也,物莫之伤,大浸稽天而不溺⑥,大旱金石流、土山焦而不热。是其尘垢秕穅⑦,将犹陶铸尧舜者也,孰肯以物为事⑧!

宋人资章甫而适诸越⑨,越人断发文身,无所用之。尧治天下之民,平海内之政,往见四子藐姑射之山,汾水之阳⑩,窅然丧其天下焉⑪。"

惠子谓庄子曰⑫:"魏王贻我大瓠之种⑬,我树之成而实五石⑭,以盛水浆,其坚不能自举也。剖之以为瓢,则瓠落无所容⑮。非不呺然大也⑯,吾为其无用而掊之⑰。"

---

① 瞽(gǔ)者:盲人,没有眼珠的瞎子。文章:错杂的色彩或花纹。
② 时:通"是",此。女:通"汝",指肩吾。
③ 旁礴:"旁"亦作"磅",混同,一说广被之意。
④ 蕲(qí):通"祈",期望。乱:治,太平,这是古代同词义反的语言现象。陈鼓应先生认为,"乱"字宜从其原义解,"世蕲乎乱",意指世人争功求名,纷纷扰扰,党派倾轧,勾心斗角,所以说求乱不已。
⑤ 弊弊:辛苦疲惫的样子。
⑥ 大浸稽天:大水滔天。大浸:大水。浸:水。稽:及,至。
⑦ 尘垢秕穅:庄子认为道在万事万物之中,此指道之粗者。
⑧ 孰肯以物为事:陈鼓应先生依《淮南子·俶真训》"分分然"三字而为"孰肯分分然以物为事",意为怎肯纷纷扰扰以俗物为务呢。
⑨ 资:贩卖。章甫:殷代的一种礼帽。
⑩ 四子:旧注指王倪、啮缺、被衣、许由四人,实为庄子寓言虚构的人物。汾水:在今山西省境内,为黄河支流。阳:山南水北为阳。
⑪ 窅(yǎo)然:怅然若失的样子。丧:忘掉。
⑫ 惠子:宋人,姓惠名施,做过梁惠王宰相,是庄子的朋友,"名家"的重要人物。他认为万物流变无常,因此一个东西不可能有相当固定的时候。他说:"日方中方睨,物主生方死。"他认为任何东西的性质都是相对的,因此事物之间,也就没有绝对的区别,"天与地卑,山与泽平",主张"泛爱万物,天地一体"。
⑬ 魏王:即魏惠王,因魏都迁大梁,所以称梁惠王,战国时魏国的国君,惠是谥号。贻:赠送。瓠(hù):葫芦。
⑭ 树:种植、培育。实:结的葫芦。石:重量单位,十斗为一石。
⑮ 瓠落无所容:指瓢太大无处可容。瓠落:又写作"廓落",大,空廓的样子。
⑯ 呺(xiāo)然:庞大而又中空的样子。
⑰ 掊(pǒu):打碎。

"Well," answered Lien Shu, "you don't ask a blind man's opinion of a picture, nor do you invite a deaf man to a concert. And blindness and deafness are not physical① only. There is blindness and deafness of the mind, diseases from which I fear you yourself are suffering. The good influence of that man fills all creation②. Yet because a paltry③ generation cries for reform, you would have him condescend④ to the details of an empire!

"Objective existences⑤ cannot harm him. In a flood which reached to the sky, he would not be drowned. In a drought⑥, though metals ran liquid and mountains were scorched⑦ up, he would not be hot. Out of his very dust and sifting⑧ you might fashion⑨ two such men as Yao and Shun. And you would have him occupy himself with⑩ adjectives!"

A man of the Sung State carried some sacrificial⑪ caps into the Yüeh State, for sale. But the men of Yüeh used to cut off their hair and paint their bodies, so that they had no use for such things. And so, when the Emperor Yao, the ruler of all under heaven and pacificator⑫ of all within the shores of ocean, paid a visit to the four sages of the Miao-ku-she Mountain, on returning to his capital at Fen-yang, the empire existed for him no more.

---

① physical/ˈfɪzɪkl/*adj*. 身体的，物质的（与精神相对）
② creation/kriːˈeɪʃn/*n*. 所有的创造物，天地万物
③ paltry/ˈpɔːltrɪ/*adj*. 微不足道的
④ condescend/ˌkɒndɪˈsend/*v*. 俯就，屈尊
⑤ existence/ɪɡˈzɪstəns/*n*. 实体，存在物
⑥ drought/draut/*n*. 干旱
⑦ scorch/skɔːtʃ/*v*. 烧焦，烤焦
⑧ sifting/ˈsɪftɪŋ/*n*. 筛；过滤
⑨ fashion/ˈfæʃn/*v*. 形成，铸成，把……塑造成
⑩ occupy oneself with 从事于……，忙于……，专心于……
⑪ sacrificial/ˌsækrɪˈfɪʃl/*adj*. 献祭的，抛售的
⑫ pacificator/pəˈsɪfɪkeɪtə/*n*. 平定者，调解人，仲裁者

Hui Tzu said to Chuang Tzu, "The Prince of Wei gave me a seed of a large-sized kind of gourd①. I planted it, and it bore a fruit as big as a five-bushel② measure. Now had I used this for holding liquids, it would have been too heavy to lift; and had I cut it in half for ladles③, the ladles would have been ill adapted for such purpose. It was uselessly large, so I broke it up."

---

① gourd/gʊəd/ n. 葫芦
② bushel/ˈbuʃl/ n. 蒲式耳(计量谷物及水果的单位,等于 8 加仑或大约 36.4 升)
③ ladle/ˈleɪdl/ n. 长柄杓

庄子曰："夫子固拙于用大矣。宋人有善为不龟手之药者^①，世世以洴澼絖为事^②。客闻之，请买其方以百金。聚族而谋曰：'我世世为洴澼絖，不过数金；今一朝而鬻技百金^③，请与之。'客得之，以说吴王。越有难^④，吴王使之将，冬与越人水战，大败越人，裂地而封之^⑤。能不龟手，一也；或以封，或不免于洴澼絖，则所用之异也。今子有五石之瓠，何不虑以为大樽而浮于江湖^⑥，而忧其瓠落无所容？则夫子犹有蓬之心也夫^⑦！"

惠子谓庄子曰："吾有大树，人谓之樗^⑧。其大本拥肿而不中绳墨^⑨，其小枝卷曲而不中规矩，立之涂^⑩，匠者不顾。今子之言，大而无用，众所同去也。"

庄子曰："子独不见狸狌乎^⑪？卑身而伏，以候敖者^⑫；东西跳梁^⑬，不辟高下^⑭；中于机辟^⑮，死于罔罟^⑯。今夫斄牛^⑰，其大若垂天之云。此能为大矣，而不能执鼠。今子有大树，患其无用，何不树之于无何有之乡，广莫之野，彷徨乎无为其侧^⑱，逍遥乎寝卧其下。不夭斤斧，物无害者，无所可用，安所困苦哉！"

---

① 龟(jūn)：通"皲"，皮肤冻裂。
② 洴澼絖：漂洗丝絮。洴(píng)：浮。澼(pì)：在水中漂洗。絖(kuàng)：丝絮。
③ 鬻(yù)：卖，出售。
④ 越有难：越国兵难侵吴。难：乱事，指军事行动。
⑤ 裂地：割地，划地。
⑥ 樽：一种形如酒器，可以缚在腰上，浮水渡河的东西。
⑦ 蓬：草名，其状弯曲不直。有蓬之心：喻心灵茅塞不通。
⑧ 樗(chū)：落叶乔木，木材皮粗质劣。成玄英《疏》云："樗，栲漆之类，嗅之甚臭，恶木者也。"
⑨ 拥肿：木瘤盘结。
⑩ 涂：通"途"，道路。
⑪ 狸(lí)：野猫。狌(shēng)：黄鼠狼。
⑫ 敖：通"遨"，遨翔。敖者：翱翔之物，指鸡鼠之类。
⑬ 跳梁：亦作"跳踉"，跳跃。
⑭ 辟：同"避"。
⑮ 机辟：捕兽器。
⑯ 罔：同"网"。罟(gǔ)：网的总称。
⑰ 斄(lí)牛：牦牛。
⑱ 彷徨：徘徊，悠游自适。无为：无所事事。

"Sir," replied Chuang Tzu, "it was rather you who did not know how to use large things. There was a man of Sung who had a recipe① for salve② for chapped③ hands，his family having been silk-washers for generations. Well，a stranger who had heard of it，came and offered him 100 oz④ of silver for this recipe；whereupon he called together his clansmen⑤ and said，'We have never made much money by silk-washing. Now，we can make 100 oz. in a single day. Let the stranger have the recipe.'

"So the stranger got it，and went and informed the Prince of Wu who was just then at war with the Yüeh State. Accordingly，the Prince used it in a naval battle fought at the beginning of winter with the Yüeh State，the result being that the latter was totally defeated. The stranger was rewarded with territory and a title. Thus，while the efficacy⑥ of salve to cure chapped hands was in both cases the same，its application was different. Here，it secured a title；there，a capacity for washing silk.

"Now as to your five-bushel gourd，why did you not make a boat of it，and float about over river and lake? You could not then have complained of its not holding anything! But I fear you are rather wooly⑦ inside."

Hui Tzu said to Chuang Tzu，"Sir，I have a large tree, of a worthless kind. Its trunk is so irregular and knotty that it cannot be measured out for planks；while its branches are so twisted as to

---

① recipe/'resəpɪ/ n. 处方,秘方
② salve/sælv/ n. 药膏,软膏
③ chap/tʃæp/ v. (皮肤)皲裂
④ oz＝ounce,盎司,英两(常衡＝1/16 磅；金衡及药衡＝1/12 磅＝31.104 克)
⑤ clansman/'klænzmən/ n. 同宗的人,族人
⑥ efficacy/'efɪkəsɪ/ n. 功效,效力
⑦ wooly/'wulɪ/ adj. (头脑、观念等)模糊的,不清楚的

admit of no geometrical① subdivision whatever. It stands by the roadside, but no carpenter will look at it. And your words, sir, are like that tree-big and useless, not wanted by anybody."

"Sir", rejoined② Chuang Tzu, "have you never seen a wild cat, crouching down in wait for its prey? Right and left it springs from bough to bough, high and low alike, -until perchance③ it gets caught in a trap or dies in a snare④. On the other hand, there is the yak⑤ with its great huge body. It is big enough in all conscience, but it cannot catch mice.

"Now if you have a big tree and are at a loss what to do with it, why not plant it in the domain of non-existence, whither you might betake⑥ yourself to inaction by its side, to blissful repose⑦ beneath its shade? There it would be safe from the axe and from all other injury; for being of no use to others, itself would be free from harm."

---

① geometrical/ˌdʒiːəˈmetrɪkl/*adj*. 几何的

② rejoin/ˌriːˈdʒɔɪn/*v*. 回答，答辩

③ perchance/pəˈtʃɑːns/*adv*. 意外地，偶然

④ snare/sneə(r)/*n*. 陷阱，罗网

⑤ yak/jæk/*n*. 牦牛

⑥ betake/bɪˈteɪk/*v*. (to)投身于，专心[致力]于

⑦ repose/rɪˈpəʊz/*n*. 歇息，静卧

【推荐阅读】

一、中文版本及注疏

陈鼓应注译.庄子今注今译(最新修订版).北京：商务印书馆,2007
 年版。

方勇译注.庄子.北京：中华书局,2010 年。

郭庆藩撰,王孝鱼点校.庄子集释.北京：中华书局,2013 年。

郭象注,成玄英疏,曹础基、黄兰华点校.南华真经注疏.北京：中华书
 局,1998 年。

孙通海译注.庄子.北京：中华书局,2007 年。

王先谦.庄子集解.北京：中华书局,1987 年。

二、英文译本

Balfour, Frederic Henry, tr. 1881. *The Divine Classic of Nan-hua,
 Being the Works of Chuang Tsze, Taoist Philosopher*. Shanghai：
 Kelly and Walsh.

Giles, Herbert A., tr. 1888. *Chuang Tzu：Mystic, Moralist, and
 Social Reformer*. London：Bernard Quaritch. 2nd revised edition
 Shanghai：Kelly and Walsh, 1926. Reprinted as *Chuang Tze：
 Taoist Philosopher and Chinese Mystic*. London：George Alan and
 Unwin, 1961.

Legge, James, tr. 1891. "The Writings of Kuang-Tze." In *The
 Sacred Books of China：The Texts of Taoism*. London：Humphrey
 Milford.

Fung, Yu-lan, tr. 1933. *Chuang Tzu：A New Selected Translation
 with an Exposition of the Philosophy of Kuo Hsiang*. Shanghai：
 Commercial Press. Reprint New York：Paragon, 1964.

Lin, Yutang, tr. 1942. "Chuang-tzu：Mystic and Humorist." In
 The Wisdom of China and India, 625 - 691. New York：Random

House.

Chan, Wing-tsit. 1963. "The Mystical Way of Chuang Tzu." In *A Source Book in Chinese Philosophy*, 177 - 210. Princeton: Princeton University Press.

Watson, Burton, tr. 1964. *Chuang Tzu, Basic Writings*. New York: Columbia University Press.

Merton, Thomas. 1969. *The Way of Chuang Tzu*. New York: New Directions.

Watson, Burton, tr. 1968. *The Complete Works of Chuang Tzu*. New York: Columbia University Press.

Feng, Gia-fu, and Jane English, tr. 1974. *Chuang Tsu, Inner Chapters*. New York: Knopf; New York: Vintage.

Graham, A. C. 1981. *Chuang-tzu: The Seven Inner Chapters and Other Writing from the Book of Chuang-tzu*. London: Allan & Unwin.

Mair, Victor H. 1994. *Wandering on the Way: Early Taoist Tales and Parables of Chuang Tzu*. New York: Bantam.

Ziporyn, Brook. 2009. *Zhuangzi: The Essential Writings with Selections from Traditional Commentaries*. Indianapolis: Hackett Publishing.

第九单元 　《荀子》

【导言】

《荀子》今存三十二篇,《四库全书》收入子部儒家类,大部分为荀子所作,据唐人杨倞考,《大略》《宥坐》《子道》《法行》《哀公》《尧问》诸篇为其学生记述。《解蔽》《正名》《劝学》等篇集中反映了荀况的唯物主义认识论思想,《性恶》《修身》《礼论》等篇集中反映了荀况的伦理思想,《王制》《富国》《王霸》《君道》《臣道》《强国》等篇集中反映了荀况的政治和经济思想。全书长于说理论辩,思想深邃,行文缜密,分析透辟,善于取譬,多用排比,行文气势磅礴,富有说服力和感染力。

荀子名况,字卿,又称孙卿,战国末期赵国人(今河北邯郸),生卒年不可确考。是我国古代著名的思想家、文学家、政治家,儒家代表人物之一。曾周游齐、楚、赵、秦等国,试图说服诸国诸侯接受他以王道统一天下的抱负,晚年隐居楚国兰陵,著《荀子》一书。荀子在孔子的"仁"、孟子的"义"的基础上提出了"礼"和"法";荀子既重视天道,又强调人为,提出了"天人之分"的自然观,主张"制天命而用之";荀子认为人能认识客观事物,认为行比知重要;在人性问题上,荀子认为"人性恶",强调后天人为和教育的作用,主张隆礼重法,以法辅礼。

《荀子》的重要注本有唐朝杨倞的《荀子注》,清朝王先谦的《荀子集解》,今人梁启雄的《荀子简释》等。其中《荀子集解》汇集清代学者训诂考订之成就,内容翔实;《荀子简释》"简易、简明、简要",综合诸家校释成果。此外还有章诗同的《荀子简注》、熊公哲的《荀子今注今释》等。

《荀子》的英译,目前已知最早始于理雅各(James Legge)1893 年出版的《中国经典》(*The Chinese Classics*),理雅各翻译了《性恶篇》(*That the Nature is Evil*),将其作为附录附在《孟子》的英译文之后。1924 年,荷兰汉学家戴闻达(J. J. L. Duyvendak)发表了《正名篇》(*Hsun-tzu on the Rectification of Names*)的英译文。1927 年美国汉学家德效骞(Homer H. Dubs)出版了《荀子的著作》(*The Works of Hsuntze*),共选译《荀子》32 篇中的 19 篇。1963 年,华兹生(Burton Waston)发表《荀子读本》,翻译了《荀子》中的 11 篇,其译本为后来很

多美国学者所参考。1988—1994 年，美国迈阿密大学哲学教授和汉学家约翰·诺布洛克(John Knoblock)完整翻译出版了《荀子：全译与研究》(*Xunzi：A Translation and Study of the Complete Works*)。全书共分三卷，分别于 1988、1990、1994 年出版。

性恶篇①

　　人之性恶，其善者伪也②。今人之性，生而有好利焉，顺是③，故争夺生而辞让亡焉④；生而有疾恶焉⑤，顺是，故残贼生而忠信亡焉⑥；生而有耳目之欲，有好声色焉，顺是，故淫乱生而礼义文理亡焉⑦。然则从人之性⑧，顺人之情，必出于争夺，合于犯分乱理而归于暴⑨。故必将有师法之化，礼义之道，然后出于辞让，合于文理，而归于治。用此观之，人之性恶明矣⑩，其善者伪也。

　　故枸木必将待檃栝、烝矫然后直⑪；钝金必将待砻厉然后利⑫。今人之性恶，必将待师法然后正⑬，得礼义然后治。

---

① 选自《荀子》第二十三篇。该篇系统阐述荀子的"性恶论"。全篇围绕"人之性恶，其善者伪也"的观点展开。荀子认为人的天性是恶的，需要通过礼义法度来治理、改变天性。荀子提出"涂之人可以为禹"，认为普通人与圣人天性一致，只要"伏术为学，专心一志，思索孰察，加日县久，积善而不息"是可以和圣人一样，达到"通于神明，参于天地"的境界的。
② 伪：人为。
③ 顺：任情，放任。
④ 争夺：争斗夺取。辞让：谦逊推让。
⑤ 疾恶(jí wù)：嫉妒，憎恨。
⑥ 残贼：残忍暴虐。
⑦ 礼义：礼法道义。礼，谓人所履。义，谓事之宜。文理：礼仪。
⑧ 从：同"纵"，放纵。
⑨ 犯分：僭越等级名分。理：名分。
⑩ 然则：连词，连接句子，表示连贯关系。犹言"如此……那么"或"那么"。
⑪ 枸(gōu)木：曲木；枸：弯曲。檃栝(yǐn kuò)：亦作"檃括"，矫正竹木邪曲的工具，泛指矫正；揉曲叫檃，正方称括。烝(zhēng)：后作"蒸"，用蒸汽加热。
⑫ 钝金：不锋利的兵器。砻(lóng)厉：亦作"砻砺"，磨，磨炼。
⑬ 师法：师长传授之法。

Man's Nature Is Evil

Translated by Burton Watson[1]

Man's nature is evil; goodness is the result of conscious activity.

The nature of man is such that he is born with a fondness for profit. If he indulges[2] this fondness, it will lead him into wrangling[3] and strife[4], and all sense of courtesy[5] and humility[6] will disappear. He is born with feelings of envy and hate, and if he indulges these, they will lead him into violence and crime, and all sense of loyalty and good faith[7] will disappear. Man is born with the desires of the eyes and ears, with a fondness for beautiful sights and sounds. If he indulges these, they will lead him into license[8] and wantonness[9], and all ritual principles and correct forms will be lost. Hence, any man who follows his nature and indulges his emotions will inevitably become involved in wrangling and strife, will violate the forms and rules of society, and will end as a criminal. Therefore, man must first be transformed[10] by the instructions of a teacher and guided by ritual principles, and only then will he be able to observe the dictates[11] of courtesy and

---

① 译文选自 Watson, Burton. 1963. *Xunzi: Basic Writings*. New York, NY: Columbia University Press。

② indulge/ɪnˈdʌldʒ/ v. 纵情于,迁就,放任,沉溺

③ wrangle/ˈræŋgl/ v. 争论,口角,争吵

④ strife/straɪf/ v. 冲突,争斗,争吵

⑤ courtesy/ˈkɜːtəsɪ/ n. 礼貌,客气话,礼貌的举止

⑥ humility/hjuːˈmɪlətɪ/ n. 谦逊,谦卑,谦虚

⑦ good faith 诚实,诚恳

⑧ license/ˈlaɪsns/ n. 放肆,放纵,放荡,淫乱

⑨ wantonness/ˈwɒntənɪs/ n. 放纵,嬉戏,淫荡

⑩ transform/trænsˈfɔːm/ v. 转换,改变,转化

⑪ dictate/dɪkˈteɪt/ n. (通常作复数)(尤指在理智、良心等驱使下必须执行的)命令,指令

humility, obey the forms and rules of society, and achieve order. It is obvious from this, then, that man's nature is evil, and that his goodness is the result of conscious activity.

A warped① piece of wood must wait until it has been laid against the straightening board, steamed, and forced into shape before it can become straight; a piece of blunt② metal must wait until it has been whetted③ on a grindstone④ before it can become sharp. Similarly, since man's nature is evil, it must wait for the instructions of a teacher before it can become upright, and for the guidance of ritual principles before it can become orderly.

---

① warp/wɔːp/v. 弯曲,翘棱(尤指因收缩或伸展不均所致)
② blunt/blʌnt/adj. 不锋利的,不尖的,钝的
③ whet/wet/v. 磨(刀、斧等)(尤指用石头磨)
④ grindstone/ˈɡraɪndstəʊn/n. 磨石,砂轮

今人无师法，则偏险而不正①；无礼义，则悖乱而不治②。古者圣王以人性恶，以为偏险而不正，悖乱而不治，是以为之起礼义、制法度，以矫饰人之情性而正之③，以扰化人之情性而导之也④。使皆出于治，合于道者也。今之人，化师法⑤，积文学⑥，道礼义者为君子⑦；纵性情⑧，安恣睢而违礼义者为小人⑨。用此观之，人之性恶明矣，其善者伪也。

孟子曰："人之学者，其性善。"曰：是不然。是不及知人之性，而不察乎人之性、伪之分者也。凡性者，天之就也⑩，不可学，不可事⑪；礼义者，圣人之所生也⑫，人之所学而能⑬，所事而成者也。不可学、不可事而在人者，谓之性，可学而能、可事而成之在人者谓之伪。是性伪之分也。

今人之性，目可以见，耳可以听。夫可以见之明不离目，可以听之聪不离耳，目明而耳聪，不可学明矣。

孟子曰："今人之性善，将皆失丧其性故也。"

---

① 偏险：偏颇邪僻。偏：偏邪。险：邪恶。
② 悖（bèi）乱：惑乱，昏乱。
③ 矫饰：亦作"矫饬"，整饰，整改。情性：本性。
④ 扰化：教化。杨倞注："扰，驯也。"
⑤ 化师法：受师法的教化。
⑥ 文学：儒家学说，泛指文章经籍。
⑦ 道：遵循，实行。
⑧ 纵：放纵；听任。性情：人的禀性和气质。
⑨ 恣睢（suī）：放纵暴戾。睢：恣意。
⑩ 就：表示原来或早已是这样。
⑪ 事：从师求学；实践，从事。
⑫ 生：生产，制作。
⑬ 能：胜任，能做到。

If men have no teachers to instruct them, they will be inclined towards evil and not upright; and if they have no ritual principles to guide them, they will be perverse① and violent and lack order. In ancient times the sage kings realized that man's nature is evil, and that therefore he inclines toward evil and violence and is not upright or orderly. Accordingly② they created ritual principles and laid down certain regulations in order to reform man's emotional nature and make it upright, in order to train and transform it and guide it in the proper channels. In this way they caused all men to become orderly and to conform to the Way. Hence, today any man who takes to heart the instructions of his teacher, applies himself to his studies, and abides by ritual principles may become a gentleman, but anyone who gives free rein to③ his emotional nature, is content④ to indulge his passions, and disregards ritual principles becomes a petty⑤ man. It is obvious from this, therefore, that man's nature is evil, and that his goodness is the result of conscious activity.

Mencius states that man is capable of learning because his nature is good, but I say that this is wrong. It indicates that he has not really understood man's nature nor distinguished properly between the basic nature and conscious activity. The nature is that which is given by Heaven; you cannot learn it, you cannot acquire it by effort. Ritual principles, on the other hand, are created by sages; you can learn to apply them, you can work to bring them to completion. That part of man which cannot be learned or acquired

① perverse/pə'vɜːs/adj. (指人)固执错误的,背理的,不合常情的;(指行为)任性的,蛮不讲理的;(指感情)不近情理的,过分的
② accordingly/ə'kɔːdɪŋlɪ/adv. 于是,从而,因此
③ give free rein to 放任,放纵
④ content/kən'tent/adj. 满足,满意
⑤ petty/'petɪ/adj. 小的,不重要的;狭隘的,器量小的,小气的

by effort is called the nature; that part of him which can be acquired by learning and brought to completion by effort is called conscious activity. This is the difference between nature and conscious activity.

It is a part of man's nature that his eyes can see and his ears can hear. But the faculty[①] of clear sight can never exist separately from the eye, nor can the faculty of keen[②] hearing exist separately from the ear. It is obvious, then, that you cannot acquire clear sight and keen hearing by study.

Mencius states that man's nature is good, and that all evil arises because he loses his original nature.

---

① faculty/'fæklti/ *n*. 官能
② keen/ki:n/*adj*. 非常敏感的,敏锐的

曰：若是，则过矣。今人之性，生而离其朴①，离其资②，必失而丧之。用此观之，然则人之性恶明矣。所谓性善者，不离其朴而美之，不离其资而利之也。使夫资朴之于美③，心意之于善，若夫可以见之明不离目，可以听之聪不离耳。故曰目明而耳聪也。今人之性，饥而欲饱，寒而欲暖，劳而欲休，此人之情性也。今人饥，见长而不敢先食者，将有所让也；劳而不敢求息者，将有所代也④。夫子之让乎父，弟之让乎兄，子之代乎父，弟之代乎兄，此二行者⑤，皆反于性而悖于情也；然而孝子之道，礼义之文理也。故顺情性则不辞让矣，辞让则悖于情性矣。用此观之，人之性恶明矣，其善者伪也。

问者曰："人之性恶，则礼义恶生？⑥"

应之曰：凡礼义者，是生于圣人之伪，非故生于人之性也。故陶人埏埴而为器⑦，然则器生于陶人之伪，非故生于人之性也。故工人斲木而成器⑧，然则器生于工人之伪，非故生于人之性也。

---

① 朴：本性，本质，原本。杨倞注："朴，质也。"
② 资：禀赋，才质。杨倞注："资，材也。"
③ 资朴：天资素质。杨倞注："使质朴资材自善，如闻见之聪明常不离于耳目，此乃天性也。"
④ 代：取代，代替（长辈劳动）。
⑤ 行：行为。
⑥ 恶（wū）：疑问代词。相当于"何""安""怎么"。
⑦ 陶人：烧制陶器的匠人。埏埴：和泥制作陶器。河上公注："埏，和也；埴，土也。谓和土以为器也。"
⑧ 工人：指从事各种技艺的劳动者。斲（zhuó）木：砍削木料。

Such a view, I believe, is erroneous. It is the way with man's nature that as soon as he is born he begins to depart from his original naïveté① and simplicity, and therefore he must inevitably lose what Mencius regards as his original nature. It is obvious from this, then, that the nature of man is evil. Those who maintain that the nature is good praise and approve whatever has not departed from the original simplicity and naïveté of the child. That is, they consider that beauty belongs to the original simplicity and naïveté and goodness to the original mind in the same way that clear sight is inseparable from the eye and keen hearing from the ear. Hence, they maintain that [the nature possesses goodness] in the same way that the eye possesses clear vision or the ear keenness of hearing. Now it is the nature of man that when he is hungry he will desire satisfaction②, when he is cold he will desire warmth, and when he is weary he will desire rest. This is his emotional nature. And yet a man, although he is hungry, will not dare to be the first to eat if he is in the presence of③ his elders, because he knows that he should yield to④ them, and although he is weary, he will not dare to demand rest because he knows that he should relieve others of the burden of labor. For a son to yield to his father or a younger brother to yield to his elder brother, for a son to relieve his father of work or a younger brother to relieve his elder brother — acts such as these are all contrary to man's nature and run counter to his emotions. And yet they represent the way of filial piety and the proper forms enjoined by ritual principles. Hence, if men follow their emotional nature, there will be no courtesy or humility;

---

① naïveté/nɑːˈviːtɪ/ n. 天真烂漫, 纯真无邪
② satisfaction/ˌsætɪsˈfækʃn/ n. 欲望、需要或食欲的实现或满足
③ in the presence of 在……面前
④ yield to 让步, 屈服于

courtesy and humility in fact run counter to man's emotional nature. From this it is obvious, then, that man's nature is evil, and that his goodness is the result of conscious activity.

Someone may ask: if man's nature is evil, then where do ritual principles come from? I would reply: all ritual principles are produced by the conscious activity of the sages; essentially① they are not products of man's nature. A potter② molds③ clay④ and makes a vessel⑤, but the vessel is the product of the conscious activity of the potter, not essentially a product of his human nature. A carpenter⑥ carves a piece of wood and makes a utensil⑦, but the utensil is the product of the conscious activity of the carpenter, not essentially a product of his human nature.

---

① essentially/ɪˈsenʃəlɪ/*adv*. 本质上,本来
② potter/ˈpɒtə/*n*. 制陶工人,陶工
③ mold/məʊld/*v*. 用模子制造
④ clay/kleɪ/*n*. 黏土,泥土
⑤ vessel/ˈvesl/*n*. 容器,器皿
⑥ carpenter/ˈkɑːpəntə/*n*. 木匠,木工
⑦ utensil/juːˈtensl/*n*. 用具,器皿(尤指家庭日用的)

圣人积思虑,习伪故,以生礼义而起法度,然则礼义法度者,是生于圣人之伪,非故生于人之性也。

若夫目好色,耳好声,口好味,心好利,骨体肤理好愉佚①,是皆生于人之情性者也,感而自然②,不待事而后生之者也。夫感而不能然,必且待事而后然者,谓之生于伪。是性伪之所生,其不同之征也③。故圣人化性而起伪,伪起而生礼义,礼义生而制法度。然则礼义法度者,是圣人之所生也。故圣人之所以同于众,其不异于众者,性也;所以异而过众者,伪也。

夫好利而欲得者,此人之情性也。假之有弟兄资财而分者,且顺情性,好利而欲得,若是,则兄弟相拂夺矣④;且化礼义之文理,若是,则让乎国人矣⑤。故顺情性则弟兄争矣,化礼义则让乎国人矣。

凡人之欲为善者,为性恶也。夫薄愿厚⑥,恶愿美⑦,狭愿广,贫愿富,贱愿贵,苟无之中者,必求于外。

---

① 骨体:骨架躯体。肤理:皮肤的纹理。愉佚:亦作"愉逸",安逸,快乐。
② 自然:天然,非人为的。
③ 征:证明,表现,表示。
④ 拂夺:争夺。
⑤ 国人:古代指居住在大邑内的人;亦指国内之人,全国的人。
⑥ 愿:羡慕,倾慕,思念。
⑦ 恶:丑陋,粗劣,不好。

The sage gathers together his thoughts and ideas, experiments with various forms of conscious activity, and so produces ritual principles and sets forth[1] laws and regulations. Hence, these ritual principles and laws are the products of the conscious activity of the sage, not essentially products of his human nature.

Phenomena such as the eye's fondness for beautiful forms, the ear's fondness for beautiful sounds, the mouth's fondness for delicious flavors, the mind's fondness for profit, or the body's fondness for pleasure and ease — these are all products of the emotional nature of man. They are instinctive[2] and spontaneous[3]; man does not have to do anything to produce them. But that which does not come into being instinctively but must wait for some activity to bring it into being is called the product of conscious activity. These are the products of the nature and of conscious activity respectively[4], and the proof that they are not the same. Therefore, the sage transforms his nature and initiates conscious activity; from this conscious activity he produces ritual principles, and when they have been produced he sets up rules and regulations. Hence, ritual principles and rules are produced by the sage. In respect to[5] human nature the sage is the same as all other men and does not surpass[6] them; it is only in his conscious activity that he differs from and surpasses other men.

It is man's emotional nature to love profit and desire gain. Suppose now that a man has some wealth to be divided. If he

---

① set forth 阐明，提出，宣布

② instinctive/ɪnˈstɪŋktɪv/ adj. 本能的，直觉的，天生的

③ spontaneous/spɔnˈteɪnɪəs/ adj. 自发的，无意识的，不由自主的，非出于强制的，自然的

④ respectively/rɪˈspektɪvlɪ/ adv. 分别地，各自地

⑤ in respect to 关于，涉及

⑥ surpass/səˈpɑːs/ v. 超越，胜过

indulges his emotional nature, loving profit and desiring gain, then he will quarrel and wrangle even with his own brothers over the division. But if he has been transformed by the proper forms of ritual principle, then he will be capable of yielding even to a complete stranger. Hence, to indulge the emotional nature leads to the quarreling of brothers, but to be transformed by ritual principles makes a man capable of yielding to strangers.

Every man who desires to do good does so precisely because his nature is evil. A man whose accomplishments① are meager② longs for greatness; an ugly man longs for beauty; a man in cramped③ quarters④ longs for spaciousness⑤; a poor man longs for wealth; a humble man longs for eminence⑥. Whatever a man lacks in himself he will seek outside.

---

① accomplishment/ə'kʌmplɪʃmənt/n. 成绩,成就;社交礼仪;完成,实现
② meager/'miːgə/adj. 不足的,缺乏的,贫乏的,虚弱的
③ cramped/kræmpt/adj. 狭窄的,受拘束的
④ quarter/'kwɔːtə/n. [通常用复数]住处;军营
⑤ spaciousness/'speɪʃəsnɪs/n. 宽敞
⑥ eminence/'emɪnəns/n. 卓越,显赫

故富而不愿财,贵而不愿埶①,苟有之中者,必不及于外。用此观之,人之欲为善者,为性恶也。今人之性,固无礼义②,故强学而求有之也③;性不知礼义,故思虑而求知之也。然则性而已,则人无礼义,不知礼义。人无礼义则乱,不知礼义则悖。然则性而已,则悖乱在己。用此观之,人之性恶明矣,其善者伪也。

孟子曰:"人之性善。"

曰:是不然。凡古今天下之所谓善者,正理平治也④;所谓恶者,偏险悖乱也。是善恶之分也已。今诚以人之性固正理平治邪,则有恶用圣王,恶用礼义哉!虽有圣王礼义,将曷加于正理平治也哉⑤!今不然,人之性恶。故古者圣人以人之性恶,以为偏险而不正,悖乱而不治,故为之立君上之埶以临之⑥,明礼义以化之,起法正以治之⑦,重刑罚以禁之,使天下皆出于治,合于善也。是圣王之治,而礼义之化也。今当试去君上之埶,无礼义之化,去法正之治,无刑罚之禁,倚而观天下民人之相与也⑧。

---

① 埶(shì):"势"的古字,权力,权势。
② 固:原来,本来。
③ 强学:勤勉地学习。
④ 正:合乎法度、规律或常情。理:治理得好,与"乱"相对。平治:合法度。
⑤ 曷(hé):代词,表示疑问,相当于"何""什么"。
⑥ 临:监视,监临,引申为统治,治理。
⑦ 法正:法政,法制,礼法规矩。
⑧ 倚:立,靠。民人:人民,百姓。相与:相处,交往。

But if a man is already rich, he will not long for wealth, and if he is already eminent, he will not long for greater power. What a man already possesses in himself he will not bother to look for outside. From this we can see that men desire to do good precisely① because their nature is evil. Ritual principles are certainly not a part of man's original nature. Therefore, he forces himself to study and to seek to possess them. An understanding of ritual principles is not a part of man's original nature, and therefore he ponders and plans and thereby seeks to understand them. Hence, man in the state in which he is born neither possesses nor understands ritual principles. If he does not possess ritual principles, his behavior will be chaotic②, and if he does not understand them, he will be wild and irresponsible. In fact, therefore, man in the state in which he is born possesses this tendency towards chaos and irresponsibility. From this it is obvious, then, that man's nature is evil, and that his goodness is the result of conscious activity.

Mencius states that man's nature is good, but I say that this view is wrong. All men in the world, past and present, agree in defining goodness as that which is upright, reasonable, and orderly, and evil as that which is prejudiced③, irresponsible, and chaotic. This is the distinction between good and evil. Now suppose that man's nature was in fact intrinsically upright, reasonable, and orderly — then what need would there be for sage kings and ritual principles? The existence of sage kings and ritual principles could certainly add nothing to the situation. But because man's nature is in fact evil, this is not so. Therefore, in ancient times the sages,

---

① precisely/prɪˈsaɪslɪ/*adv*. (用作加强语气的词)恰恰
② chaotic/keɪˈɒtɪk/*adj*. 混乱,无秩序
③ prejudiced/ˈpredʒədɪst/*adj*. 怀偏见的,有成见的

realizing that man's nature is evil, that it is prejudiced and not upright, irresponsible and lacking in order, for this reason established the authority of the ruler to control it, elucidated① ritual principles to transform it, set up laws and standards to correct it, and meted② out strict punishments to restrain it. As a result, all the world achieved order and conformed to③ goodness. Such is the orderly government of the sage kings and the transforming power of ritual principles. Now let someone try doing away with④ the authority of the ruler, ignoring the transforming power of ritual principles, rejecting the order that comes from laws and standards, and dispensing with⑤ the restrictive power of punishments, and then watch and see how the people of the world treat each other.

---

① elucidate/ɪˈluːsɪdeɪt/ v. 阐明，使明晰
② mete/miːt/out v. 给予，加以（惩罚、奖励等）
③ conform to 符合，使一致，适应
④ do away with 废除，去掉
⑤ dispense with 无需，免除，省掉

若是,则夫强者害弱而夺之,众者暴寡而哗之^①,天下悖乱而相亡不待顷矣。用此观之,然则人之性恶明矣,其善者伪也。

故善言古者必有节于今^②,善言天者必有征于人。凡论者,贵其有辨合^③,有符验^④。故坐而言之,起而可设^⑤,张而可施行^⑥。今孟子曰:"人之性善。"无辨合符验,坐而言之,起而不可设,张而不可施行,岂不过甚矣哉!

故性善则去圣王,息礼义矣^⑦;性恶则与圣王^⑧,贵礼义矣。故隐栝之生,为枸木也;绳墨之起,为不直也;立君上,明礼义,为性恶也。用此观之,然则人之性恶明矣,其善者伪也。

直木不待隐栝而直者,其性直也;枸木必将待隐栝烝矫然后直者,以其性不直也。今人之性恶,必将待圣王之治,礼义之化,然后始出于治,合于善也。用此观之,人之性恶明矣,其善者伪也。

---

① 暴:欺凌,凌辱。哗:通"华",当中裂开。
② 节:证验,验证。王先谦集解引王引之曰:"节亦验也。"
③ 辨合:符合,契合。指论说的道理与事实相符。辨,通"别",别之为两。杨倞注:"辨,别也……言论议如别之合如符之验然,可施行也。"古代的一种凭信方式,将一物一分为二,各持其一,相合为验。合,合之为一。
④ 符验:应验,符合。
⑤ 设:施用。
⑥ 张:张设,陈设。
⑦ 息:停止,停息。
⑧ 与:称赞,赞扬。

He will find that the powerful impose upon[1] the weak and rob them, the many terrorize the few and extort[2] from them, and in no time[3] the whole world will be given up to[4] chaos and mutual destruction. It is obvious from this, then, that man's nature is evil, and that his goodness is the result of conscious activity.

Those who are good at discussing antiquity must demonstrate the validity[5] of what they say in terms of modern times; those who are good at discussing Heaven must show proofs from the human world. In discussions of all kinds, men value what is in accord with the facts and what can be proved to be valid. Hence if a man sits on his mat[6] propounding[7] some theory, he should be able to stand right up and put it into practice, and show that it can be extended over a wide area with equal validity. Now Mencius states that man's nature is good, but this is neither in accord with the facts, nor can it be proved to be valid. One may sit down and propound such a theory, but he cannot stand up and put it into practice, nor can he extend it over a wide area with any success at all. How, then, could it be anything but erroneous?

If the nature of man were good, we could dispense with sage kings and forget about ritual principles. But if it is evil, then we must go along with[8] the sage kings and honor ritual principles. The straightening board is made because of the warped wood; the plumb

---

① impose upon 强加
② extort/ɪkˈstɔːt/敲诈, 勒索
③ in no time 立即, 马上
④ give up to 陷入
⑤ validity/vəˈlɪdəti/ n. 有效性, 正确性
⑥ mat/mæt/ n. 席, 垫
⑦ propound/prəˈpaʊnd/ v. 提出, 提出……以供考虑
⑧ go along with 陪……一起去, 赞同, 附和

line① is employed because things are crooked②; rulers are set up and ritual principles elucidated because the nature of man is evil. From this it is obvious, then, that man's nature is evil, and that his goodness is the result of conscious activity.

A straight piece of wood does not have to wait for the straightening board to become straight; it is straight by nature. But a warped piece of wood must wait until it has been laid against the straightening board, steamed, and forced into shape before it can become straight, because by nature it is warped. Similarly, since man's nature is evil, he must wait for the ordering power of the sage kings and the transforming power of ritual principles; only then can he achieve order and conform to goodness. From this it is obvious, then, that man's nature is evil, and that his goodness is the result of conscious activity.

---

① plumb line 铅垂线,垂直线
② crooked/ˈkrukɪd/ *adj*. 歪的,扭曲的,弯曲的

问者曰："礼义积伪者①，是人之性，故圣人能生之也。"

应之曰：是不然。夫陶人埏埴而生瓦，然则瓦埴岂陶人之性也哉②？工人斫木而生器，然则器木岂工人之性也哉？夫圣人之于礼义也，辟则陶埏而生之也③，然则礼义积伪者，岂人之本性也哉？

凡人之性者，尧舜之与桀跖，其性一也；君子之与小人，其性一也。今将以礼义积伪为人之性邪？然则有曷贵尧禹，曷贵君子矣哉？凡所贵尧禹君子者，能化性，能起伪，伪起而生礼义。然则圣人之于礼义积伪也，亦犹陶埏而生之也。用此观之，然则礼义积伪者，岂人之性也哉？所贱于桀跖小人者，从其性，顺其情，安恣睢，以出乎贪利争夺。故人之性恶明矣，其善者伪也。

天非私曾、骞、孝己而外众人也④，然而曾、骞、孝己独厚于孝之实，而全于孝之名者，何也？以綦于礼义故也⑤。天非私齐鲁之民而外秦人也，然而于父子之义，夫妇之别，不如齐鲁之孝具敬文者⑥，何也？以秦人之从情性，安恣睢，慢于礼义故也，岂其性异矣哉？

---

① 积伪：累积人的作为。伪，人为。王先谦集解："礼义积伪者，积作为而起礼义也。"

② 瓦埴：把细黏土制成瓦器。埴，细黏土。

③ 辟：通"譬"，譬如，譬喻。

④ 私：偏爱。曾：曾参。骞：闵子骞。两人都是孔子的学生，以孝闻名。孝己：殷高宗之子，也有孝名。

⑤ 綦：极，很。

⑥ 敬文：注重礼节、仪式。

Someone may ask whether ritual principles and concerted[①] conscious activity are not themselves a part of man's nature, so that for that reason the sage is capable of producing them. But I would answer that this is not so. A potter may mold clay and produce an earthen pot, but surely molding pots out of clay is not a part of the potter's human nature. A carpenter may carve wood and produce a utensil, but surely carving utensils out of wood is not a part of the carpenter's human nature. The sage stands in the same relation to ritual principles as the potter to the things he molds and produces. How, then, could ritual principles and concerted conscious activity be a part of man's basic human nature?

As far as human nature goes, the sages Yao and Shun possessed the same nature as the tyrant Jie or Robber Zhi, and the gentleman possesses the same nature as the petty man. Would you still maintain, then, that ritual principles and concerted conscious activity are a part of man's nature? If you do so, then what reason is there to pay any particular honor to Yao, Shun, or the gentleman? The reason people honor Yao, Shun, and the gentleman is that they are able to transform their nature, apply themselves to conscious activity, and produce ritual principles. The sage, then, must stand in the same relation to ritual principles as the potter to the things he molds and produces. Looking at it this way, how could ritual principles and concerted conscious activity be a part of man's nature? The reason people despise Jie, Robber Zhi, or the petty man is that they give free rein to their nature, follow their emotions, and are content to indulge their passions, so that their conduct is marked by greed and contentiousness[②]. Therefore, it is

---

① concerted /kən'sɜːtɪd/ *adj*. 商议好的, 预定的, 协定的
② contentiousness /kən'tenʃəsnəs/ *n*. 好争, 爱争吵

clear that man's nature is evil, and that his goodness is the result of conscious activity.

Heaven did not bestow① any particular favor upon Zengzi, Min Ziqian, or Xiaoyi that it withheld② from other men. And yet these three men among all others proved most capable of carrying out their duties as sons and winning fame for their filial piety. Why? Because of their thorough attention to ritual principles. Heaven has not bestowed any particular favor upon the inhabitants③ of Qi and Lu which it has withheld from the people of Qin. And yet when it comes to observing the duties of father and son and the separation of roles between husband and wife, the inhabitants of Qin cannot match the filial reverence④ and respect for proper form which marks the people of Qi and Lu. Why? Because the people of Qin give free rein to their emotional nature, are content to indulge their passions, and are careless of ritual principles. It is certainly not due to any difference in human nature between the two groups.

---

① bestow/bɪˈstəu/ v. 赠予，授予
② withhold/wɪðˈhəuld/ v. 不给，不赋予，阻挡
③ inhabitant/ɪnˈhæbɪtənt/ n. 居民（居住在某地的人，尤指长期居民）
④ reverence/ˈrevərəns/ n. 尊敬，敬礼，敬重

"涂之人可以为禹①。"曷谓也?

曰：凡禹之所以为禹者，以其为仁义法正也。然则仁义法正有可知可能之理②。然而涂之人也，皆有可以知仁义法正之质，皆有可以能仁义法正之具，然则其可以为禹明矣。今以仁义法正为固无可知可能之理邪? 然则唯禹不知仁义法正，不能仁义法正也。将使涂之人固无可以知仁义法正之质，而固无可以能仁义法正之具邪? 然则涂之人也，且内不可以知父子之义，外不可以知君臣之正。今不然。涂之人者，皆内可以知父子之义，外可以知君臣之正，然则其可以知之质，可以能之具，其在涂之人明矣。今使涂之人者，以其可以知之质，可以能之具，本夫仁义之可知之理，可能之具，然则其可以为禹明矣。今使涂之人伏术为学③，专心一志，思索孰察④，加日县久⑤，积善而不息，则通于神明，参于天地矣。故圣人者，人之所积而致也。

曰："圣可积而致，然而皆不可积，何也?"

曰：可以而不可使也。故小人可以为君子而不肯为君子，君子可以为小人而不肯为小人。

---

① 涂人：普通人，路人，陌生人。涂，通"途"。

② 可能：可以实现。

③ 伏：通"服"，从事。术：方法，此处指掌握道术的方法。

④ 孰察：仔细考察、研究。

⑤ 县久：历时久长。

"The man in the street can become a Yu. What does this mean?"

What made the sage emperor Yu a Yu, I would reply, was the fact that he practiced benevolence and righteousness and abided by the proper rules and standards. If this is so, then benevolence, righteousness, and proper standards must be based upon principles which can be known and practiced. Any man in the street has the essential faculties needed to understand benevolence, righteousness, and proper standards, and the potential ability to put them into practice. Therefore it is clear that he can become a Yu. Would you maintain that benevolence, righteousness, and proper standards are not based upon any principles that can be known and practiced? If so, then even a Yu could not have understood or practiced them. Or would you maintain that the man in the street does not have the essential faculties needed to understand them or the potential ability to put them into practice? If so, then you are saying that the man in the street in his family life cannot understand the duties required of a father or a son and in public life cannot comprehend the correct relationship between ruler and subject①. But in fact this is not true. Any man in the street can understand the duties required of a father or a son and can comprehend the correct relationship between ruler and subject. Therefore, it is obvious that the essential faculties needed to understand such ethical② principles and the potential ability to put them into practice must be a part of his make-up③. Now if he takes these faculties and abilities and applies them to the principles of benevolence and righteousness, which we have already

---

① subject/'sʌbdʒɪkt/ n. 臣民，国民
② ethical/'eθɪkl/ adj. 道德的，伦理的
③ make-up 性质，天性，性格

shown to be knowable and practicable, then it is obvious that he can become a Yu. If the man in the street applies himself to training and study, concentrates his mind and will, and considers and examines things carefully, continuing his efforts over a long period of time and accumulating good acts without stop, then he can achieve a godlike understanding and form a triad[1] with Heaven and earth. The sage is a man who has arrived where he has through the accumulation of good acts.

You have said, someone may object[2], that the sage has arrived where he has through the accumulation of good acts. Why is it, then, that everyone is not able to accumulate good acts in the same way?

I would reply: everyone is capable of doing so, but not everyone can be made to do so. The petty man is capable of becoming a gentleman, yet he is not willing to do so; the gentleman is capable of becoming a petty man but he is not willing to do so.

---

① triad/'traɪæd/ *n*. 三个一组,三合体
② object/əb'dʒekt/ *v*. 反对,不赞成

小人、君子者，未尝不可以相为也，然而不相为者，可以而不可使也。故涂之人可以为禹则然，涂之人能为禹，未必然也。虽不能为禹，无害可以为禹①。足可以遍行天下，然而未尝有能遍行天下者也。夫工匠农贾，未尝不可以相为事也，然而未尝能相为事也。用此观之，然则可以为，未必能也；虽不能，无害可以为。然则能不能之与可不可，其不同远矣，其不可以相为明矣。

尧问于舜曰："人情何如？"舜对曰："人情甚不美，又何问焉？妻子具而孝衰于亲，嗜欲得而信衰于友，爵禄盈而忠衰于君。人之情乎！人之情乎！甚不美，又何问焉。唯贤者为不然。"

有圣人之知者，有士君子之知者②，有小人之知者，有役夫之知者：多言则文而类③，终日议其所以，言之千举万变，其统类一也④，是圣人之知也。少言则径而省⑤，论而法⑥，若佚之以绳⑦，是士君子之知也。

---

① 无害：不损害，不妨害。

② 士君子：有学问而品德高尚的人。

③ 文：有文才，有才华。类：有系统，有条理。

④ 统类：纲纪和条例。杨倞注："统，谓纲纪；类，谓比类。大谓之统，分别谓之类。"

⑤ 径：直接。省：少。

⑥ 论：通"伦"。法：有法度。

⑦ 佚：俞樾以为当读作"秩"，又通"程"，指事物的标准。此处用作动词。

The petty man and the gentleman are perfectly capable of changing places; the fact that they do not actually do so is what I mean when I say that they are capable of doing so but they cannot be made to do so. Hence, it is correct to say that the man in the street is capable of becoming a Yu, but it is not necessarily correct to say that he will in fact find it possible to do so. But that he does not find it possible to do so does not prove that he is incapable of doing so. A person with two feet is theoretically capable of walking to every corner of the earth, although in fact no one has ever found it possible to do so. Similarly, the artisan①, the carpenter, the farmer, and the merchant are theoretically capable of exchanging professions, although in actual practice they find it impossible to do so. From this we can see that, although someone may be theoretically capable of becoming something, he may not in practice find it possible to do so. But although he does not find it possible to do so, this does not prove that he is not capable of doing so. To find it practically possible or impossible to do something and to be capable or incapable of doing something are two entirely different things. It is perfectly clear, then, that a man is theoretically capable of becoming something else.

Yao asked Shun, "What are man's emotions like?" Shun replied, "Man's emotions are very unlovely things indeed! What need is there to ask any further? Once a man acquires a wife and children, he no longer treats his parents as a filial son should. Once he succeeds in satisfying his cravings② and desires, he neglects his duty to his friends. Once he has won a high position and a good

---

① artisan/ˌɑːtɪˈzæn/ n. 工匠，技工
② craving/ˈkreɪvɪŋ/ n. 占有欲，渴望

stipend①, he ceases to serve his sovereign② with a loyal heart. Man's emotions, man's emotions — they are very unlovely things indeed! What need is there to ask any further? Only the worthy man is different from this."

There is the understanding of the sage, the understanding of the gentleman and man of breeding③, the understanding of the petty man, and the understanding of the menial④. He speaks many words but they are graceful and well ordered; all day he discourses⑤ on his reasons, employing a thousand different and varied modes of expression, and yet all that he says is united around a single principle: such is the understanding of the sage. He speaks little but what he says is brief and to the point⑥, logical and clearly presented, as though laid out with a plumb line: such is the understanding of the gentleman and man of breeding.

---

① stipend/ˈstaɪpend/ n. 薪俸，薪金
② sovereign/ˈsɔvrɪn/ n. 最高统治者（如国王、皇帝）
③ breeding/ˈbriːdɪŋ/ n. 教养（指社交和个人举止的礼仪表现的训练）
④ menial/ˈmiːnɪəl/ n. 佣人，仆人，下人
⑤ discourse/ˈdɪskɔːs/on v. （通常长篇大论地）论说、宣扬或讲授
⑥ to the point 中肯，切中要害

其言也诇，其行也悖，其举事多悔①，是小人之知也。齐给便敏而无类②，杂能旁魄而无用③，析速粹孰而不急④，不恤是非，不论曲直，以期胜人为意，是役夫之知也。

有上勇者，有中勇者，有下勇者。天下有中，敢直其身；先王有道，敢行其意；上不循于乱世之君，下不俗于乱世之民；仁之所在无贫穷，仁之所亡无富贵；天下知之，则欲与天下同苦乐之；天下不知之，则傀然独立天地之间而不畏⑤，是上勇也。礼恭而意俭，大齐信焉而轻货财⑥，贤者敢推而尚之，不肖者敢援而废之，是中勇也。轻身而重货，恬祸而广解苟免⑦，不恤是非然不然之情，以期胜人为意，是下勇也。

繁弱、钜黍古之良弓也；然而不得排檠⑧，则不能自正。桓公之葱⑨，太公之阙⑩，文王之录，庄君之曶⑪，阖闾之干将、莫邪、钜阙、辟闾⑫，此皆古之良剑也；然而不加砥砺则不能利，不得人力则不能断。

---

① 举事：行事，办事。悔：过失。

② 齐给：敏捷。齐，通"斋"。便敏：敏捷，多指言辞、文思等。杨倞注："便，谓轻巧；敏，速也。"

③ 杂能：博杂的技能。旁魄：亦作"旁薄"，广大，宏伟。

④ 粹孰：精熟。杨倞注："粹孰，所著论甚精孰也。"不急：不切需要。

⑤ 傀（guī）然：独立貌。傀，通"块"。杨倞注："傀，傀伟，大貌也。或曰，傀与'块'同，独居之貌也。"王先谦集解引王念孙曰："后说是也。"

⑥ 大：重视。齐：庄敬。

⑦ 恬（tián）：安然，满不在乎。广解：多方解说。杨倞注："恬，安也，谓安于祸难也。而广自解说，言以辞胜人也。"苟免：苟且免于损害。

⑧ 排檠（qíng）：矫正弓弩的工具，矫正。

⑨ 葱：古剑名。下文的"阙""录""曶（hū）""干将""莫邪""巨阙""辟闾"均为古剑名。

⑩ 太公：姜太公。

⑪ 庄君：楚庄王。

⑫ 阖闾（hé lǘ）：春秋末吴的国君。

His words are all flattery①, his actions irresponsible; whatever he does is shot② through with error: such is the understanding of the petty man. His words are rapid and shrill③ but never to the point; his talents are varied and many but of no practical use; he is full of subtle distinctions and elegant turns of phrase that serve no practical purpose; he ignores right or wrong, disdains④ to discuss crooked or straight, but seeks only to overpower⑤ the arguments of his opponent: such is the understanding of the menial.

There is superior valor⑥, there is the middle type of valor, and there is inferior valor. When proper standards prevail⑦ in the world, to dare to bring your own conduct into accord with them; when the Way of the former kings prevails, to dare to follow its dictates⑧; to refuse to bow before the ruler of a disordered age, to refuse to follow the customs of the people of a disordered age; to accept poverty and hardship if they are in the cause of⑨ benevolent action; to reject wealth and eminence if they are not consonant⑩ with benevolent action; if the world recognizes you, to share in the world's joys; if the world does not recognize you, to stand alone and without fear: this is superior valor. To be reverent in bearing⑪ and modest in intention; to value honor and make light of⑫ material

---

① flattery/ˈflætərɪ/ n. 谄媚,巴结,阿谀
② shot/ʃɒt/(through with) adj. 很有(某特质),充满着
③ shrill/ʃrɪl/ adj. 尖锐的,刺耳的
④ disdain/dɪsˈdeɪn/ v. 鄙视,轻视,蔑视
⑤ overpower/ˌəʊvəˈpaʊə/ v. 制服,压倒
⑥ valor/ˈvælə/ n. 英勇,勇敢
⑦ prevail/prɪˈveɪl/ v. 盛行,流行
⑧ dictate/dɪkˈteɪt/ n. 命令,指示
⑨ in the cause of 为了
⑩ consonant/ˈkɒnsənənt/(with) 一致的,适合的,符合的
⑪ bearing/ˈbeərɪŋ/ n. 行为,举止
⑫ make light of 轻视,不在乎

goods; to dare to promote and honor the worthy, and reject and cast off① the unworthy: such is the middle type of valor. To ignore your own safety in the quest for wealth; to make light of danger and try to talk your way out of every difficulty; to rely on lucky escapes; to ignore right and wrong, just and unjust, and seek only to overpower the arguments of your opponents: such is inferior valor.

Fanruo and Jushu were famous bows of ancient times, but if they had not first been subjected to presses and straighteners, they would never have become true of themselves. Cong of Duke Huan of Qi, Que of Taigong of Qi, Lu of King Wen of the Zhou, Hu of Lord Zhuang of Chu, and Ganjiang, Moye, Juque, and Bilü of King Helü of Wu were all famous swords of antiquity, but if they had not been subjected to the grindstone, they would never have become sharp, and if men of strength had not wielded② them, they would never have been able to cut anything.

---

① cast off 丢弃
② wield/wiːld/ v. 使用,运用,挥舞

骅骝、骐骥、纤离、绿耳，此皆古之良马也；然而必前有衔辔之制，后有鞭策之威，加之以造父之驭①，然后一日而致千里也。

夫人虽有性质美而心辩知，必将求贤师而事之，择良友而友之。得贤师而事之，则所闻者尧舜禹汤之道也；得良友而友之，则所见者忠信敬让之行也。身日进于仁义而不自知也者，靡使然也②。今与不善人处，则所闻者欺诬诈伪也，所见者污漫淫邪贪利之行也，身且加于刑戮而不自知者，靡使然也。传曰："不知其子视其友，不知其君视其左右。"靡而已矣！靡而已矣！

---

① 造父：古之善御者，赵之先祖。因献八骏幸于周穆王。穆王使之御，西巡狩，见西王母，乐而忘归。时徐偃王反，穆王日驰千里马，大破之，因赐造父以赵城，由此为赵氏。

② 靡：潜移默化，沾染。

Hualiu，Qiji，Xianli，and Luer were famous horses of antiquity，but if they had not been subjected to the restraint of bit① and bridle and the threat of the whip，and driven by a master driver like Zaofu，they would never have succeeded in traveling a thousand *li* in one day.

In the same way a man，no matter how fine his nature or how keen② his mind，must seek a worthy teacher to study under and good companions to associate③ with. If he studies under a worthy teacher，he will be able to hear about the ways of Yao，Shun，Yu，and Tang，and if he associates with good companions，he will be able to observe conduct that is loyal and respectful. Then，although he is not aware of it，he will day by day progress in the practice of benevolence and righteousness，for the environment he is subjected to will cause him to progress. But if a man associates with men who are not good，then he will hear only deceit and lies and will see only conduct that is marked by wantonness，evil，and greed. Then，although he is not aware of it，he himself will soon be in danger of severe punishment，for the environment he is subjected to will cause him to be in danger. An old text says，"If you do not know a man，look at his friends；if you do not know a ruler，look at his attendants④." Environment is the important thing! Environment is the important thing!

---

① bit/bɪt/ *n.* 马勒，嚼子
② keen/kiːn/ *adj.* （指头脑）敏捷的，精明的
③ associate/əˈsəuʃɪət/ *v.* 结交，交往，打交道
④ attendant/əˈtendənt/ *n.* 服务员，侍者；（复数）随员，随从，陪侍

【推荐阅读】

一、中文版本及注疏

梁启雄.荀子简释.北京：中华书局,1956 年版。

王先谦.荀子集解.北京：中华书局,1988 年版。

王天海.荀子校释(上下).上海：上海古籍出版社,2005 年版。

熊公哲.荀子今注今释.重庆：重庆出版集团,2009 年版。

章诗同.荀子简注.上海：上海人民出版社,1974 年版。

二、英文译本

Hutton, Eric L. 2014. *Xunzi：The Complete Text*. Princeton, NJ：
Princeton University Press.

Knoblock, John. 1988. *Xunzi：A Translation and Study of the
Complete Works*, vol.1. Stanford：Stanford University Press.

Knoblock, John. 1990. *Xunzi：A Translation and Study of the
Complete Works*, vol.2. Stanford：Stanford University Press.

Knoblock, John. 1994. *Xunzi：A Translation and Study of the
Complete Works*, vol.3. Stanford：Stanford University Press.

Legge, James. 1895. *The Chinese Classics：With a Translation,
Critical and Exegetical Notes, Prolegomena, and Copious Incexes*,
Vol.II. Oxford：Clarendon Press.

Watson, Burton. 1963. *Xunzi：Basic Writing*s. New York, NY：
Columbia University Press.

第十单元　《孙子》

【导言】

《孙子》即《孙子兵法》,又称《孙武兵法》《吴孙子兵法》,中国古代最杰出的军事著作,中国现存最早的兵书。从战国开始,《孙子兵法》为历代兵家所推崇,被尊为"兵经",与德国克劳塞维茨(Karl Philip Gottfried von Clausewitz)的《战争论》、日本宫本武藏的《五轮书》并称世界三大兵书。《孙子兵法》分为计篇、作战篇、谋攻篇、形篇、势篇、虚实篇、军争篇、九变篇、行军篇、地形篇、九地篇、火攻篇、用间篇共十三篇。全书以权谋为经,以决定战争胜负之要素为纬,阐述战略和战术原理,揭示战争与政治、经济、地理等之间的密切关系。

孙子(约公元前 545—前 470 年),名武,字长卿,春秋时期著名军事家和政治家,出生于齐国名将世家,自幼喜研兵法。公元前 532 年离开齐国,去吴国隐居,潜心研究兵法。在伍子胥的举荐下,吴王阖闾拜请孙子出山,呈上其所著兵书十三篇。司马迁《史记·孙子吴起列传》云:"(吴国)西破强楚,入郢,北威齐、晋,显名诸侯,孙子与有力焉"。

历代对《孙子兵法》进行校勘、考证、注释和通解著作众多,仅留下姓名者就有 200 余家。三国时曹操的《孙子注》是现存最早注本;唐宋时期注家最多,涌现出众多单注本、集注本及合刻本,其中以宋朝的《武经七书》和《十一家注孙子》影响最大;明正统年间《孙子兵法》收入《道藏》;清代孙星衍校《孙子十家注》流传最广,影响最大。

《孙子兵法》亦风靡西方,尤以英国对《孙子兵法》的研究最深,英美出版的英译本影响最大。百余年来,《孙子兵法》已有 30 余种英译本问世。1905 年,英国皇家骑兵团卡尔斯罗普上尉(Everard Ferguson Calthrop)在东京出版的由日文版转译的《孙子兵法》英译本为《孙子兵法》的首个英译本;1908 年卡尔斯罗普再据汉语底本重译,题曰《兵书——远东兵学经典》(*The Book of War*, *The Military Classic of the Far East*),由伦敦约翰·默莱公司出版;1910 年,翟林奈(Lionel Giles)以孙星衍《孙子十家注》为底本,以《孙子兵法:世界最古老的兵书》(*Sun Tzǔ: on the Art of War: The Oldest Military Treatise in the*

World)为题首次比较准确地全译了《孙子兵法》十三篇,在欧美被公认为严谨的学术型译本;1963 年,美国海军准将格里菲思(Samuel B. Griffith)的《孙子——战争艺术》(*Sun Tzu：The Art of War*)参照权威注疏本《宋本十一家注孙子》翻译而成,被西方知名人士和军事院校广泛采用并转译成其他文字;1993 年拉尔夫·索耶(Ralph D. Sawyer)翻译出版了包含《孙子兵法》的《武经七书》;1999 年,加里·加葛里亚蒂(Gary Gagliardi)的《兵法：孙子之言》被确定为指导其他亚洲语言著作英译的范本,获得"独立出版商多元文化非小说类图书奖"。此外,《孙子兵法》的英译者还有：柯立瑞(Thomas Cleary,1988)、安乐哲(Roger T. Ames,1993)、闵福德(John Minford,2002)、梅维恒(Victor H. Mair,2007)等。2001 年国内资深学者林茂荪翻译出版的英文译本(*Sun Zi：The Art of War. Sun Bin：The Art of War*)在中国典籍对外传播中也产生了不小的影响。

《孙子》(节选)①

计篇第一

孙子曰：兵者②，国之大事，死生之地③，存亡之道，不可不察也④。

故经之以五事⑤，校之以计⑥，而索其情⑦：一曰道⑧，二曰天⑨，三曰地⑩，四曰将⑪，五曰法⑫。

道者，令民与上同意也⑬，故可以与之死，可以与之生，而不畏危。天者，阴阳、寒暑、时制也⑭。地者，远近、险易、广狭、死生也⑮。将者，智、信、仁、勇、严也。法者，曲制、官道、主用也⑯。凡此五者，将莫不闻⑰，知之者胜，不知者不胜。

---

① 本单元汉语原文参校曹操等注，杨丙安校理.《十一家注孙子校理》.北京：中华书局，1999年。

② 兵：军事，战争。

③ 死生之地：关系着人的生和死。一说地形上的生地和死地。

④ 察：明辨，详审，知道，理解。

⑤ 经：治理，管理。五事：指下文的道、天、地、将、法五个方面。翟林奈的中文为"经之以五"。

⑥ 校(jiào)：通"较"，比较。计：计谋，考虑。

⑦ 索：探索。情：实际情况。

⑧ 道：道义，品德，指政治上清明。

⑨ 天：天时，即气候、时令方面的条件。

⑩ 地：地理条件。

⑪ 将：将令，指统率作战的将帅的谋略、智慧以及指挥作战的方法等。

⑫ 法：法令，指军队的编制、将帅的执掌、军备物资的供给等。

⑬ 上：国君。同意：同心。

⑭ 阴阳：指昼夜、晴雨等气象变化。时制：指春、夏、秋、冬四季更替。

⑮ 险易：地势的险阻平坦。死生：指死地和生地，即有利于进退和不利于进退的地形环境。

⑯ 曲制：军队编制的制度，亦用以指军队。曹操注："曲制者，部曲旛帜、金鼓之制也。"官道：指军队中将官的职权划分等制度。梅尧臣注："官道，裨校首长，统率必有道也。"主用：指对军队后勤军需的管理。主：主持，掌管。

⑰ 闻：知道，了解。

Sun Tzǔ : On The Art of War (Excerpt)

Translated by Lionel Giles①

I. Laying Plans

Sun Tzǔ said: The art of war is of vital importance to the State. It is a matter of life and death, a road either to safety or to ruin. Hence it is a subject of inquiry② which can on no account③ be neglected.

The art of war, then, is governed by five constant④ factors, to be taken into account in one's deliberations⑤, when seeking to⑥ determine the conditions obtaining in the field. These are: (1) The Moral Law; (2) Heaven; (3) Earth; (4) The Commander; (5) Method and discipline⑦.

The MORAL LAW causes the people to be in complete accord with⑧ their ruler, so that they will follow him regardless of⑨ their lives, undismayed⑩ by any danger. HEAVEN signifies⑪ night and day, cold and heat, times and seasons. EARTH comprises distances, great and small; danger and security; open ground and narrow passes; the chances of life and death. The COMMANDER

---

① 英语译文选自 Giles, Lionel, tr. 1910. *Sun Tzǔ : On the Art of War*. London: Luzac and Company。

② inquiry/ɪnˈkwaɪərɪ/ *n*. 调查,查究

③ on no account 决不,绝对不

④ constant/ˈkɒnstənt/ *adj*. 不变,恒定,稳定

⑤ deliberation/dɪˌlɪbəˈreɪʃn/ *n*. 熟虑

⑥ seek to 谋求,设法,力图

⑦ 此处译者并未准确传达道、天、地、将、法的涵义。

⑧ in accord with 与……一致

⑨ regardless of 不管,不顾

⑩ undismay/ˌʌndɪsˈmeɪ/ *v*. 不畏惧,不受惊吓

⑪ signify/ˈsɪɡnɪfaɪ/ *v*. 表示,表明,意味

stands for the virtues of wisdom, sincerity, benevolence, courage and strictness. By METHOD AND DISCIPLINE are to be understood the marshaling① of the army in its proper subdivisions②, the graduations③ of rank among the officers, the maintenance④ of roads by which supplies⑤ may reach the army, and the control of military expenditure⑥. These five heads⑦ should be familiar to every general: he who knows them will be victorious; he who knows them not will fail.

---

① marshal/'mɑːʃl/ v. 整顿,集结,配置
② subdivision/ˌsʌbdɪ'vɪʒən/ n. 再分,细分;分支,分部
③ graduation/ˌgrædʒʊ'eɪʃn/ n. 分级(排列或分成不同等级或程度)
④ maintenance/'meɪntənəns/ n. 维护,保养,维修
⑤ supply/sə'plaɪ/ n. 补给,供应品,供给
⑥ expenditure/ɪk'spendɪtʃə/ n. 支出,支出额,费用
⑦ head/hed/ n. (被认为是)最重要的一端

故校之以计,而索其情,曰:主孰有道①? 将孰有能? 天地孰得? 法令孰行? 兵众孰强? 士卒孰练②? 赏罚孰明? 吾以此知胜负矣。

将听吾计③,用之必胜,留之;将不听吾计,用之必败,去之。

计利以听④,乃为之势⑤,以佐其外⑥。势者,因利而制权也⑦。

兵者,诡道也⑧。故能而示之不能⑨,用而示之不用⑩,近而示之远,远而示之近。利而诱之⑪,乱而取之⑫,实而备之⑬,强而避之,怒而挠之⑭,卑而骄之⑮,佚而劳之⑯,亲而离之⑰。攻其无备,出其不意⑱。此兵家之胜⑲,不可先传也⑳。

---

① 主:君王,国君。旧史家以正统为帝,偏安为主。如陈寿《三国志》以魏为正统,故称魏为帝,吴、蜀为主;朱熹《资治通鉴纲目》以蜀为正统,故称蜀为帝,魏吴为主。
② 练:精壮;干练,训练有素。
③ 将:将领。一说,含假设关系的助词,相当于"如果"。计:计谋,计策。
④ 计利:指有利的计策。一说指分析后觉得对我有利。以:通"已",指已经。听:听从,采纳。
⑤ 为之势:制造某种态势。势:态势,如战略形势、战术态势、战场优势等。
⑥ 佐:辅助。外:国境之外。古时用兵多在境外。
⑦ 制权:根据实际利害关系而灵活应变。权:权变,灵活应对。
⑧ 兵:指用兵打仗。诡道:诡诈之术。诡:诡诈。道:方法、计谋。
⑨ 示:显示,表现出。
⑩ 用:指采取某种行动,此处指出兵打仗。
⑪ 利而诱之:对于贪利的敌人就用利益来引诱它。一说指用利益来引诱敌人。
⑫ 取:攻取。
⑬ 实:充实,有实力。备:防备,有准备。
⑭ 挠:挑逗,扰乱。
⑮ 卑:卑弱而谨慎。
⑯ 佚:安逸,休整充分。劳:使疲劳。
⑰ 亲:亲密。离:离间。
⑱ 不意:空虚无防备。
⑲ 胜:佳妙,克敌制胜的诀窍。
⑳ 传:传授,泄露。一说,指规定。

Therefore, in your deliberations, when seeking to determine the military conditions, let them be made the basis of a comparison, in this wise①: (1) Which of the two sovereigns② is imbued③ with the Moral law? (2) Which of the two generals has most ability? (3) With whom lie the advantages derived from Heaven and Earth? (4) On which side is discipline most rigorously④ enforced? (5) Which army is stronger? (6) On which side are officers and men more highly trained? (7) In which army is there the greater constancy⑤ both in reward and punishment? By means of these seven considerations I can forecast victory or defeat.

The general that hearkens⑥ to my counsel⑦ and acts upon it, will conquer: — let such a one be retained⑧ in command! The general that hearkens not to my counsel nor acts upon it, will suffer defeat: — let such a one be dismissed⑨!

While heading the profit of my counsel, avail⑩ yourself also of any helpful circumstances over and beyond the ordinary rules. According as⑪ circumstances are favorable, one should modify one's plans.

All warfare is based on deception⑫. Hence, when able to attack, we must seem unable; when using our forces, we must seem

---

① in this wise 既然这样,这样地
② sovereign/'sɔvrɪn/n. 最高统治者(如国王、皇帝)
③ imbue/ɪm'bjuː/v. 充满
④ rigorously/'rɪɡərəslɪ/adv. 严格地,严厉地
⑤ constancy/'kɔnstənsɪ/n. 坚定,始终如一
⑥ hearken (to)/'hɑːkən/vt. 倾听
⑦ counsel/'kaʊnsl/n. 劝告,建议
⑧ retain/rɪ'teɪn/v. 保持,保留,记住
⑨ dismiss/dɪs'mɪs/v. 拒绝,拒绝接受,抛弃
⑩ avail (of)/ə'veɪl/v. 利用
⑪ according as 倘若,取决于
⑫ deception/dɪ'sepʃn/n. 欺骗,诡计

inactive; when we are near, we must make the enemy believe we are far away; when far away, we must make him believe we are near. Hold out baits① to entice② the enemy. Feign③ disorder, and crush④ him. If he is secure at all points, be prepared for him. If he is in superior strength, evade⑤ him. If your opponent is of choleric⑥ temper, seek to irritate him. Pretend to be weak, that he may grow arrogant⑦. If he is taking his ease, give him no rest. If his forces are united, separate them. Attack him where he is unprepared, appear where you are not expected. These military devices, leading to victory, must not be divulged⑧ beforehand.

---

① bait/beɪt/ n. 诱饵,诱惑物
② entice/ɪnˈtaɪs/ v. 诱使,引诱
③ feign/feɪn/ vt. 假装,捏造
④ crush/krʌʃ/ v. 消灭,击溃,制服
⑤ evade/ɪˈveɪd/ v. 逃避,躲避
⑥ choleric/ˈkɒlərɪk/ adj. 易怒的
⑦ arrogant/ˈærəgənt/ adj. 傲慢的,自负的,自大的
⑧ divulge/daɪˈvʌldʒ/ v. 泄露,暴露

夫未战而庙算胜者①,得算多也②;未战而庙算不胜者,得算少也。多算胜,少算不胜,而况于无算乎! 吾以此观之,胜负见矣。

虚实篇第六

孙子曰:凡先处战地而待敌者佚③,后处战地而趋战者劳④。故善战者,致人而不致于人⑤。能使敌人自至者,利之也;能使敌人不得至者,害之也⑥。故敌佚能劳之,饱能饥之,安能动之。

出其所不趋⑦,趋其所不意⑧。行千里而不劳者,行于无人之地也。攻而必取者,攻其所不守也;守而必固者,守其所不攻也⑨。故善攻者,敌不知其所守;善守者,敌不知其所攻。微乎微乎⑩,至于无形;神乎神乎,至于无声,故能为敌之司命⑪。

进而不可御者⑫,冲其虚也⑬;退而不可追者,速而不可及也。故我欲战,敌虽高垒深沟,不得不与我战者,攻其所必救也;

----

① 庙算:亦作"庙筭",指朝廷或帝王对战事进行的谋划。古代在用兵打仗之前,都要在宗庙里举行仪式,并商讨作战计划,故称庙算。
② 得算:得计,计谋成功。算:谋划,通"筭",古代计数用的筹码。
③ 先处:先期到达、占据。处:居止。佚:安逸,从容。
④ 趋战:仓促应战。趋:急行。劳:劳顿,疲劳。
⑤ 致人:控制别人,此处意为调动敌人。
⑥ 害:妨碍,阻挠。
⑦ 出:出兵。不趋:不能奔赴,敌人无法迅速救援的地方。翟林奈中文为"出其所必趋"。
⑧ 趋:奔赴。其所不意:出乎敌方意料之外。
⑨ 不攻:指不敢进攻的地方。
⑩ 微乎:精微,微妙。
⑪ 司命:命运的主宰。
⑫ 御:抵御。
⑬ 冲:冲击。虚:空虚,这里指防守薄弱。

Now the general who wins a battle makes many calculations in his temple ere① the battle is fought. The general who loses a battle makes but few calculations beforehand. Thus do many calculations lead to victory, and few calculations to defeat: how much more no calculation at all! It is by attention to this point that I can foresee who is likely to win or lose.

VI. Weak Points and Strong

Sun Tzǔ said: Whoever is first in the field and awaits the coming of the enemy, will be fresh for the fight; whoever is second in the field and has to hasten to battle, will arrive exhausted. Therefore the clever combatant② imposes③ his will on the enemy, but does not allow the enemy's will to be imposed on him. By holding out advantages to him, he can cause the enemy to approach of his own accord④; or, by inflicting damage, he can make it impossible for the enemy to draw near. If the enemy is taking his ease, he can harass⑤ him; if well supplied with food, he can starve him out; if quietly encamped⑥, he can force him to move.

Appear at points which the enemy must hasten to defend; march swiftly to places where you are not expected. An army may march great distances without distress⑦, if it marches through country where the enemy is not. You can be sure of succeeding in your attacks if you only attack places which are undefended. You can ensure the safety of your defense if you only hold positions that cannot be attacked. Hence that general is skillful in attack whose

---

① ere/eə/ *conj. prep.* 在……之前
② combatant/ˈkɒmbətənt/ *n.* 参战者
③ impose/ɪmˈpəʊz/ *v.* 把……强加于
④ of his own accord 自愿地(主动地)
⑤ harass/ˈhærəs/ *v.* 不断打扰,不断骚扰
⑥ encamp/ɪnˈkæmp/ *v.* 宿营;扎营
⑦ distress/dɪˈstres/ *n.* 忧虑,身体不适,苦恼,痛苦

opponent does not know what to defend; and he is skillful in defense whose opponent does not know what to attack. O divine art of subtlety① and secrecy! Through you we learn to be invisible, through you inaudible②, and hence we can hold the enemy's fate in our hands.

You may advance and be absolutely irresistible, if you make for the enemy's weak points; you may retire and be safe from pursuit if your movements are more rapid than those of the enemy. If we wish to fight, the enemy can be forced to an engagement③ even though he be sheltered behind a high rampart④ and a deep ditch. All we need do is attack some other place that he will be obliged to⑤ relieve.

---

① subtlety/'sʌtltɪ/ n. 精明,微妙
② inaudible/ɪn'ɔːdəbl/ adj. 听不见的
③ engagement/ɪn'geɪdʒmənt/ n. 战斗,交战
④ rampart/'ræmpɑːt/ n. 垒,壁垒,城墙,防御
⑤ be obliged to 不得不,被迫

我不欲战,画地而守之①,敌不得与我战者,乖其所之也②。

故形人而我无形③,则我专而敌分④。我专为一,敌分为十,是以十攻其一也,则我众而敌寡,能以众击寡者,则吾之所与战者,约矣⑤。吾所与战之地不可知⑥,不可知则敌所备者多⑦;敌所备者多,则吾所与战者,寡矣。故备前则后寡⑧,备后则前寡;备左则右寡,备右则左寡;无所不备,则无所不寡。寡者,备人者也;众者,使人备己者也⑨。

故知战之地,知战之日,则可千里而会战⑩。不知战地,不知战日,则左不能救右,右不能救左,前不能救后,后不能救前,而况远者数十里,近者数里乎?以吾度之⑪,越人之兵虽多⑫,亦奚益于胜败哉⑬?故曰:胜可为也⑭,敌虽众,可使无斗⑮。

---

① 画地:在地上画界线。
② 乖其所之:改变敌人的去向。乖:违背,这里指改变。之:到,往。
③ 形人:指使敌人暴露形迹。
④ 专:集中。分:分散。
⑤ 约:穷困,困窘。一说少。
⑥ 与战:与敌军作战。
⑦ 备:准备,指兵力防备。
⑧ 备前则后寡:用兵力防备了前面,后面的兵力便少了。
⑨ 使人备己:使别人防备自己,使敌人防备我军。
⑩ 会战:敌对双方主力在一定地区和时间内进行的决战。
⑪ 度(duó):推测,判断。
⑫ 越人:越国人。越国是春秋时期的诸侯国,与吴国相邻。
⑬ 奚:为何。
⑭ 为:指人为造成,创造。
⑮ 无斗:指没有战斗力,无法战斗。

If we do not wish to fight, we can prevent the enemy from engaging① us even though the lines of our encampment be merely traced out② on the ground. All we need do is to throw something odd and unaccountable in his way.

By discovering the enemy's dispositions③ and remaining invisible ourselves, we can keep our forces concentrated, while the enemy's must be divided. We can form a single united body, while the enemy must split up into fractions④. Hence there will be a whole pitted against⑤ separate parts of a whole, which means that we shall be many to the enemy's few. And if we are able thus to attack an inferior force with a superior one, our opponents will be in dire straits⑥. The spot where we intend to fight must not be made known; for then the enemy will have to prepare against a possible attack at several different points; and his forces being thus distributed in many directions, the numbers we shall have to face at any given point will be proportionately⑦ few. For should the enemy strengthen his van⑧, he will weaken his rear⑨; should he strengthen his rear, he will weaken his van; should he strengthen his left, he will weaken his right; should he strengthen his right, he will weaken his left. If he sends reinforcements⑩ everywhere, he will everywhere be weak. Numerical weakness comes from having to prepare against possible attacks; numerical strength, from

---

① engage/ɪnˈɡeɪdʒ/ v. 与……交战
② trace out 描绘出,探寻出
③ disposition/ˌdɪspəˈzɪʃn/ n. 排列,布置,配置
④ fraction/ˈfrækʃn/ n. 片断,碎片
⑤ pit against 使竞争,使对杀
⑥ in dire straits 陷入岌岌可危的境地
⑦ proportionately/prəˈpɔːʃnətlɪ/ adv. 相称地,成比例地
⑧ van/væn/ n. (部队的)先锋,前卫,前锋
⑨ rear/rɪə/ n. 后部,后方
⑩ reinforcement/ˌriːɪnˈfɔːsmənt/ n. (通常用复数)援军,增援

compelling our adversary① to make these preparations against us.

Knowing the place and the time of the coming battle，we may concentrate from the greatest distances in order to fight. But if neither time nor place be known，then the left wing will be impotent② to succor③ the right，the right equally impotent to succor the left，the van unable to relieve the rear，or the rear to support the van. How much more so if the furthest portions of the army are anything under a hundred *li* apart，and even the nearest are separated by several *li*！Though according to my estimate the soldiers of Yüueh exceed our own in number，that shall advantage them nothing in the matter of victory. I say then that victory can be achieved. Though the enemy be stronger in numbers，we may prevent him from fighting.

---

① adversary/ˈædvəsərɪ/ *n*. 敌手，对手
② impotent/ˈɪmpətənt/ *adj*. 无力的，虚弱的，无助的
③ succor/ˈsʌkə/ *v*. 救援

故策之而知得失之计①,作之而知动静之理②,形之而知死生之地③,角之而知有余不足之处④。故形兵之极⑤,至于无形;无形,则深间不能窥⑥,智者不能谋。因形而错胜于众⑦,众不能知。人皆知我所以胜之形⑧,而莫知吾所以制胜之形。故其战胜不复⑨,而应形于无穷⑩。

夫兵形象水⑪,水之形,避高而趋下,兵之形,避实而击虚。水因地而制流,兵因敌而制胜。故兵无常势⑫,水无常形,能因敌变化而取胜者,谓之神⑬。故五行无常胜⑭,四时无常位,日有短长,月有死生⑮。

---

① 策:策算,分析。得失之计:敌方计谋的得失。
② 作:触动,挑动,指诱使敌人行动。
③ 形:侦察地形。一说,指陈师布阵的势态。
④ 角:较量。有余不足:指兵力配置的强和弱。
⑤ 形兵:使军队的部署呈现某种状态,这里指排兵布阵时用来迷惑敌人的假象。
⑥ 深间:深藏的间谍。
⑦ 错胜:制胜。错:同"措",指放置。
⑧ 形:情状,一说指方法。
⑨ 复:重复。
⑩ 应:适应。形:形势。
⑪ 形:规律,特点。
⑫ 常势:固定不变的常态。常:永恒不变。
⑬ 神:神奇,玄妙。
⑭ 五行无常胜:五行中没有哪一种因素是永远能克制别的因素的。胜:克。
⑮ 月有生死:月亮在一月之中有盈有亏。古人所谓"生霸""死霸"。"生霸"指月亮有光明,"死霸"指月亮的光明由明转晦。

Scheme① so as to discover his plans and the likelihood of their success. Rouse② him, and learn the principle of his activity or inactivity. Force him to reveal himself, so as to find out his vulnerable③ spots. Carefully compare the opposing army with your own, so that you may know where strength is superabundant④ and where it is deficient⑤. In making tactical dispositions⑥, the highest pitch⑦ you can attain is to conceal them; conceal your dispositions, and you will be safe from the prying⑧ of the subtlest⑨ spies, from the machinations⑩ of the wisest brains. How victory may be produced for them out of the enemy's own tactics — that is what the multitude⑪ cannot comprehend. All men can see the tactics whereby I conquer, but what none can see is the strategy out of which victory is evolved⑫. Do not repeat the tactics which have gained you one victory, but let your methods be regulated by the infinite variety of circumstances.

Military tactics are like unto⑬ water; for water in its natural course⑭ runs away from high places and hastens downwards. So in war, the way is to avoid what is strong and to strike at what is weak. Water shapes its course according to the nature of the ground

---

① scheme/skiːm/ v. 策划,密谋,图谋
② rouse/rauz/ v. 激起(愤怒或行动),煽动
③ vulnerable/'vʌlnərəbl/ adj. 易受伤害的,脆弱的
④ superabundant/ˌsuːpərə'bʌndənt/ adj. 过多的,有余的
⑤ deficient/dɪ'fɪʃnt/ adj. 有缺陷的,不足的,缺乏的,有缺点的
⑥ tactical disposition 战略安排
⑦ pitch/pɪtʃ/ 最高点,顶点,程度
⑧ pry/praɪ/ v. 窥探,刺探,打听
⑨ subtle/'bʌtl/ adj. 诡秘的,隐蔽进行的,阴险的
⑩ machination/ˌmæʃɪ'neɪʃn/ n. 阴谋,图谋
⑪ multitude/'mʌltɪtjuːd/ n. 大量,多数
⑫ evolve/ɪ'vɔlv/ v. 逐渐形成
⑬ unto/'ʌntʊ/ prep. 对,给,于;直到;在…旁边
⑭ course/kɔːs/ n. 道路,路线,水道

over which it flows; the soldier works out his victory in relation to the foe whom he is facing. Therefore, just as water retains no constant shape, so in warfare there are no constant conditions. He who can modify his tactics in relation to his opponent and thereby succeed in winning, may be called a heaven-born captain. The five elements① are not always equally predominant②; the four seasons make way for③ each other in turn. There are short days and long; the moon has its periods of waning and waxing.

---

① five elements 五行
② predominant/prɪˈdɔmɪnənt/ *adj.* 有势力的,占优势的
③ make way for 让路,为……开路

九变篇第八

孙子曰：凡用兵之法，将受命于君，合军聚众①，圮地无舍②，衢地交合③，绝地无留④，围地则谋⑤，死地则战⑥。涂有所不由⑦，军有所不击，城有所不攻，地有所不争，君命有所不受。

故将通于九变之地利者⑧，知用兵矣；将不通于九变之利者，虽知地形，不能得地之利矣。治兵不知九变之术，虽知五利⑨，不能得人之用矣⑩。

是故智者之虑⑪，必杂于利害⑫。杂于利，而务可信也⑬；杂于害，而患可解也⑭。

是故屈诸侯者以害⑮，役诸侯者以业⑯，趋诸侯者以利⑰。

---

① 合军：集结军队。聚众：聚集人众。
② 圮(pǐ)地：难以通行的地方。《孙子·九地》："行山林、险阻、沮泽，凡难行之道者，为圮地。"圮：塌坏，毁坏。舍：住舍，这里指驻扎。
③ 衢地：四通八达的地方。交合：结交，交好。
④ 绝地无留：在缺乏生存条件或地形十分险恶的地方，部队不能停留。绝地：指极险恶而无出路的境地。《九地篇》云：去国越境而师者，绝地也。即离开本国到别的国家境内去打仗，就是绝地。
⑤ 围地：指出入通道狭窄，易被敌人围攻之地。《孙子·九地》："所由入者隘，所从归者迂，彼寡可以击吾之众者，为'围地'。"杜牧注："出入艰难，易设奇伏覆胜也。"杜佑注："所从入阸险，归道远也，持久则粮乏。故敌可以少击吾众者，为围地也。"谋：计谋。
⑥ 死地：前无进路、后有追兵，必得死战之地。
⑦ 涂：通"途"，道路。由：经过。
⑧ 九变之地利：指精通各种地形的灵活利用。九变之地，指《九地篇》中所说的散地、轻地、争地、交地、衢地、重地、圮地、围地、死地九种地形。
⑨ 五利：指五变之利，具体指"涂有所不由"到"君命有所不受"的五变之利。
⑩ 得人之用：指充分发挥军队的战斗力。
⑪ 智者之虑：聪明的人思考问题。
⑫ 杂：掺杂，兼顾。
⑬ 务可信：能顺利完成战斗任务。务：战斗任务。信，通"伸"，指伸展，顺利发展。
⑭ 患：灾祸。解：解除，免除。
⑮ 屈：使屈服。
⑯ 役：役使。业：事业，功业，此处指自己的实力。
⑰ 趋：归附。

VIII. Variation of Tactics

Sun Tzǔ said: In war, the general receives his commands from the sovereign, collects his army and concentrates his forces. When in difficult country, do not encamp①. In country where high roads② intersect③, join hands with your allies. Do not linger④ in dangerously isolated positions. In hemmed-in⑤ situations, you must resort to⑥ stratagem⑦. In desperate position, you must fight. There are roads which must not be followed, armies which must not be attacked, towns which must not be besieged, positions which must not be contested⑧, commands of the sovereign which must not be obeyed.

The general who thoroughly understands the advantages that accompany variation of tactics knows how to handle his troops. The general who does not understand these, may be well acquainted with the configuration⑨ of the country, yet he will not be able to turn his knowledge to practical account. So, the student of war who is unversed⑩ in the art of war of varying his plans, even though he be acquainted with the Five Advantages, will fail to make the best use of his men.

Hence in the wise leader's plans, considerations of advantage and of disadvantage will be blended together. If our expectation of

① encamp/ɪnˈkæmp/ v. 扎营
② high road 最佳的途径, 大路, 公路, 捷径
③ intersect/ˌɪntəˈsekt/ v. 横断, 相交, 交叉
④ linger/ˈlɪŋgə/ vi. 徘徊, 逗留
⑤ hemmed-in 被包围
⑥ resort to 诉诸于
⑦ stratagem/ˈstrætədʒəm/ n. 战略, 计谋
⑧ contest/kənˈtest/ v. (参与并)争取赢得
⑨ configuration/kənˌfɪgəˈreɪʃn/ n. 形状, 外貌
⑩ unversed/ˌʌnˈvɜːst/ adj. 不熟练的, 无经验的

advantage be tempered① in this way, we may succeed in accomplishing the essential part of our schemes. If, on the other hand, in the midst of difficulties we are always ready to seize an advantage, we may extricate② ourselves from misfortune.

Reduce the hostile chiefs by inflicting③ damage on them; make trouble for them, and keep them constantly engaged; hold out specious④ allurements⑤, and make them rush to any given point.

---

① temper/'tempə/ v. 调和,使温和,使协调
② extricate/'ekstrɪkeɪt/ v. 使解脱,救出
③ inflict/ɪn'flɪkt/ v. 使遭受(打击、惩罚等)
④ specious/'spiːʃəs/ adj. 似是而非的
⑤ allurement/ə'luəmənt/ n. 引诱,诱惑

故用兵之法：无恃其不来①，恃吾有以待也②；无恃其不攻，恃吾有所不可攻也。

故将有五危③：必死④，可杀也；必生⑤，可虏也；忿速⑥，可侮也；廉洁⑦，可辱也；爱民⑧，可烦也。凡此五者，将之过也⑨，用兵之灾也。覆军杀将，必以五危，不可不察也。

---

① 恃：依赖，依靠。
② 有以待：有对付敌人的办法。
③ 危：指带来危险的弱点。
④ 必死：只知死拼。
⑤ 必生：贪生怕死。
⑥ 忿速：容易发怒。
⑦ 廉洁：过于追求好名声。
⑧ 爱民：溺爱民众。
⑨ 将之过也：将领的过失。

The art of war teaches us to rely not on the likelihood of the enemy's not coming, but on our own readiness to receive him; not on the chance of his not attacking, but rather on the fact that we have made our position unassailable①.

There are five dangerous faults which may affect a general: (1) Recklessness②, which leads to destruction; (2) cowardice③, which leads to capture; (3) a hasty temper, which can be provoked by insults; (4) a delicacy of honor which is sensitive to shame; (5) over-solicitude④ for his men, which exposes him to worry and trouble. These are the five besetting⑤ sins of a general, ruinous to the conduct of war. When an army is overthrown and its leader slain⑥, the cause will surely be found among these five dangerous faults. Let them be a subject of meditation⑦.

---

① unassailable/ˌʌnə'seɪləbl/ *adj.* 攻不破的,无懈可击的
② recklessness/'rekləsnəs/ *n.* 不顾后果,鲁莽
③ cowardice/'kaʊədɪs/ *n.* 胆小,懦弱,
④ over-solicitude 过分关心
⑤ besetting/bɪ'setɪŋ/ *adj.* 不断侵袭的,(念头等)老是缠着人的
⑥ slay/sleɪ/ *vt.* (slew, slain)杀害
⑦ meditation/medɪ'teɪʃn/ *n.* 沉思,冥想

【推荐阅读】

一、中文版本及注疏

曹操等注,杨丙安校理.十一家注孙子校理.北京：中华书局,1999 年。

冯国超著.孙子兵法.北京：商务印书馆,2009 年。

郭化若.孙子译注.上海：上海古籍出版社,2006 年。

李零.《孙子》十三篇综合研究.北京：中华书局,2006 年.

骈宇骞等译注.孙子兵法・孙膑兵法(中华经典藏书).北京：中华书局,2007 年。

吴如嵩.孙子兵法十五讲.北京：中华书局,2010 年。

银雀山汉墓竹简整理小组.银雀山汉墓竹简——孙子兵法.北京：文物出版社.1976 年。

中国人民解放军军事科学院战争理论研究部.孙子兵法新注.北京：中华书局,2011 年。

二、英文译本

Calthrop, E. F., tr. 1908. *The Book of War：The Military Classic of the Far East*. London：John Murray.

Giles, Lionel, tr. 1910. *Sun Tzǔ：On the Art of War*. London：Luzac and Company.

Griffith, Samuel B., tr. 1960. *Sun Tzu：The Art of War*. Oxford：Oxford University Press.

Mair, Victor H. 2007. *The Art of War：Sunzi's Military Methods*. New York：Columbia University Press.

孙武著,林茂荪译.孙子兵法・孙膑兵法.北京：外文出版社,2001 年。

第十一单元　《六祖坛经》

【导言】

《六祖坛经》,亦称《坛经》,为佛教禅宗六祖慧能大师于韶州大梵寺讲堂传法授戒的记录,由六祖慧能口述,弟子法海等记录整理而成,是中国僧人著述中唯一被尊为"经"者。《坛经》以通俗的文字,丰富的内容,记载了慧能一生得法传法,引导启迪门徒的事迹,它以"佛性"回答人为什么能成佛,以"悟性"回答成佛的途径,以"心性"回答怎样成佛,不但完整介绍了慧能的禅宗思想,还为禅宗的发展奠定了理论基础,为禅宗正式形成的标志。

慧能(638—713 年),一作惠能,俗姓卢,范阳(今北京大兴)人,自幼随父流放岭南新州(今广东新兴),父亡后,随母移居南海(今广东南海),以卖柴为生。二十四岁时,在蕲州黄梅(今湖北黄梅县)得五祖弘忍大师传授衣钵,后建立南宗,弘扬"直指人心,见性成佛"的顿教法门。他是中国佛教最后一位嫡传佛祖,被誉为中国禅宗的真正创始人,是中国历史上有重大影响的佛教高僧之一,享有至高无上的地位。慧能禅师的真身,供奉于广东韶关南华寺灵照塔中。

《坛经》有四大系统,二十余种版本,包括:(1)传宗本(敦煌本),一卷,弟子法海集记,题为《南宗顿教最上乘摩诃般若波罗蜜经六祖惠能大师于韶州大梵寺施法坛经》,约一万二千字;(2)惠昕本,二卷,禅僧惠昕于宋乾德五年(967 年)改编、删定,题为《六祖坛经》,约一万四千字;(3)契嵩本,亦称德异本、曹溪原本,三卷,宋代禅师契嵩于宋仁宗至和三年(1056 年)依据曹溪古本校定刊行,题为《六祖大师法宝坛经曹溪原本》,约二万一千字;(4)宗宝本,不分卷,由元代禅师宗宝于元至元二十八年(1291 年)校订,题为《六祖大师法宝坛经》。这些版本体例字数虽异,但内容大都包括三个方面:一是慧能自述生平;二是慧能开坛授戒说六波罗蜜;三是慧能一生以机锋、三十六对等调教弟子及临终嘱咐等。关于《坛经》的注释解说,古代有:契嵩的《法宝坛经赞》、天柱的《注法宝坛经海水一滴》、袁宏道的《法宝坛经节录》、李贽的《六祖法宝坛经解》、恒璇的《法宝坛经要解》、益淳的《法宝坛经肯綮》、青峦的《法宝坛经讲义》、道忠的《六祖坛经生苔帚》等数种。近代以来,国内外的《坛经》注释之书亦不下数十种,其中丁福保的《六祖坛经笺注》为"内容最为丰富、征引最为广泛、解说相当全面、理解较为可靠的一种"(陈兵)。中华书局 1983 年出版的郭朋《坛经校释》为近年最为流行的版本。

　　《六祖坛经》在西方世界的译介始于十八世纪。1930 年,黄茂林居士应狄平子之邀将其翻译为英文由上海有正书局出版,此为《坛经》首个英文译本。1932 年,美国传教士德怀特·戈达德(Dwight Goddard)在黄茂林译本的基础上对其进行了改译,收于美国 Thetford Vermont 出版的《佛教圣典》(A Buddhist Bible)。1953 年,韩福里(Christmas Humphreys)对黄译进行完善,在新加坡、马来西亚等地出版发行。至 2017 年,《坛经》英文译本共 15 种,其中不乏出自著名学者之手的译本,如:陈荣捷(Wing-tsit Chan)(1963)、扬波斯基(Philip B. Yampolsky)(1967)、林光明(2004)、星云大师(2010)等。

行由品第一①

时，大师至宝林②。韶州韦刺史与官僚入山③，请师出，于城中大梵寺讲堂④，为众开缘说法⑤。

师升座次⑥，刺史官僚三十余人，儒宗学士三十余人⑦，僧尼道俗一千余人，同时作礼，愿闻法要⑧。

大师告众曰："善知识⑨，菩提自性⑩，本来清净⑪。但用此心，直了成佛。善知识，且听惠能行由法事意⑫。"

---

① 原文选自：杨曾文校敦博本第4—10节。行由：丁福保笺注云：述六祖一代之行状由来，故曰行由。

② 宝林：宝林寺。丁福保笺注云：时六祖自广州法性寺至宝林寺，即曹溪南华寺是也。

③ 刺史：官名。隋唐之刺史，犹清之知府及直隶州知州。官僚：官与僚属。山：指南华山，在曲江县南六十里，宝林即在此山。

④ 讲堂：讲经说法之堂舍。

⑤ 开缘说法：启发人之因缘而为说妙法。

⑥ 座次：坐的地方。

⑦ 儒宗：儒者的宗师，汉以后亦泛指为读书人所宗仰的学者。学士：读书人，学者。

⑧ 作礼：举手施礼，行礼。法要：佛法的要义。

⑨ 善知识：佛教语，梵语意译，闻名为"知"，见形为"识"，即善友、好伴侣之意。后亦以泛指高僧。《法华文句》云："闻名为知，见形为识，是人益我菩提之道，名善知识。"《涅盘经》云："能救众生远离十恶，修行十善，谓之善知识。"

⑩ 菩提：梵文Bodhi的音译，意译"觉""智""道"等，指豁然彻悟的境界，又指觉悟的智慧和觉悟的途径。《名义集》云："道之极者，称之曰菩提。"自性：诸法各自不变不改之性。

⑪ 本来：无始以来名本来。清静：远离身口意三业恶行之过失，烦恼之垢染，名清静。

⑫ 得法：获得正确的方法或找到窍门。事意：事情，事务；事情的意义；用意，意图。

Sutra Spoken by the Sixth Patriarch on the High Seat of "The Treasure of the Law"

Chapter I. Autobiography

Translated by Wong Mou-lam & Christmas Humphreys①

Once，when the Patriarch had arrived at Pao Lam Monastery②，Prefect③ Wai of Shiu Chow and other officials went there to ask him to deliver public lectures on Buddhism in the hall of Tai Fan Temple in the City（of Canton）.

In due course④，there were assembled（in the lecture hall）Prefect Wai，government officials and Confucian scholars，about thirty each，and Bhikkhus⑤，Bhikkhunis⑥，Taoists and laymen⑦，to the number of about one thousand. After the Patriarch had taken his seat，the congregation⑧ in a body⑨ paid him homage⑩ and asked him to preach⑪ on the fundamental laws⑫ of Buddhism.

---

① 译文选自：Humphreys，Christmas. 1953. *The Sutra of Wei Lang（or Hui-neng）*. London：Luzac and Company，pp. 1 - 16。sutra/'suːtrə/ *n*. 经，经典(经文性的叙述文，尤指传统上认为是释迦牟尼讲道的文本)。patriarch/'peɪtrɪɑːk/ *n*. 祖先(在太古时代的从亚当到诺亚的人类祖先之一)；(罗马天主教中)大主教，教皇；(东正教中)总主教，教长

② monastery/'mɔnəstrɪ/ *n*. 修道院

③ prefect/'priːfekt/ *n*. 长官，地方行政长官

④ in due course 顺次，及时地，在适当时

⑤ Bhikkhu/'bɪku/ *n*. 比丘(梵语的译音。意译"乞士"，以上从诸佛乞法，下就俗人乞食得名，为佛教出家"五众"之一。指已受具足戒的男性，俗称和尚。)

⑥ Bhikkhuni/'bɪkunɪ/ *n*. 比丘尼(梵语译音。佛教出家"五众"之一，指已受具足戒的女性，俗称尼姑。)

⑦ laymen/'leɪmən/ *n*. 俗人(非教士之人)

⑧ congregation/ˌkɔŋgrɪ'geɪʃn/ *n*. (参加宗教礼拜式的)会众

⑨ in a body 全体一致地

⑩ homage/'hɔmɪdʒ/ *n*. 尊崇，效忠，尊敬；pay sb. homage/pay homage to sb.：(对……)表敬意

⑪ preach/priːtʃ/ *v*. 讲道，布道

⑫ law/lɔː/ *n*. 训诫(用来表示神意愿的一系列法规或概念，尤指体现在《圣经》中的)

Whereupon①, His Holiness delivered the following address:

Learned Audience, our Essence of Mind (literally, self-nature) which is the seed or kernel② of enlightenment (Bodhi) is pure by nature, and by making use of this mind alone we can reach Buddhahood directly. Now let me tell you something about my own life and how I came into possession of the esoteric③ teaching of the Dhyana④(or the Zen) School.

---

① whereupon/ˌweərəˈpɒn/*adv*. 于是,因此
② kernel/ˈkɜːnl/*n*. 仁,核,种仁
③ esoteric/ˌesəʊˈterɪk/*adj*. 只有内行才懂的,神秘的,难懂的
④ Dhyana/ˈdjɑːnə/*n*. 禅,禅定

惠能严父①，本贯范阳，左降流于岭南②，作新州百姓③。此身不幸④，父又早亡。老母孤遗，移来南海⑤，艰辛贫乏⑥。于市卖柴。时有一客买柴，使令送至客店⑦。客收去，惠能得钱，却出门外。见一客诵经，惠能一闻经语，心即开悟⑧。遂问客诵何经。客曰："《金刚经》⑨。"复问："从何所来，持此经典？"客云："我从蕲州黄梅县东禅寺来。其寺是五祖弘忍大师在彼主化⑩，门人一千有余。我到彼中礼拜，听受此经。大师常劝僧俗：但持《金刚经》，即自见性⑪，直了成佛。"

惠能闻说，宿昔有缘⑫，乃蒙一客取银十两与惠能，令充老母衣粮，教便往黄梅参礼五祖。惠能安置母毕，即便辞违⑬。不经三十余日，便至黄梅。礼拜五祖。

祖问曰："汝何方人？欲求何物？"惠能对曰："弟子是岭南新州百姓，远来礼师，惟求作佛，不求余物。"祖言："汝是岭南人，又是獦獠⑭，若为堪作佛⑮？"惠能曰："人虽有南北，佛性本无南北；獦獠身与和尚不同，佛性有何差别？"五祖更欲与语，且见徒众总在左右，乃令随众作务。

---

① 严父：父亲，旧谓父严母慈，故多称父为"严父"。《孝经》云："严父莫大乎配天。"

② 左降：贬官。多指京官降职到州郡。左：即左迁，降职。流：流放，为五刑之一，把罪人放逐到远方。

③ 作：为，充当，担任某种职务。

④ 不幸：表示不希望发生而竟然发生。《说文》："夭死之事，故死谓之不幸。"

⑤ 南海：古代指极南地区。此处指广州。

⑥ 贫乏：穷困，贫困。

⑦ 使令：差遣，使唤。

⑧ 开悟：领悟，解悟，（心窍）开通。

⑨ 《金刚经》：大乘佛教经典，全名《金刚般若波罗蜜多经》。

⑩ 五祖：佛教禅宗指"东土第五祖"唐代弘忍禅师。弘忍俗姓周，七岁出家，改用《金刚经》传法，开"东山法门"。下传慧能、神秀，衍生南、北二宗。

⑪ 见性：悟彻清净的佛性。

⑫ 宿昔有缘：犹言前世因缘也。宿昔：从前，往日。

⑬ 辞违：辞别。别本作"辞亲"。

⑭ 獦獠(gé liáo)：古代对南方少数民族的称呼，亦以泛指南方人。

⑮ 若为堪作佛：如何能作得佛。若为：怎样，怎堪，怎能。

My father, a native of Fan Yang, was dismissed from his official post and banished to be a commoner[①] in Sun Chow in Kwangtung. I was unlucky in that my father died when I was very young, leaving my mother poor and miserable. We moved to Kwang Chow (Canton) and were then in very bad circumstances.

I was selling firewood in the market one day, when one of my customers ordered some to be brought to his shop. Upon delivery[②] being made and payment received, I left the shop, outside of which I found a man reciting a Sutra. As soon as I heard the text of this Sutra my mind at once became enlightened. Thereupon[③] I asked the man the name of the book he was reciting and was told that it was the Diamond Sutra (Vajracchedika or Diamond Cutter). I further enquired whence he came and why he recited this particular Sutra. He replied that he came from Tung Tsan Monastery in Wong Mui District of Kee Chow; that the Abbot[④] in charge of this temple was Hwang Yan, the Fifth Patriarch; that there were about one thousand disciples under him; and that when he went there to pay homage to the Patriarch, he attended lectures on this Sutra. He further told me that His Holiness[⑤] used to encourage the laity[⑥] as well as the monks to recite this scripture, as by doing so they might realise their own Essence of Mind, and thereby reach Buddhahood directly.

It must be due to my good karma[⑦] in past lives that I could hear

---

① commoner/ˈkɔmənə/n. 平民，没有贵族等级或头衔的人

② delivery/dɪˈlɪvərɪ/n. 交付，交货

③ thereupon/ˌðeərəˈpɔn/adv. 于是，因此，随即

④ abbot/ˈæbət/n. 男修道院院长，大寺院男住持，方丈

⑤ His Holiness 对宗教领袖的尊称

⑥ laity/ˈleɪətɪ/n. （别于神职人员的）俗人，普通信徒

⑦ karma/ˈkɑːmə/n. 业（音译"羯磨"，意为个人行为的总和可决定其来世的命运），因果报应，命运

about this, and that I was given ten taels[1] for the maintenance of my mother by a man who advised me to go to Wong Mui to interview the Fifth Patriarch. After arrangements had been made for her, I left for Wong Mui, which took me less than thirty days to reach.

I then went to pay homage to the Patriarch, and was asked where I came from and what I expected to get from him. I replied, "I am a commoner from Sun Chow of Kwangtung. I have travelled far to pay you respect and I ask for nothing but Buddhahood." "You are a native of Kwangtung, a barbarian[2]? How can you expect to be a Buddha?" asked the Patriarch. I replied, "Although there are northern men and southern men, north and south make no difference to their Buddha-nature. A barbarian is different from Your Holiness physically, but there is no difference in our Buddha-nature." He was going to speak further to me, but the presence of other disciples made him stop short[3]. He then ordered me to join the crowd to work.

---

[1] tael/teɪl/ n. 两,东亚之重量单位,尤指用于中国者,等于十六分之一斤,约 38 克
[2] barbarian/bɑːˈbeərɪən/ n. 原始人,未开化的人,野蛮人
[3] stop short 突然中止

惠能曰:"惠能启和尚①:弟子自心常生智慧②,不离自性③,即是福田④。未审和尚教作何务?"

祖云:"这猺獠,根性大利⑤! 汝更勿言,著槽厂去。"惠能退至后院,有一行者⑥,差惠能破柴踏碓⑦。经八月余。

祖一日忽见惠能,曰:"吾思汝之见可用,恐有恶人害汝,遂不与汝言,汝知之否?"惠能曰:"弟子亦知师意,不敢行至堂前,令人不觉。"

祖一日唤诸门人总来:"吾向汝说:世人生死事大⑧。汝等终日只求福田,不求出离生死苦海⑨。自性若迷,福何可救? 汝等各去,自看智慧,取自本心般若之性⑩,各作一偈⑪,来呈吾看。若悟大意,付汝衣法⑫,为第六代祖。火急速去! 不得迟滞。思量即不中用⑬,见性之人⑭,言下须见。若如此者,轮刀上阵⑮,亦得见之。"

---

① 启:启奏,禀告。

② 弟子:《行事钞》云:"学在我后,名之为弟。解从我生,名之为子。"智慧:梵语"般若"的意译,佛教谓超越世俗虚幻的认识,达到把握真理的能力。

③ 自性:指诸法各自具有的不变不灭之性;个性,本性。

④ 福田:佛教以为供养布施,行善修德,能受福报,犹如播种田亩,有秋收之利,故称。《无量寿经净影疏》云:"生世福善,如田生物,故云福田。"

⑤ 根性:本性,本质。佛家认为气力之本曰根,善恶之习曰性,人性有生善恶作业之力,故称"根性"。《辅行》云:"能生为根,数习为性。"大,过也。利,锐也。

⑥ 行者:禅院侍者。《禅林象器笺》云:"有发而依止僧寺,称为行者。"

⑦ 踏碓(tà duì):踩踏杵杆一端使杵头起落舂米。

⑧ 世人生死事大:世间之人,当以追求解脱、出离生死为本分大事。这是弘忍教导他的弟子们,都要厌离人世,期求解脱。

⑨ 不求出离生死苦海:这是弘忍责备弟子们只求世间福,不求出生死。佛教宣称人世生死,苦深如海。苦海:佛教指尘世间的烦恼和苦难。

⑩ 般若(bō rě):梵语译音。或译为"波若",意译"智慧"。佛教用以指如实理解一切事物的智慧,为表示有别于一般所指的智慧,故用音译。大乘佛教称之为"诸佛之母"。

⑪ 偈(jì):梵语"偈佗"(Gatha)的简称,即佛经中的唱颂词,通常以四句为一偈。

⑫ 衣法:"衣"指出家人的袈裟,"法"指佛陀的教法。丁福保笺注云:"传正法而更授以师之袈裟也。"

⑬ 思量:思虑事理而量度之。

⑭ 见性:彻见自心之佛性。《永平道元法语》云:"见性,即佛性也。万法之实想也。亦即众生之心性也。"

⑮ 轮刀上阵:丁福保笺注云:言舞刀如车轮之转而入军阵作战也。

"May I tell Your Holiness," said I, "that Prajna① (transcendental Wisdom) often rises in my mind. When one does not go astray② from one's own Essence of Mind, one may be called the 'field of merits③' (a title of honour given to monks, as they afford the best opportunities to others to sow the 'seed' of merits). I do not know what work Your Holiness would ask me to do?"

"This barbarian is too bright," he remarked. "Go to the stable④ and speak no more." I then withdrew myself to the backyard and was told by a lay brother⑤ to split firewood and to pound rice.

More than eight months after, the Patriarch saw me one day and said, "I know your knowledge of Buddhism is very sound⑥; but I have to refrain⑦ from speaking to you, lest evil doers should do you harm. Do you understand?" "Yes Sir, I do," I replied. "To avoid people taking notice of me, I dare not go near your hall."

The Patriarch one day assembled all his disciples and said to them, "The question of incessant⑧ rebirth is a momentous⑨ one. Day after day, instead of trying to free yourselves from this bitter sea of life and death, your men seem to go after tainted⑩ merits only (i.e., merits which will cause rebirth). Yet merits will be of no help, if your Essence of Mind is obscured⑪. Go and seek for

---

① Prajna/'prʊdʒnə/ n. 般若
② go astray 走失,迷路,走入歧途
③ merit/'merɪt/ n. (常作 merits)功过
④ stable/'steɪbl/ n. 马厩,马棚
⑤ lay brother 修道院做杂役的僧侣,凡人修士,庶务修士(修会中从事庶务工作的修士)
⑥ sound/saʊnd/ adj. 健全的,合理的,可靠的
⑦ refrain/rɪ'freɪn/ v. 忍住,克制,抑制
⑧ incessant/ɪn'sesnt/ adj. 不停的,连续的,不断的
⑨ momentous/məʊ'mentəs/ adj. 极为重要的
⑩ tainted/'teɪntɪd/ adj. 受玷污的
⑪ obscure/əb'skjʊə/ v. 使变模糊,隐藏

Prajna (wisdom) in your own mind and then write me a stanza (gatha①) about it. He who understands what the Essence of Mind is will be given the robe (the insignia② of the Patriarchate③) and the Dharma④(i. e. , the esoteric teaching of the Dhyana School), and I shall make him the Sixth Patriarch. Go away quickly. Delay not in writing the stanza, as deliberation⑤ is quite unnecessary and of no use. The man who has realised the Essence of Mind can speak of it at once, as soon as he is spoken to about it; and he cannot lose sight of it, even when engaged in a battle. "

① gatha/ɡɑːθɑː/ n. 偈颂
② insignia/ɪnˈsɪɡnɪə/ n. 官阶识别符号,象征(如国王或王后的王冠及权杖);标记
③ patriarchate/ˈpeɪtrɪɑrkɪt/ n. 主教的职位
④ Dharma/ˈdɑːmə/ n. 达摩,(佛教)法,约束天地万物的规则或法律
⑤ deliberation/dɪˌlɪbəˈreɪʃn/ n. 仔细的考虑或商议

　　众得处分①,退而递相谓曰②:"我等众人,不须澄心用意作偈③,将呈和尚④,有何所益? 神秀上座⑤,现为教授师⑥,必是他得。我辈谩作偈颂⑦,枉用心力⑧。"诸人闻语,总皆息心,咸言我等已后,依止秀师⑨,何烦作偈?

　　神秀思惟⑩:"诸人不呈偈者,为我与他为教授帅。我须作偈,将呈和尚,若不呈偈,和尚如何知我心中见解深浅? 我呈偈意,求法即善,觅祖即恶,却同凡心夺其圣位奚别? 若不呈偈,终不得法。大难⑪!大难!"

　　五祖堂前,有步廊三间,拟请供奉卢珍画《楞伽经》变相及五祖血脉图⑫,流传供养⑬。

　　神秀作偈成已,数度欲呈。行至堂前,心中恍惚,遍身汗流,拟呈不得。前后经四日,一十三度呈偈不得。

---

① 处分:吩咐;处置,安排。

② 递:交替,轮流。

③ 澄心:清心,静心,使心思进入感悟佛理以便作偈子的境界。

④ 将:如,若。

⑤ 神秀(公元606—公元706年):唐代高僧,禅宗五祖弘忍弟子,北宗禅创始人。俗姓李,汴州尉氏(今河南开封尉氏)人。上座:亦作"上坐",一寺之长,"三纲"(佛寺有上座、维那、典座,皆为主要职务,称三纲)之首,多由朝廷任命年高德劭者担任。

⑥ 教授师:五种阿阇梨之第三种,教授弟子威仪、作法等。《辅行》云:"宣传圣言,名之为教;训诲于义,名之为授。"

⑦ 谩:通"漫",胡乱,随便。

⑧ 枉用心力:劳而无功曰枉。心力:谓人所以运用其心思之能力也。

⑨ 依止:依托,依附。

⑩ 思惟:思量。

⑪ 大难:异常艰难。

⑫ 供奉:官名,唐时凡有一材一艺者,得供奉内廷,故有翰林、供奉诸名。至宋时,尚有东西两头供奉官。清代之在南书房行走者,亦自称内庭供奉。卢珍:宫廷画家。《楞伽经》:全称《楞伽阿跋多罗宝经》,亦称《入楞伽经》《大乘入楞伽经》。其译名分别出自南朝宋元嘉二十年(443年)的求那跋陀罗、北魏的菩提流支、唐代于阗(今新疆和田)僧人实叉难陀。各译为四卷本、十卷本、七卷本。由于求那跋陀罗的译本最早,更接近本经的原始义,因此流传广、影响大。变相:敷演佛经的内容而绘成的具体图相,一般绘制在石窟、寺院的墙壁上或纸帛上,多用几幅连续的画面表现故事的情节,是广泛传播教义的佛教通俗艺术。

⑬ 供养:奉养。后世称献佛及饭僧亦曰供养。

Having received this instruction, the disciples withdrew and said to one another, "It is of no use for us to concentrate our mind to write the stanza and submit it to His Holiness, since the Patriarchate is bound to be won by Shin Shau, our instructor. And if we write perfunctorily①, it will only be a waste of energy." Upon hearing this, all of them made up their minds not to write and said, "Why should we take the trouble? Hereafter, we will simply follow our instructor, Shin Shau, wherever he goes; and look upon him for guidance."

Meanwhile, Shin Shau reasoned② thus with himself. "Considering that I am their teacher, none of them would take part in the competition. I wonder whether I should write a stanza and submit it to His Holiness. If I do not, how can the Patriarch know how deep or superficial③ my knowledge is? If my object is to get the Dharma, my motive is a pure one. If I were after the Patriarchate, then it would be bad. In that case, my mind would be that of a worldling④ and my action would amount to⑤ robbing the Patriarch's holy seat. But if I do not submit the stanza, I shall never have a chance of getting the Dharma. A very difficult point to decide, indeed!"

In front of the Patriarch's hall there were three corridors, the walls of which were to be painted by a court artist, named Lo Chun, with pictures from the Lankavatara (Sutra) depicting⑥ the transfiguration⑦ of

① perfunctorily/pəˈfʌŋktrɪlɪ/adv. 敷衍地,随便地,马虎地
② reason/ˈriːzn/v. 推论,思考
③ superficial/ˌsuːpəˈfɪʃl/adj. 表面的,浅薄的,肤浅的
④ worldling/ˈwɜːldlɪŋ/n. 俗人,凡人,被世俗的追求和享乐吸引的人
⑤ amount to 相当于
⑥ depict/dɪˈpɪkt/v. 描绘,描述,描写
⑦ transfiguration/ˌtrænsfɪɡjəˈreɪʃn/n. 变形,变容,变貌

the assembly①, and with sceneries② showing the genealogy③ of the five Patriarchs for the information and veneration④ of the public.

When Shin Shau had composed his stanza he made several attempts to submit⑤ it to the Patriarch; but as soon as he went near the hall his mind was so perturbed⑥ that he sweated all over. He could not screw up⑦ courage to submit it, although in the course of four days he had altogether made thirteen attempts to do so.

---

① assembly/əˈsemblɪ/ n. 汇编,集群
② scenery/ˈsiːnərɪ/ n. 风景,景色,舞台布景
③ genealogy/ˌdʒɪnɪˈælədʒɪ/ n. 宗谱,家谱,谱系
④ veneration/ˌvenəˈreɪʃn/ n. 尊敬,崇拜
⑤ submit/səbˈmɪt/ v. 提交,呈递
⑥ perturb/pəˈtɜːb/ v. 烦扰,使混乱,使不安
⑦ screw up 鼓舞,振作

秀乃思惟："不如向廊下书著,从他和尚看见。忽若道好,即出礼拜,云是秀作。若道不堪,枉向山中数年,受人礼拜,更修何道?"

是夜三更①,不使人知,自执灯,书偈于南廊壁间,呈心所见。偈曰:

身是菩提树②,心如明镜台。

时时勤拂拭,勿使惹尘埃。

秀书偈了,便却归房,人总不知。秀复思惟："五祖明日见偈欢喜,即我与法有缘;若言不堪,自是我迷③,宿业障重④,不合得法。"圣意难测⑤,房中思想,坐卧不安,直至五更⑥。

祖已知神秀入门未得,不见自性。

天明,祖唤卢供奉来,向南廊壁间绘画图相。忽见其偈,报言:"供奉却不用画,劳尔远来。经云:'凡所有相,皆是虚妄⑦。'但留此偈,与人诵持。依此偈修,免堕恶道⑧;依此偈修,有大利益。"

---

① 三更:指半夜十一时至翌晨一时。
② 菩提树:"菩提"一词是梵文 Bodhi 的音译,意思是觉悟、智慧。佛教用以指豁然彻悟的境界,又指觉悟的智慧和途径。菩提是大彻大悟,明心见性,证得了最后的光明的自性,也就是达到了涅槃的程度。涅槃对凡夫来讲是人死了,实际上就是达到了无上菩提。菩提树是印度的一种桑科无花果树,树冠圆形或倒卵形,枝叶扶疏,浓荫覆地,传说释迦牟尼在此树下禅坐而觉悟成佛,故称作菩提树。用菩提表示对佛教真谛的彻悟或功德圆满,修道成佛。
③ 迷:谓心闇于事理而不悟也。
④ 宿业障重:前世业障太重。宿业:为作于前世善恶之业因也。宿:指过去,前世。障:烦恼之异名。重:严重。
⑤ 圣意:圣人及其经典的意旨;神灵的启示。
⑥ 五更:旧时自黄昏至拂晓一夜间分为甲、乙、丙、丁、戊五段,谓之"五更"。又称五鼓、五夜。北齐颜之推《颜氏家训·书证》:"或问:'一夜何故五更? 更何所训?'答曰:'汉魏以来,谓为甲夜、乙夜、丙夜、丁夜、戊夜;又云鼓,一鼓、二鼓、三鼓、四鼓、五鼓;亦云一更、二更、三更、四更、五更;皆以五为节……更,历也,经也,故曰五更尔。'"
⑦ 凡所有相,皆是虚妄:出自《金刚经》,意为:凡是所有一切的相,都要将它当成是虚妄的,只要不去执着它,就会产生智慧。《六祖坛经》讲的无相,是说一切相都是虚妄相,不是真实相。现象虽然有,但那只是幻境、幻象,是因缘有而自性空,只因为因缘的凑合而有了现象;如果另外的因缘产生,现在的现象就会改变,形成另一种现象,所以称它为虚妄相。
⑧ 恶道:佛教谓六道轮回中作恶业者受生的三个去处。即:地狱、饿鬼、畜生三道。入恶道者无缘佛法。

Then he suggested to himself，"It would be better for me to write it on the wall of the corridor and let the Patriarch see it himself. If he approves it，I shall come out to pay homage，and tell him that it is done by me；but if he disapproves it，then I shall have wasted several years in this mountain in receiving homage from others which I by no means deserve! In that case，what progress have I made in learning Buddhism?"

At 12 o'clock that night，he went secretly with a lamp to write the stanza on the wall of the south corridor，so that the Patriarch might know what spiritual insight① he had attained. The stanza read：

Our body is the Bodhi-tree，

And our mind a mirror bright.

Carefully we wipe them hour by hour，

And let no dust alight②.

As soon as he had written it he left at once for his room；so nobody knew what he had done. In his room he again pondered③："When the Patriarch sees my stanza tomorrow and is pleased with it，I shall be ready for the Dharma；but if he says that it is badly done，it will mean that I am unfit for the Dharma，owing to my misdeeds④ in previous lives which thickly becloud⑤ my mind. It is difficult to know what the Patriarch will say about it!" In this vein⑥ he kept on thinking until dawn，as he could neither sleep nor sit at ease.

---

① insight/'ɪnsaɪt/ n. 洞察力，见识
② alight/ə'laɪt/ v. 下来，飘落，飞落
③ ponder/'pɒndə/ v. (长时间地仔细)考虑(尤指以便作出决定)，深思
④ misdeed/ˌmɪs'diːd/ n. (通常作复数)恶行，罪行
⑤ becloud/bɪ'klaud/ v. 遮蔽，掩盖，使混乱
⑥ vein/veɪn/ n. 情绪，心境的起伏

But the Patriarch knew already that Shin Shau had not entered the door of enlightenment, and that he had not known the Essence of Mind.

In the morning, he sent for Mr. Lo, the court artist, and went with him to the south corridor to have the walls there painted with pictures. By chance, he saw the stanza. "I am sorry to have troubled you to come so far," he said to the artist. "The walls need not be painted now, as the Sutra says, 'All forms or phenomena are transient① and illusive②.' It will be better to leave the stanza here, so that people may study it and recite it. If they put its teaching into actual practice, they will be saved from the misery of being born in these evil realms of existence (*gatis*). The merit gained by one who practises it will be great indeed!"

---

① transient/ˈtrænʃənt/*adj*. 短暂的，转瞬即逝的
② illusive/ɪˈluːsɪv/*adj*. 幻影的，错觉的，迷惑人的

令门人炷香礼敬,尽诵此偈,即得见性①。门人诵偈,皆叹善哉。

祖三更唤秀入堂,问曰:"偈是汝作否?"秀言:"实是秀作,不敢妄求祖位,望和尚慈悲②,看弟子有少智慧否?"

祖曰:"汝作此偈,未见本性,只到门外,未入门内。如此见解,觅无上菩提③,了不可得。无上菩提,须得言下识自本心,见自本性,不生不灭。于一切时中④,念念自见⑤,万法无滞,一真一切真,万境自如如⑥。如如之心,即是其实。若如是见,即是无上菩提之自性也。汝且去一两日思惟,更作一偈,将来吾看。汝偈若入得门,付汝衣法。"

神秀作礼而出。又经数日,作偈不成,心中恍惚,神思不安,犹如梦中,行坐不乐。

---

① 见性:谓悟彻清净的佛性。
② 慈悲:与乐为慈,拔苦为悲。《智度论》云:"大慈与一切众生乐,大悲拔一切众生苦。"
③ 无上菩提:最高之觉悟境界。
④ 一切时:自无始以来相续者,名一切时。
⑤ 念念:谓极短的时间,犹言刹那。凡物变化于极短之时间,若心念然者。
⑥ 如如:诸法皆平等不二的法性理体;永恒存在的真如;引申为永存,常在。

He then ordered incense① to be burnt，and all his disciples to pay homage to it and to recite it，so that they might realise the Essence of Mind. After they had recited it，all of them exclaimed，"Well done！"

In midnight，the Patriarch sent for Shin Shau to come to the hall and asked him whether the stanza was written by him or not. "It was，Sir，" replied Shin Shau. "I dare not be so vain② as to expect to get the Patriarchate，but I wish Your Holiness would kindly tell me whether my stanza shows the least grain③ of wisdom."

"Your stanza，" replied the Patriarch，"shows that you have not yet realised the Essence of Mind. So far you have reached the 'door of enlightenment,' but you have not yet entered it. To seek for supreme enlightenment with such an understanding as yours can hardly be successful.

"To attain the supreme enlightenment，one must be able to know spontaneously④ one's own nature or Essence of Mind，which is neither created nor can it be annihilated⑤. From Ksana⑥ to Ksana (momentary sensations⑦)，one should be able to realise the Essence of Mind all the time. All things will then be free from restraint (i.e. emancipated⑧). Once the Tathata⑨(Suchness⑩，another name

---

① incense/'ɪnsens/ n. （宗教仪式上用的）香
② vain/veɪn/ adj. （对自己的才、貌等）自视过高的，自负的
③ grain/greɪn/ n. 一点儿，少许或最小的可能的量
④ spontaneously/spɒn'teɪnɪəslɪ/ adv. 自发地，无意识地，不由自主地
⑤ annihilate/ə'naɪəleɪt/ v. 歼灭，消灭，毁灭
⑥ Ksana/sɑːnə/ n. 刹那，极短的时间。依《俱舍论》，一刹那合 1/75 秒，佛经中说弹一下指头的时间有 60 刹那。刹那生灭，就是一刹那具足生、住、异、灭。
⑦ sensation/sen'seɪʃn/ n. 感觉，知觉
⑧ emancipate/ɪ'mænsɪpeɪt/ v. 释放，解放
⑨ Tathata/tætə'tɑː/ n. 真如
⑩ suchness/'sʌtʃnɪs/ n. 本质，本性

for Essence of Mind) is known, one will be free from delusion① for ever; and in all circumstances, one's mind will be in a state of 'Thusness②.' Such a state of mind is absolute truth. If you can see things in such a frame of mind, you would have known the Essence of Mind which is supreme enlightenment.

"You had better go back to think it over again for a couple of days, and then submit me another stanza. If your stanza shows that you have entered the 'door of enlightenment,' I will transmit you the robe and the Dharma."

Shin Shau made obeisance③ to the Patriarch and left. For several days, he tried in vain to write another stanza. This upset his mind so much that he was as ill at ease as if he were in a nightmare, and he could find comfort neither in sitting nor in walking.

---

① delusion/dɪˈluːʒn/ n . 幻想，妄想，迷惑，错觉
② thusness/ˈðʌsnɪs/ n . 这个样子，如此，如是
③ obeisance/əuˈbeɪsəns/ n . 尊敬，顺从

复两日，有一童子①于碓坊过②，唱诵其偈。惠能一闻，便知此偈未见本性。虽未蒙教授，早识大意③。

遂问童子曰："诵者何偈?"童子曰："尔这獦獠不知，大师言：世人生死事大，欲得传付衣法，令门人作偈来看，若悟大意，即付衣法，为第六祖。神秀上座于南廊壁上书无相偈④，大师令人皆诵，依此偈修，免堕恶道。依此偈修，有大利益。"

惠能曰："我亦要咏此，结来生缘。上人⑤，我此踏碓八个余月，未曾行到堂前，望上人引至偈前礼拜。"童子引至偈前礼拜，惠能曰："惠能不识字，请上人为读。"

时有江州别驾⑥，姓张，名日用，便高声读。惠能闻己，遂言："亦有一偈，望别驾为书。"别驾言："汝亦作偈，其事希有!"惠能向别驾言："欲学无上菩提，不得轻于初学。下下人有上上智，上上人有没意智。若轻人，即有无量无边罪。"别驾言："汝但诵偈，吾为汝书。汝若得法，先须度吾，勿忘此言。"

惠能偈曰：

菩提本无树，明镜亦非台，

本来无一物，何处惹尘埃。

---

① 童子：未成年的仆役。

② 碓坊：舂米作坊。

③ 识大意：明白要点，明白大体意思，但此处意为明白最终意义，真实的意义，而非表面肤浅的意义。

④ 无相偈：无相就是指人们本身具备的佛性，不是指别的东西。无相偈意指如何发现、体验自己的真心，并将此体验用颂词的形式传递给他人。

⑤ 上人：对僧人的尊称。

⑥ 别驾：官名，别驾从事史或别驾从事的简称。汉置，为州刺史的佐官。隋初废郡存州，改别驾为长史。唐初改郡丞为别驾，高宗又改别驾为长史，另以皇族为别驾，后废置不常。宋各州的通判，职任似别驾，后世因以别驾为通判之习称。

Two days after, it happened that a young boy who was passing by the room where I was pounding recited loudly the stanza written by Shin Shau. As soon as I heard it, I knew at once that the composer of it had not yet realised the Essence of Mind. For although I had not been taught about it at that time, I already had a general idea① of it.

"What stanza is this?" I asked the boy. "You barbarian," he replied, "don't you know about it? The Patriarch told his disciples that the question of incessant rebirth was a momentous one, that those who wished to inherit his robe and Dharma should write him a stanza, and that the one who had an understanding of the Essence of Mind would get them and be made the Sixth Patriarch. Elder Shin Shau wrote this 'Formless' Stanza on the wall of the south corridor and the Patriarch told us to recite it. He also said that those who put its teaching into actual practice would attain great merit, and be saved from the misery of being born in the evil realms of existence."

I told the boy that I wished to recite the stanza too, so that I might have an affinity② with its teaching in future life. I also told him that although I had been pounding rice there for eight months, I had never been to the hall, and that he would have to show me where the stanza was to enable me to make obeisance to it.

The boy took me there and I asked him to read it to me, as I am illiterate③. A petty officer of the Kong Chau District named Chang Yat Yung, who happened to be there, read it out to me When he had finished reading, I told him that I also had composed a stanza,

---

① general idea 大意,梗概。此译是对原文"大意"的误读。
② affinity/ə'fɪnətɪ/ n. 共鸣,吸引,自然的吸引或亲密的感情
③ illiterate/ɪ'lɪtərət/ adj. 不会读或不会写的,不识字的,没受教育的

and asked him to write it for me. "Extraordinary indeed!" he exclaimed "that you also can compose a stanza!"

"Don't despise① a beginner," said I, "if you are a seeker of supreme enlightenment. You should know that the lowest class may have the sharpest② wit, while the highest may be in want of③ intelligence. If you slight④ others, you commit a very great sin."

"Dictate⑤ your stanza," said he. "I'll take it down for you. But do not forget to deliver⑥ me, should you succeed in getting the Dharma!"

My stanza read:

There is no Bodhi-tree,

Nor stand of a mirror bright.

Since all is void,

Where can the dust alight?

---

① despise/dɪ'spaɪz/ v. 鄙视，藐视，看不起
② sharp/ʃɑːp/ adj. （智力上）敏锐的，精明的
③ in want of 缺少，需要
④ slight/slaɪt/ v. 轻视
⑤ dictate/dɪk'teɪt/ v. 口授，口述，读出
⑥ deliver/dɪ'lɪvə/ v. 拯救，解救，释放

书此偈已，徒众总惊，无不嗟讶。各相谓言："奇哉！不得以貌取人。何得多时使他肉身菩萨①！"

祖见众人惊怪，恐人损害，遂将鞋擦了偈，曰："亦未见性。"众以为然。

次日，祖潜至碓坊，见能腰石舂米，语曰："求道之人，为法忘躯，当如是乎？"乃问曰："米熟也未②？"惠能曰："米熟久矣，犹欠筛在。"祖以杖击碓三下而去。

惠能即会祖意。三鼓入室③。祖以袈裟遮围，不令人见，为说《金刚经》。至"应无所住④，而生其心"，惠能言下大悟，"一切万法⑤，不离自性。"

遂启祖言："何期自性⑥，本自清净；何期自性，本不生灭；何期自性，本自具足⑦；何期自性，本无动摇；何期自性，能生万法。"

祖知悟本性，谓惠能曰："不识本心，学法无益；若识自本心，见自本性，即名丈夫、天人师、佛⑧。"

----

① 肉身菩萨：谓即生修成的菩萨，亦为大善知识的尊称。菩萨：梵文菩提萨埵（Bodhi-sattva）之省，原为释迦牟尼修行而未成佛时的称号，后泛用为对大乘思想的实行者的称呼。
② 熟：经过加工或处理过的；成熟。
③ 三鼓：三更，晚上十一点至一点期间。
④ 无所住：不被任何意念、事物所拘执。
⑤ 万法：梵语"dharma"，意译"法"，指事物及其现象，也指理性、佛法等。"万法"指一切事物。
⑥ 何期：犹言岂料，表示没有想到。
⑦ 具足：具备，充足。
⑧ 丈夫：指有所作为的人。天人师：释迦牟尼佛的别号，以其为天与人之师，故名。亦指皈佛成正果者。

When he had written this, all disciples and others who were present were greatly surprised. Filled with admiration, they said to one another, "How wonderful! No doubt we should not judge people by appearance. How can it be that for so long we have made a Bodhisattva incarnate① work for us?"

Seeing that the crowd was overwhelmed with amazement, the Patriarch rubbed off the stanza with his shoe, lest jealous ones should do me injury. He expressed the opinion, which they took for granted, that the author of this stanza had also not yet realized the Essence of Mind.

Next day the Patriarch came secretly to the room where the rice was pounded. Seeing that I was working there with a stone pestle②, he said to me, "A seeker of the Path risks his life for the Dharma. Should he not do so?" Then he asked, "Is the rice ready?" "Ready long ago," I replied, "only waiting for the sieve③." He knocked the mortar④ thrice with his stick and left.

Knowing what his message meant, in the third watch of the night, I went to his room. Using the robe as a screen so that none could see us, he expounded⑤ the *Diamond Sutra* to me. When he came to the sentence, "One should use one's mind in such a way that it will be free from any attachment," I at once became thoroughly enlightened, and realised that all things in the universe are the Essence of Mind itself.

"Who would have thought," I said to the Patriarch, "that the

---

① incarnate/ɪnˈkɑrneɪt/ *adj*. 化身的
② pestle/ˈpestl/ *n*. 碾槌，杵
③ sieve/sɪv/ *n*. 筛子
④ mortar/ˈmɔːtər/ *n*. 臼
⑤ expound/ɪkˈspaund/ *v*. 详加解释，详述

Essence of Mind is intrinsically① pure! Who would have thought that the Essence of Mind is intrinsically free from becoming or annihilation! Who would have thought that the Essence of Mind is intrinsically self-sufficient! Who would have thought that the Essence of Mind is intrinsically free from change! Who would have thought that all things are the manifestation② of the Essence of Mind!"

Knowing that I had realized the Essence of Mind, the Patriarch said, "For him who does not know his own mind, there is no use learning Buddhism. On the other hand, if he knows his own mind and sees intuitively③ his own nature, he is a Hero, a 'Teacher of gods and men,' 'Buddha'."

---

① intrinsically/ɪnˈtrɪnsɪkəlɪ/*adv*. 本质上,内存地,固有地
② manifestation/ˌmænɪˈfesteɪʃn/*n*. 显示,表现,表现形式
③ intuitively/ɪnˈtuːɪtɪvlɪ/*adv*. 直觉地,直观地

三更受法①，人尽不知，便传顿教及衣钵②。云："汝为第六代祖，善自护念③，广度有情④。流布将来，无令断绝。听吾偈曰：

有情来下种，因地果还生。

无情亦无种，无性亦无生。

祖复曰："昔达摩大师，初来此土，人未之信，故传此衣，以为信体，代代相承。法则以心传心，皆令自悟自解。自古，佛佛惟传本体⑤，师师密付本心；衣为争端⑥，止汝勿传。若传此衣，命如悬丝⑦。汝须速去，恐人害汝。"

惠能启曰："向甚处去？"祖云："逢怀则止⑧，遇会则藏⑨。"

惠能三更领得衣钵，云："能本是南中人，素不知此山路，如何出得江口？"五祖言，"汝不须忧，吾自送汝。"

祖相送至九江驿⑩，祖令上船，五祖把橹自摇。惠能言，"请和尚坐，弟子合摇橹。"祖云："合是吾渡汝。"惠能云："迷时师度，悟了自度。度名虽一，用处不同。

---

① 受法：此处的"法"等同于"传法"或"传授师傅言教的许可"。

② 顿教：不依次第，快速到达觉悟之教法，称为顿教，是禅门南宗的标志。与之相对的是北宗长时间修行而到达悟境之教法，称为渐教。此划分引发南北两宗的激烈争论，南方慧能系主张速疾直入突极之悟，世称"南顿"；北方神秀系则强调依序渐进之悟，世称"北渐"，此即禅宗之顿渐二教。衣钵：本义为佛教僧尼的袈裟与饭盂，佛家以衣钵为师徒传授之法器，因引申指师传的思想、学问、技能等。

③ 护念：令外恶不入为护，内善得生为念。

④ 有情：梵语"sattva"的意译，也译为"众生"，指人和一切有情识的动物。

⑤ 佛佛：佛佛者，前佛后佛也。本体：诸法之根本自性也。

⑥ 争端：引起双方争执的事由。

⑦ 命如悬丝：生命都像悬着的丝，随时有危险。

⑧ 怀：怀集，县名。明清属广西梧州府，今属广西苍梧县。

⑨ 会：四会，县名。明清皆属广东肇庆府，今属广东粤海道。

⑩ 九江驿："驿"指驿站。《清会典》云："腹地为驿，军报所设为站，皆为交通递送之用。"《大明一统志》云："九江驿即九江府浔阳驿也。"

Thus, to the knowledge of no one, the Dharma was transmitted to me at midnight, and consequently I became the inheritor of the teaching of the 'Sudden' School as well as of the robe and the begging bowl.

"You are now the Sixth Patriarch," said he, "Take good care of yourself, and deliver as many sentient① beings as possible. Spread and preserve the teaching, and don't let it come to an end. Take note of my stanza:

Sentient beings who sow the seeds of enlightenment

In the field of Causation② will reap③ the fruit of Buddhahood.

Inanimate④ objects void of Buddha-nature

Sow not and reap not.

He further said, "When Patriarch Bodhidharma first came to China, most Chinese had no confidence in him, and so this robe was handed down as a testimony⑤ from one Patriarch to another. As to the Dharma, this is transmitted from heart to heart, and the recipient⑥ must realise it by his own efforts. From time immemorial⑦, it has been the practice for one Buddha to pass to his successor the quintessence⑧ of the Dharma, and for one Patriarch to transmit to another the esoteric teaching from heart to heart. As the robe may give cause for dispute, you are the last one to inherit it. Should you hand it down to your successor, your life would be in

---

① sentient/'senʃnt/adj. 有感觉能力的,有感觉力的,有意识的

② causation/kɔː'zeɪʃn/n. 原因,起因

③ reap/riːp/v. 收割,获得,收获

④ inanimate/ɪn'ænɪmət/adj. 无生命的

⑤ testimony/'testɪmənɪ/n.（对某事物的）见证或证明

⑥ recipient/rɪ'sɪpɪənt/n. 接受者

⑦ time immemorial：太古时代,远古

⑧ quintessence/kwɪn'tesns/n. 精华,精髓

imminent danger①. Now leave this place as quickly as you can, lest some one should do you harm."

"Whither② should I go?" I asked. "At Wei you stop and at Wui you seclude yourself," he replied.

Upon receiving the robe and the begging bowl in the middle of the night, I told the Patriarch that, being a Southerner, I did not know the mountain tracks, and that it was impossible for me to get to the mouth of the river (to catch a boat). "You need not worry," said he. "I will go with you."

He then accompanied me to Kiukiang, and there ordered me into a boat. As he did the rowing himself, I asked him to sit down and let me handle the oar. "It is only right for me to carry you across," he said. To this I replied, "While I am under illusion, it is for you who get me across; but after enlightenment, I should cross it by myself. Although the term 'to go across' is the same, it is used differently in each case.

---

① imminent danger 迫近的危险
② whither/ˈwɪðə/ adv. 何处, 到哪里

　　惠能生在边方，语音不正，蒙师传法，今已得悟，只合自性自度。"

　　祖云："如是，如是。以后佛法，由汝大行。汝去三年，吾方逝世。汝今好去，努力向南，不宜速说，佛法难起。"

　　惠能辞违祖已，发足南行①。两月中间，至大庾岭②。（祖归，数月不上堂。众疑，诣问曰③："和尚少病少恼否？"曰："病即无，衣法已南矣。"问："谁人传授？"曰："能者得之。"众乃知焉。）④逐后数百人来，欲夺衣钵。

　　一僧俗姓陈，名惠明，先是四品将军⑤，性行粗糙⑥，极意参寻⑦，为众人先，趁及惠能⑧。惠能掷下衣钵于石上，曰："此衣表信，可力争耶？"能隐草莽中。惠明至，提掇不动⑨，乃唤云："行者⑩！行者！我为法来，不为衣来。"

　　惠能遂出，盘坐石上。惠明作礼云："望行者为我说法。"

　　惠能云："汝既为法而来，可屏息诸缘⑪，勿生一念，吾为汝说。"明良久，惠能云："不思善，不思恶，正与么时⑫，那个是明上座本来面目⑬？"

————————

① 发足：起程，出发。

② 大庾岭：在江西大庾县南，与广东南雄县分界。一名台岭，亦名庾岭，为五岭之一，当赣粤之要冲，极险峻。

③ 诣问：前往叩问。

④ 黄译漏掉此部分。根据契嵩本原文及顾瑞荣本《坛经》补全。

⑤ 将军：将兵者之通称。

⑥ 性行：本性与行为。粗糙：粗暴鲁莽。粗，不精也。糙，米谷杂也。

⑦ 极意参寻：极意，尽意也。参，参究也。寻，追寻也。

⑧ 趁：逐也，自后追及之也。

⑨ 掇：拾取。

⑩ 行者：出家而未经剃度的佛教徒。

⑪ 屏息：抑止，停息。诸缘：指色香等百般世相。此种种世相，皆为我心识攀缘之所，故称诸缘。

⑫ 与么时：此时。

⑬ 那个：俗语，指不思善，不思恶。一说，哪个。上座：僧人之尊称，在最高之位者。本来面目：指自己之本分。

As I happen to be born on the frontier, even my speaking is incorrect in pronunciation; (but in spite of this) I have had the honour to inherit the Dharma from you. Since I am now enlightened, it is only right for me to cross the sea of birth and death myself by realising my own Essence of Mind. "

"Quite so, quite so," he agreed. "Beginning from you, Buddhism (meaning the Dhyana School) will become very popular. Three years after your departure from me I shall leave this world. You may start on your journey now. Go as fast as you can towards the South. Do not preach too soon, as Buddhism (of the Dhyana School) is not so easily spread. "

After saying good-bye, I left him and walked towards the South. In about two months' time, I reached the Tai Yu Mountain. (The Patriarch returned and made no appearance in the hall for several days. The disciples suspected and asked whether the Patriarch was ill or in worries. They were answered: no illness, but the robe and the bowl had been carried to the South. They asked again who inherited them. Hui Neng was the answer, and the disciples were all apprehensive.)[1] There I noticed that several hundred men were in pursuit of me with the intention of robbing me of my robe and begging bowl.

Among them there was a monk named Wei Ming whose lay surname was Chen. He was a general of the fourth rank in lay life. His manner was rough and his temper hot. Of all the pursuers, he was the most vigilant[2] in search of me. When he was about to overtook[3] me, I threw the robe and the begging bowl on a rock,

---

① 黄译本漏译。此处根据顾瑞荣本《坛经》补全。

② vigilant/ˈvɪdʒɪlənt/ *adj.* 警醒的，警惕的

③ overtake/ˌəʊvəˈteɪk/ *v.* 追上，超越

saying, "This robe is nothing but a symbol. What is the use of taking it away by force?" I then hid myself. When he got to the rock, he tried to pick them up, but found he could not. Then he shouted out, "Lay Brother, Lay Brother, (for the Patriarch had not yet formally joined the order) I come for the Dharma, not for the robe."

Whereupon I came out from my hiding place and squatted① on the rock. He made obeisance and said, "Lay Brother, preach to me, please."

"Since the object of your coming is the Dharma," said I, "refrain from thinking of anything and keep your mind blank. I will then teach you." When he had done this for a considerable② time, I said "When you are thinking of neither good nor evil, what is at that particular moment, Venerable Sir, your real nature (literally, original face)?"

---

① squat/skwɔt/ v. 蹲,收膝而坐
② considerable/kən'sɪdərəbl/ adj. 相当大的数量、数目、距离等

惠明言下大悟。复问云："上来密语密意外①,还更有密意否?"惠能云："与汝说者,即非密也。汝若返照②,密在汝边。"

明曰："惠明虽在黄梅,实未省自己面目,今蒙指示,如人饮水,冷暖自知。今行者即惠明师也。"

惠能曰："汝若如是,吾与汝同师黄梅,善自护持。"

明又问："惠明今后向甚处去?"惠能曰："逢袁则止,遇蒙则居。"明礼辞。

(明回至岭下,谓趁众曰："向陟崔嵬③,竟无踪迹,当别道寻之。"趁众咸以为然。惠明后改道明,避师上字。)④

惠能后至曹溪,又被恶人寻逐。乃于四会,避难猎人队中,凡经一十五载。

时与猎人随宜说法。猎人常令守网,每见生命,尽放之。每至饭时,以菜寄煮肉锅。或问,则对曰:"但吃肉边菜。"

一日思惟:"时当弘法⑤,不可终遁。"遂出至广州法性寺。

---

① 上来:上代祖师以来。密语:以密意而说之语。
② 返照:用佛性对照检查自己。
③ 崔嵬(cuī wéi):山顶,有石头的土山。
④ 此段缺,根据《坛经》契嵩本补全。
⑤ 弘法:弘扬流通佛法。

As soon as he heard this, he at once became enlightened. But he further asked, "Apart from those esoteric sayings and esoteric ideas handed down by the Patriarch from generation to generation, are there any other esoteric teachings?" "What I can tell you is not esoteric," I replied. "If you turn your light① inwardly, you will find what is esoteric within you."

"In spite of my staying in Wong Mui," said he, "I did not realize my self-nature. Now, thanks to your guidance, I know it as a water-drinker knows how hot or how cold the water is. Lay Brother, you are now my teacher."

I replied, "If that is so, then you and I are fellow disciples of the Fifth Patriarch. Take good care of yourself."

In answering his question whither he should go thereafter, I told him to stop at Yuen and to take up his abode② in Mong. He paid homage and departed.

(Wei Ming went down the hills and told the purchasers③, "I have been up to the mountain and failed to find him. We ought to try another road to search." The purchasers all agreed. Later, Wei Ming changed his name into Tao Ming to avoid repeating Hui Neng's first name.)④

Sometime after, I reached Tso Kai. There the evil-doers again persecuted⑤ me and I had to take refuge⑥ in Sze Wui, where I stayed with a party of⑦ hunters for a period as long as fifteen years.

Occasionally I preached to them in a way that befitted their

---

① light /laɪt/ n. 领悟
② abode /əˈbəud/ n. 住处,住所
③ purchaser /ˈpɜːtʃəsə/ n. 顾译本有误,应为 chaser。
④ 黄译缺此段,译文根据顾瑞荣本《坛经》补全。
⑤ persecute /ˈpɜːsɪkjuːt/ v. 迫害,残害,困扰,为难
⑥ refuge /ˈrefjuːdʒ/ n. 躲避,避难,避难所
⑦ a party of 一群

understanding. They used to put me to watch their nets; but whenever I found living creatures therein[1] I set them free. At meal times I put vegetables in the pan in which they cooked their meat. Some of them questioned me, and I explained to them that I would eat vegetables only, after they had been cooked with the meat.

One day I bethought myself that I ought not to pass a secluded[2] life all the time, and that it was high time for me to propagate[3] the Law. Accordingly I left there and went to Fat Shing Temple in Canton.

---

① therein/ˌðeər'ɪn/ *adv*. 在那里
② secluded/sɪ'kluːdɪd/ *adj*. 与世隔绝的，隐居的
③ propagate/'prɒpəgeɪt/ *v*. 传播，扩散

值印宗法师讲《涅槃经》①。时有风吹幡②动,一僧曰:"风动。"一僧曰:"幡动。"议论不已,惠能进曰:"不是风动,不是幡动,仁者心动③。"一众骇然。印宗延至上席④,征诘奥义⑤。

见惠能言简理当,不由文字。宗云:"行者定非常人,久闻黄梅衣法南来,莫是行者否?"

惠能曰:"不敢!"宗于是作礼,告请传来衣钵,出示大众。

宗复问曰:"黄梅付嘱,如何指授⑥?"惠能曰:"指授即无,惟论见性,不论禅定⑦解脱⑧。"宗曰:"何不论禅定解脱?"能曰:"为是二法,不是佛法。佛法是不二之法⑨。"

宗又问:"如何是佛法不二之法?"惠能曰:"法师讲《涅槃经》,明佛性是佛法不二之法。如高贵德王菩萨白佛言:犯四重禁⑩,作五逆罪⑪,及一阐提等⑫,当断善根佛性否⑬?佛言:善根有二:一者常,二者无常⑭,佛性非常非无常,是故不断,名为不二;

---

① 值:遇到,碰上。
② 幡(fān):旗帜。
③ 仁者:佛教语。对人的尊称。
④ 上席:受尊敬的席位,座中之第一位。
⑤ 征:求。诘:问。
⑥ 指授:指导,传授。
⑦ 禅定:佛教禅宗修行方法之一。一心审考为禅,息虑凝心为定。佛教修行者以为静坐敛心,专注一境,久之达到身心安稳、观照明净的境地,即为禅定。又禅为色界天之法,定为无色界天之法。依其入定程度的浅深,并有四禅(色界定)、四定(无色界定)的区分。
⑧ 解脱:摆脱苦恼,得到自在。
⑨ 不二之法:平等而无差异之至道。
⑩ 四重禁:全称四重禁戒,略作四重,又作四重罪、四波罗夷罪。即:(一)杀生;(二)偷盗;(三)邪淫,指与人或畜牲行淫事之不净行;(四)妄语,即伪言体证上人法。上述为戒律所禁之四种根本重罪。
⑪ 五逆罪:亦省作"五逆",指杀父、杀母、害阿罗汉、斗乱众僧、起恶意于如来所等五种将招致堕无间地狱报应的恶业大罪。
⑫ 一阐提:梵语 Icchantika 的音译,亦译"一阐提迦",略称"阐提",意为"不具信",或称"断善根"。佛教用以称呼不具信心、断了成佛善根的人。《涅盘经·梵行品》云:"一阐提者,断灭一切诸善根本,心不攀缘一切善法。"
⑬ 善根:梵语意译,人所以为善之根性。善根指身、口、意三业之善法而言,善能生妙果,故谓之根。
⑭ 无常:谓世间一切事物不能久住,都处于生灭变异之中。

At that time Bhikku Yen Chung, Master of the Dharma, was lecturing on the *Maha Parinirvana Sutra* in the Temple. It happened that one day, when a pennant① was blown about by the wind, two Bhikkus entered into a dispute as to what it was that was in motion②, the wind or the pennant. As they could not settle their difference I submitted to them that it was neither, and that what actually moved was their own mind. The whole assembly was startled by what I said, and Bhikku Yen Chung invited me to take a seat of honour and questioned me about various knotty③ points in the Sutras.

Seeing that my answers were precise and accurate, and that they showed something more than book-knowledge, he said to me, "Lay Brother, you must be an extraordinary man. I was told long ago that the inheritor of the Fifth Patriarch's robe and Dharma had come to the South. Very likely you are the man."

To this I politely assented④. He immediately made obeisance and asked me to show the assembly the robe and the begging bowl which I had inherited.

He further asked what instructions I had when the Fifth Patriarch transmitted me the Dharma. "Apart from a discussion on the realisation of the Essence of Mind," I replied, "he gave me no other instruction, nor did he refer to Dhyana and Emancipation." "Why not?" he asked. "Because that would mean two ways," I replied. "And there cannot be two ways in Buddhism. There is one way only."

He asked what was the only way. I replied, "The *Maha*

---

① pennant/ˈpenənt/ *n*. 三角旗
② in motion 运动中
③ knotty/ˈnɑtɪ/ *adj*. 难解决的，棘手的
④ assent/əˈsent/ *v*. 赞成，同意

Parinirvana Sutra which you expound explains that Buddha-nature is the only way. For example，in that Sutra King Ko Kwai Tak，a Bodhisattva，asked Buddha whether or not those who commit the four paragika，(acts of gross misconduct：murder，stealing，incontinence①，and falsehood of serious nature)，or the five deadly sins (i. e. Patricide②，Matricide③，Setting the Buddhist Order in discord④，Killing an Arhat⑤，and Causing blood to flow from the body of a Buddha)，and those who are Icchantika (heretics⑥)，etc.，would eradicate⑦ their 'element of goodness' and their Buddha-nature. Buddha replied，"There are two kinds of 'element of goodness'：the eternal and the non-eternal. Since Buddha-nature is neither eternal nor non-eternal，therefore their 'element of goodness' is not eradicated. Now Buddhism is known as having no two ways.

---

① incontinence/ɪnˈkɒntɪnəns/ *n.* 不能自制，失禁，无节制
② patricide/ˈpætrɪsaɪd/ *n.* 弑父
③ matricide/ˈmætrɪsaɪd/ *n.* 弑母
④ discord/ˈdɪskɔːd/ *n.* 不和，纷争
⑤ Arhat/ˈɑːhət/ *n.* 阿罗汉（达到涅槃境界的僧人）
⑥ heretic/ˈherətɪk/ *n.* 异教徒，异端者
⑦ eradicate/ɪˈrædɪkeɪt/ *v.* 根除，消灭

一者善，二者不善，佛性非善非不善，是名不二。蕴之与界①，凡夫见二，智者了达其性无二②。无二之性，即是佛性。"

印宗闻说，欢喜合掌，言："某甲讲经③，犹如瓦砾；仁者论义，犹如其金。"于是为惠能剃发，愿事为师。

"惠能遂于菩提树下，开东山法门④。

惠能于东山得法，辛苦受尽，命似悬丝。今日得与使君⑤、官僚、僧尼、道俗⑥同此一会，莫非累劫之缘⑦？亦是过去生中供养诸佛，同种善根，方始得闻如上顿教，得法之因。教是先圣所传，不是惠能自智。愿闻先圣教者，各令净心。闻了各自除疑，如先代圣人无别。"

一众闻法，欢喜作礼而退。

---

① 蕴：即色、受、想、行、识五蕴。界：即十八界，梵文的意译。佛教以人的认识为中心，对世界一切现象所作的分类。人的一身即具此十八界，包括能发生认识功能的六根（眼界、耳界、鼻界、舌界、身界、意界），作为认识对象的六境（色界、声界、香界、味界、触界、法界）和由此生起的六识（眼识界、耳识界、鼻识界、舌识界、身识界、意识界）。

② 了达：彻悟，通晓。

③ 某甲：自称之代词。

④ 东山法门：禅宗四祖道信、五祖弘忍俱住湖北省黄梅县东山说法，称"东山法门"。宋赞宁《宋高僧传·唐荆州当阳山度门寺神秀传》云："昔魏末有天竺沙门达磨者，得禅宗妙法……以法付慧可，可付粲，粲付道信，信付忍（弘忍）。忍与信俱住东山，故谓其法为东山法门。"

⑤ 使君：对人的尊称，亦指对州郡长官的尊称。

⑥ 道俗：出家之人与世俗之人。

⑦ 劫：梵文 kalpa 的音译，"劫波"（或"劫簸"）的略称。意为极久远的时节。古印度传说世界经历若干万年毁灭一次，重新再开始，这样一个周期叫做一"劫"。"劫"的时间长短，佛经有各种不同的说法。一"劫"包括"成""住""坏""空"四个时期，叫做"四劫"。到"坏劫"时，有水、火、风三灾出现，世界归于毁灭。后人借指天灾人祸。

There are good ways and evil ways, but since Buddha-nature is neither, therefore Buddhism is known as having no two ways. From the point of view of ordinary folks, the component parts① of a personality (skhandhas) and factors of consciousness (Dhatus) are two separate things; but enlightened men understand that they are not dual② in nature. Buddha-nature is non-duality."

Bhikku Yen Chung was highly pleased with my answer. Putting his two palms together as a sign of respect, he said, "My interpretation of the Sutra is as worthless as a heap of debris③, while your discourse is as valuable as genuine gold." Subsequently he conducted the ceremony of hair-cutting for me (i.e., the ceremony of Initiation into the Order) and asked me to accept him as my pupil.

Thenceforth④, under the Bodhi-tree I preached the teaching of the Tung Shan School (the School of the Fourth and the Fifth Patriarchs, who lived in Tung Shan).

Since the time when the Dharma was transmitted to me in Tung Shan, I had gone through many hardships and my life often seemed to be hanging by a thread. Today, I have had the honour of meeting you in this assembly, and I must ascribe⑤ this to our good connection in previous kalpas⑥ (cyclic periods), as well as to our common accumulated merits in making offerings to various Buddhas in our past incarnations; otherwise, we should have had no chance of hearing the above teaching of the 'Sudden' School, and thereby

① component parts 组成部分,构件
② dual/'dju:əl/adj. 双的,双重的
③ debris/'deibri:/n. 碎片,残骸
④ thenceforth/ðens'fɔ:θ/adv. 此后,从那时
⑤ ascribe/ə'skraib/v. 归因于
⑥ kalpas/'kælpə/n. 劫(指宇宙从创始到毁灭的一个周期,约四十三亿二千万年)

laying the foundation of our future success in understanding the Dharma.

This teaching was handed down from the past Patriarchs，and it is not a system of my own invention. Those who wish to hear the teaching should first purify their own mind；and after hearing it they should each clear up their own doubts in the same way as the Sages did in the past. "

At the end of the address，the assembly felt rejoiced①，made obeisance and departed.

---

① rejoice/rɪ'dʒɔɪs/ v. 极欢喜，极高兴

【推荐阅读】

一、中文版本

丁福保笺注,陈兵导读,哈磊整理. 坛经. 上海：上海古籍出版社,
　　2011 年。

郭朋. 坛经校释. 北京：中华书局,1983 年。

铃木大拙(D. T. Suzuki). 敦煌出土六祖坛经. 东京：森江书店出版,
　　1934 年。

吴平. 坛经讲读. 上海：华东师范大学出版社,2014 年。

星云大帅. 六祖坛经讲话. 北京：新世界出版社,2008 年。

杨曾文. 新版敦煌新本六祖坛经. 北京：宗教文化出版社,2001 年。

二、英文译本

Chan，Wing-tsit. 1963. *The Platform Scripture*. New York：St.
　　John's University Press.

Cleary，T. 1998. *The Sutra of Hui-neng，Grand Master of Zen：
　　with Hui-neng's Commentary on the Diamond Sutra*，Shambhala
　　Publications.

Goddard，D. 1992. *A Buddhist Bible*. Boston：Beacon Press.

Humphreys，Christmas. 1953. *The Sutra of Wei Lang（or Hui-
　　neng）*. London：Luzac and Company.

Kuo，U. C. R.，Shih，H. Y. & Triptaka，M. H. 1977. *The Sixth
　　Patriarch's Dharma Jewel Platform Sutra*，the Sino-American
　　Buddhist Association，Buddhist Text Translation Society.

Lin Guangming. 2012. *Chinese Classics of the Mandala Sutra*.
　　Beijing：Religion Culture Press.

Mcrae，J. R. 2000. *The Platform Sutra of the Sixth Patriarch*.
　　Numata Center for Buddhist Translation and Research.

Pine，R. 2008. *The Platform Sutra：The Zen Teaching of Hui-neng*.

Counterpoint Press.

Price, A. & Wong, M. L. 1990. *Diamond Sutra and the Sutra of Hui-Neng*. Shambhala Publications.

Suzuki, D. T. 2011. *Manual of Zen Buddhism*. Grove Press.

Wong, M. L. 1930. *Sutra Spoken by the Sixth Patriarch*, *Wei Lang*, *on the High Seat of the Gem of Law* (Message from the East). Shanghai: Yu Ching Press.

Yampolsky, Philip B. 1967. *The Platform Sutra of the Sixth Patriarch*: *The Text of the Tun-Huang Manuscript with Translation*, *Introduction*, *and Notes*. New York: Columbia University Presss.

第十二单元　《黄帝内经》

【导言】

　　《黄帝内经》为中国古代医家托轩辕黄帝之名所作,是我国现存最早的较为系统和完整的中医典籍,分为《素问》和《灵枢》两部分,各八十一篇。全书以黄帝、岐伯、雷公对话、问答形式阐述病机病理。其中《素问》基于阴阳五行思想,重点论述有关生理、病理、诊断、治疗等,强调人与自然密切相关和人体内部的高度统一;《灵枢》除论述脏腑功能、病因、病机外,重点阐述经络腧穴、针具、刺法及治疗原则等。《黄帝内经》中还包含着不少朴素唯物主义和辩证法思想,在中国思想史上亦占有重要地位。

　　关于《黄帝内经》的成书,历来说法各异,但大多认为其成于周秦之间或战国至两汉时期。《黄帝内经》之名始见于刘歆的《七略》,《汉书·艺文志》亦有著录。《素问》传本较多,篇目颇不一致。现存最早、最完整的《素问》注本是六朝齐梁间全元起注本,其祖本是《素问》9卷本(南宋以后失传);唐代王冰在全氏注本基础上对该书进行整理的注释本,将其改为24卷,北宋林亿对王冰注本进行校勘,改称《重广补注黄帝内经素问》,24卷,此刊本成为后世诸本的祖本。《灵枢》现传本系南宋史崧据其家藏旧本编定,24卷,注释有山东中医学院的《灵枢经语释》等。

　　《黄帝内经》自汉代开始即传入日本、朝鲜、越南邻国,其在西方的译介则晚至明清耶稣会士来华之际,英译则更晚。1925年,珀西·米勒·道森(Percy Millard Dawson)的《素问》节译本(Sun-Wen, the Basis of Chinese Medicine)在美国《医学史年鉴》(*Annuals of Medical History*)杂志发表。该文从医学史的角度对《黄帝内经》进行评介并做概要性介绍,此为《黄帝内经》英译之滥觞。至2020年,英文译本达20个,其中不乏英译精品,如,爱尔萨·威斯(Ilza Veith)的 *The Yellow Emperor's Classic of Internal Medicine*(1949)、吕聪明(Henry C. Lu)的《内、难全集》(*A Complete Translation of Nei Ching and Nan Ching*)(1978)、倪毛信(Maoshing Ni)编译的 *The Yellow Emperor's Classic of Medicine：A New Translation of the Neijing Suwen with*

Commentary (1995)、吴连胜、吴奇父子的《黄帝内经》汉英对照全译本（Yellow Emperor's Canon of Internal Medicine）(1997)、周春才、韩亚洲等的漫画版《〈黄帝内经〉养生图典》（The Illustrated Yellow Emperor's Canon of Medicine）(1997)、吴景暖的全译本《灵枢》（Ling Shu：or The Spiritual Pivot）(2002)、文树德（Paul Unschuld）的《素问》评述译本（Huang Di Nei Jing Su Wen：Nature，Knowledge，Imagery in an Ancient Chinese Medical Text）(2003)、李照国的汉英对照本《素问》(2005)和《灵枢》(2008)、江润祥（Kong Yun Cheung）的 Huang Di Nei Jing：A Synopsis with Commentaries (2010)、伯钦格（Richard Bertschinger）的 Essential Texts in Chinese Medicine：The Single Idea in the Mind of the Yellow Emperor (2014)、杨明山的英汉对照本《黄帝内经素问新译》(2015)等。

黄帝内经·素问(节选)

阴阳应象大论篇①

黄帝曰：阴阳者，天地之道也，万物之纲纪②，变化之父母③，生杀之本始④，神明之府也⑤。治病必求于本⑥。故积阳为天，积阴为地。阴静阳躁⑦，阳生阴长，阳杀阴藏⑧。阳化气，阴成形⑨。寒极生热，热极生寒。寒气生浊，热气生清⑩。清气在下，则生飧泄⑪；浊气在上，则生䐜胀⑫。此阴阳反作⑬，病之逆从也⑭。

故清阳为天，浊阴为地；地气上为云，天气下为雨；雨出地气，云出天气。故清阳出上窍⑮，浊阴出下窍⑯；清阳发腠理⑰，浊阴走五脏⑱；清

---

① 本单元原文参考郭霭春主编《黄帝内经素问校注》(1992 年版)校核。《阴阳应象大论篇》是《黄帝内经》阐述中医学基本理论最重要的篇章，故称"大论"。该篇说明人体的阴阳与天地四时的阴阳是息息相通的。认为人体生理、病理以及养生、诊断治疗皆应法于阴阳。

② 纲纪：大纲要领。纲：本义为提网的总绳。纪：本义为丝缕的头绪。"总之曰纲，周之曰纪。万物得是阴阳，而统之为纲，散之为纪。"

③ 变化：事物的生灭转化。"变者化之渐，化者变之成。"父母：指万物化生的根源。

④ 生杀：指萌生凋落、昭苏伏蛰、阴阳消长等自然规律。本始：根本、原本。

⑤ 神明：推动万物生成和变化的力量称为神明，"阴阳不测谓之神，神之昭昭谓之明"。一说，神明指人的神态、知觉、精神活动的功能。府：宫府，宅第，住所，聚集之处。

⑥ 本：根源，根本，此处指阴阳。

⑦ 静：安静，平静；静止，不动，寂静无声。躁：急躁，浮躁，不安定。

⑧ 杀：收割，砍伐。藏：收藏，储藏。

⑨ 气：指能力，力量。形：指形体、物质。"阳动而散，故化气；阴静而凝，故成形。"

⑩ 清：清澈不浑。

⑪ 飧(sūn)泄：指大便泄泻清稀，并有不消化的食物残渣。多因肝郁脾虚，清气不升所致。热气在下则谷不化，故飧泄。

⑫ 䐜(chēn)胀：上腹部胀满。䐜，起也，胀，通"张"，腹满也。寒气在上则气不散，故䐜胀。

⑬ 阴阳反作：《千金方》为"反㑅"，阴阳反其位。"清气在下，浊气在上，正阴阳反其位也。

⑭ 逆：病的异常称"逆证"。从：病的正常称"顺证"。

⑮ 上窍：指耳、目、鼻、口诸窍。

⑯ 下窍：指肛门与阴部。

⑰ 发：流出。腠(còu)理：中医指皮下肌肉之间的空隙和皮肤、肌肉的纹理，为渗泄及气血流通灌注之处。

⑱ 走：流动，经由。五脏：指心、肝、脾、肺、肾五种器官。

阳实四支①,浊阴归六腑②。

---

① 实：充满,堵塞,充实。四支：四肢。
② 六腑：指胃、胆、三焦、膀胱、大肠、小肠。

Huang Di's Inner Classic: *Basic Questions* (Excerpt)

Translated by Paul U. Unschuld and Hermann Tessenow
in collaboration with Zheng Jinsheng①
Comprehensive Discourse on Phenomena
Corresponding to② Yin and Yang

Huang Di: "As for yin and yang, they are the Way of heaven and earth, the fundamental principles [governing] the myriad③ beings, father and mother to all changes and transformations④, the basis and beginning of generating life and killing, the palace of spirit brilliance. To treat diseases, one must search for the basis. Hence, the accumulation of yang, that is heaven; the accumulation of yin, that is the earth. Yin is tranquillity⑤, yang is agitation⑥. Yang gives life, yin stimulates growth. Yang kills, yin stores. Yang transforms qi, yin completes physical appearance. Cold at its maximum generates⑦ heat; heat at its maximum generates cold. Cold qi generates turbidity⑧; heat qi generates clarity. When clear qi is in the lower [regions of the body], then this generates outflow⑨ of [undigested] food. When turbid⑩ qi is in the upper

---

① 译文选自：Unschuld, Paul U. & Hermann Tessenow in collaboration with Zheng Jinsheng. 2011. *Huang Di Nei Jing Su Wen*: *An Annotated Translation of Huang Di's Inner Classic — Basic Questions*. Berkeley and Los Angeles, Ca.: University of California Press。

② corresponding to 对应于，与……相一致

③ myriad/'mɪrɪəd/ n. [古语]一万；无数，巨大的数目，无穷大

④ transformation/ˌtrænsfə'meɪʃn/ n. 转变，变化

⑤ tranquillity/træŋ'kwɪlətɪ/ n. 平静，宁静

⑥ agitation/ˌædʒɪ'teɪʃn/ n. 激动，不安，焦虑，扰乱

⑦ generate/'dʒenəreɪt/ v. 产生，形成，造成，生成

⑧ turbidity/tɜr'bɪdətɪ/ n. 浑浊，浓密，混乱

⑨ outflow/'aʊtfləʊ/ n. [通常作单数]流出，流出物，流出量

⑩ turbid/'tɜːbɪd/ adj. 混浊的，不清的；混乱的，紊乱的

[regions], then this generates bloating①. These [are examples of] activities of yin and yang [qi] contrary [to their normal patterns], and of diseases opposing [the patterns of] compliance②.

The fact is, the clear yang is heaven; the turbid yin is the earth. The qi of the earth rises and turns into clouds; the qi of heaven descends and becomes rain. Rain originates from the qi of the earth; clouds originate from the qi of heaven. Hence, the clear yang exits through the upper orifices③; the turbid yin exits through the lower orifices. The clear yang is effused④ through the interstice⑤ structures; the turbid yin moves to the five depots⑥. The clear yang replenishes⑦ the four limbs; the turbid yin turns to the six palaces.

---

① bloat/bləʊt/ v. 膨胀，肿胀
② compliance/kəmˈplaɪəns/ n. 顺从，屈从，依从
③ orifice/ˈɔrɪfɪs/ n. 窍，(身体等的)外孔，外口
④ effuse/ɪˈfjuːz/ v. 流出，泻出
⑤ interstice/ɪnˈtɜːstɪs/ n. 空隙(两个物体或部位之间的空间，特指小而狭窄的空间)
⑥ depot/ˈdepəʊ/ n. 仓库，储藏处，补给站
⑦ replenish/rɪˈplenɪʃ/ v. 补充，把……再装满

水为阴,火为阳。阳为气①,阴为味②。味归形③,形归气。气归精,精归化④。精食气⑤,形食味⑥。化生精,气生形。味伤形⑦,气伤精。精化为气,气伤于味。

阴味出下窍,阳气出上窍。味厚者为阴⑧,薄为阴之阳。气厚者为阳,薄为阳之阴。味厚则泄,薄则通。气薄则发泄,厚则发热。壮火之气衰⑨,少火之气壮⑩。壮火食气,气食少火。壮火散气,少火生气。气味,辛甘发散为阳,酸苦涌泄为阴⑪。

阴胜则阳病,阳胜则阴病。阳胜则热,阴胜则寒。重寒则热,重热则寒。寒伤形,热伤气;气伤痛,形伤肿。故先痛而后肿者,气伤形也;先肿后痛者,形伤气也。风胜则动⑫,热胜则肿,燥胜则干,寒胜则浮⑬,湿胜则濡泻⑭。

天有四时五行⑮,以生长收藏,以生寒暑燥湿风。人有五脏化五气⑯,以生喜怒悲忧恐。故喜怒伤气,寒暑伤形。暴怒伤阴,暴喜伤阳。

---

① 气:指体内流动的精微物质,能力。
② 味:泛指一切食物。
③ 归:归结,产生。形:形体,包括脏腑、肌肉、血脉、筋骨、皮毛等。
④ 化:化生。
⑤ 食(sì):与"蚀"通,指侵蚀、消耗。
⑥ 形食味:形体仰赖食物的营养。
⑦ 味伤形:饮食太过会损伤身体。
⑧ 味厚者为阴:根据中医学理论,药物之性包括四气五味。四气源于一年四季寒热温凉的变化,所以药气分为温热凉寒四大类。五味源于地气,分为酸、苦、甘、辛、咸五大类。因四气源于天所以属阳,五味源于地所以属阴。但气味又有厚薄的不同。气厚的为纯阳,味厚的为纯阴,气薄的为阳中之阴,味薄的为阴中之阳。
⑨ 壮火:过于亢盛的阳气,这种火不是生理性的而是病理性的邪火。
⑩ 少火:微少的阳气,这种火属于生理性的,是人体生命活动的动力。
⑪ 涌泄:喷涌外泄。
⑫ 风:中医学谓人体的病因之一。"六淫"之一,为阳邪。外感风邪常致风寒、风热、风湿等症。亦指急症。如中风、痛风等。
⑬ 浮:浮肿。
⑭ 濡泻:湿泻。濡:湿。
⑮ 四时:春、夏、秋、冬。五行:水、火、木、金、土。
⑯ 五气:五脏之气。气:指脏腑的功能活动。一说,中医谓寒、暑、燥、湿、风五气;一说,五气,谓喜怒悲忧恐。

Water is yin; fire is yang. Yang is qi; yin is flavor[①]. Flavor turns to physical appearance. Physical appearance turns to qi. Qi turns to essence. Essence turns to transformation. Essence is nourished by qi. Physical appearance is nourished by flavor. Transformations generate essence. Qi generates physical appearance. Flavor harms physical appearance. Qi harms essence. Essence transforms into qi. Qi is harmed by flavor.

Flavor is yin and exits through the lower orifices. Qi is yang and exits through the upper orifices. That which is of strong flavor is yin; that with weak [flavor] is yang of yin. That which is of strong qi is yang; that with weak qi is yin of yang. When the flavor is strong, then outflow [results]; when it is weak, then penetration [results]. When the qi is weak, then it brings forth outflow; when it is strong, then it brings forth heat. The qi of strong fire weakens. The qi of a small fire gains in strength. Strong fire feeds on qi. Qi feeds on small fire. A strong fire disperses[②] qi. A small fire generates qi. Qi and flavor: acrid [flavor] and sweet [flavor] are effused and disperse and are yang, sour [flavor] and bitter [flavor] cause gushing[③] up and outflow and are yin.

When yin dominates[④], then the yang is ill; when yang dominates, then the yin is ill. When the yang dominates, then there is heat; when the yin dominates, then there is cold. Doubled cold results in heat; doubled heat results in cold. Cold harms the physical appearance; heat harms the qi. Harmed qi causes pain; a harmed physical appearance causes swelling. Hence, when there is pain first

① flavor/ˈfleɪvə/n. [古语]气味,香味;有特色的味道,滋味
② disperse/dɪˈspɜːs/v. 消散,驱散
③ gush/gʌʃ/v. 喷涌,涌出,迅速大量外流
④ dominate/ˈdɒmɪneɪt/v. 支配,控制,处于支配地位

and swelling① afterwards，qi has harmed the physical appearance. When there is swelling first and pain comes afterwards，the physical appearance has harmed the qi. When wind dominates，then there is movement；when heat dominates，then there is swelling. When dryness dominates，then there is aridity②；when cold dominates，then there is surface [swelling]. When dampness③ dominates，then there is soggy④ outflow.

Heaven has the four seasons and the five agents. It is through [the former that heaven causes] generation，growth，gathering，and storage. It is through [the latter that it] generates cold，summerheat⑤，dryness，dampness，and wind. Man has the five depots；they transform the five qi，thereby generating joy，anger，sadness，anxiety，and fear. The fact is，joy and anger harm the qi；cold and summerheat harm the physical appearance. Violent anger harms the yin；violent joy harms the yang.

---

① swelling/ˈswelɪŋ/ n. 肿胀，膨胀，肿块
② aridity/æˈrɪdətɪ/ n. 干旱，干燥
③ dampness/ˈdæmpnɪs/ n. 潮湿，湿气
④ soggy/ˈsɒgɪ/ adj. 透湿的，湿热的
⑤ summerheat 暑热

厥气上行①,满脉去形。喜怒不节②,寒暑过度,生乃不固③。故重阴必阳,重阳必阴。故曰:冬伤于寒,春必温病④;春伤于风,夏生飧泄;夏伤于暑,秋必痎疟⑤;秋伤于湿,冬生咳嗽。

帝曰:余闻上古圣人,论理人形⑥,列别脏腑⑦,端络经脉⑧,会通六合⑨,各从其经;气穴所发⑩,各有处名;谿谷属骨⑪,皆有所起;分部逆从⑫,各有条理⑬;四时阴阳,尽有经纪⑭;内外之应,皆有表里。其信然乎?

岐伯对曰:东方生风,风生木,木生酸,酸生肝,肝生筋,筋生心,肝主目。其在天为玄,在人为道,在地为化。化生五味,道生智,玄生神。神在天为风,在地为木,在体为筋,在脏为肝,在色为苍⑮,在音为角⑯,在声为呼⑰,在变动为握⑱,在窍为目,在味为酸,在志为怒⑲。怒伤肝,悲胜怒;风伤筋,燥胜风;酸伤筋,辛胜酸。

---

① 厥气:逆行之气。王冰注:"厥,谓气逆上也。"
② 不节:不遵法度;无节制。
③ 生乃不固:有伤害生命的危险。固:稳固,安定。
④ 温病:感受风寒而引起的热病的总称。
⑤ 痎(jiē)疟:疟疾的通称,亦指经年不愈的老疟。痎:隔日发作的疟疾。
⑥ 论理:议论道理。
⑦ 列别:分别,分辨。列:分。
⑧ 端:审。络:联系。端络经脉:审察经脉的相互联系。
⑨ 会通:张介宾云:"两经交至为之会,他经相贯谓之通。"六合:太阴、阳明为一合,少阴、太阳为一合,厥阴、少阳为一合,手足之脉各三合,共为六合。"六合"亦指天地四方,阴阳家以月建与日辰的地支相合为吉日,即子与丑合,寅与亥合,卯与戌合,辰与酉合,巳与申合,午与未合,总称六合。
⑩ 气穴:经气输注之孔穴。
⑪ 谿(xī)谷:指肢体肌肉之间相接之缝隙或凹陷部位,为经络气血输注出入的处所。小的凹陷为之谿,大的缝隙谓之谷。王冰注:"大经所会,谓之大谷也……小络所会,谓之小谿也。"属骨:骨肉相连处。
⑫ 分部逆从:张志聪云:"分部者,皮之分部也。皮部中之浮络,分三阴三阳,有顺有逆,各有条理也。"
⑬ 条理:脉络,层次,秩序。
⑭ 经纪:天文进退迟速的度数,引申为法度,规律。
⑮ 苍:青色(包括蓝色和绿色)。
⑯ 音:音乐。角(jué):我国古代五声音阶中的五个音级之一,与五行、五方相配,角属东方。五音:宫、商、角、徵、羽。
⑰ 呼:中医诊察病情的五声之一。五声即:呼、笑、歌、哭(或为悲)和呻。
⑱ 握:屈指成拳。姚止庵云:"敛掌拳指曰握。肝主筋,筋之为用,人怒则握拳以击是也。"
⑲ 志:意志,感情。

Receding① qi moves upwards; it fills the vessels② and leaves the physical appearance. If joy and anger are unrestrained, if cold and summerheat exceed the norms, life no longer exists on a solid [foundation]. Hence, doubled yin must [become] yang; doubled yang must [become] yin. Hence it is said: If [a person] is harmed in winter by cold, he will [suffer from] warmth disease in spring. If he is harmed in the spring by wind, he will develop outflow of [undigested] food in summer. If he is harmed in summer by summerheat, he will suffer from *jie* and malaria③ in autumn. If he is harmed in autumn by dampness, he will develop cough in winter."

[Huang] Di: "I have heard, the sages of high antiquity in discussing and structuring the physical appearance of man, they arranged and distinguished among the depots and palaces, they traced and connected the conduit④ vessels and they combined [them to set up] the six unions. In each case they followed the respective conduits. The qi holes where [the qi] are effused, all their locations have a name. The ravines⑤, valleys, and the joints, all have a place where they emerge. The divisions and the sections, opposition and compliance, all have their regular structures. The four seasons and yin and yang, all have their normal arrangements. The correspondences⑥ of outer and inner, all have exterior⑦ and

---

① recede/rɪ'siːd/ v. 退,后退
② vessel/'vesl/ n. 血管,脉管
③ malaria/mə'leərɪə/ n. 疟疾:一种传染性疾病,症状为周期性地感到冷、热和发汗,病因是寄生于红血球的一种疟原虫属原生动物,这种动物通过已感染病菌的雌性疟蚊传播。
④ conduit/'kɔndɪt/ n. 导管,水管
⑤ ravine/rə'viːn/ n. 沟壑,既深且狭、坡度很大的山谷
⑥ correspondence/ˌkɔrɪ'spɔndəns/ n. 一致,相符,相应
⑦ exterior/ɪk'stɪərɪə/ n. 外部,外面,表面

interior①. Is this true?"

Qi Bo responded: "The East generates wind; wind generates wood; wood generates sour [flavor]; sour [flavor] generates the liver; the liver generates the sinews②; the sinews generate the heart; The liver rules the eyes. In heaven it is darkness, in man it is the Way, on the earth it is transformation. Transformation generates the five flavors; the Way generates wisdom; darkness generates the spirit. The spirit, in heaven it is wind, on the earth it is wood, in man's body it is sinews. Among the depots it is the liver; among the colors it is greenish③; among the tones it is *jue*; among the voices it is shouting; among the movements [indicating] changes it is grasping; among the orifices it is the eye; among the flavors it is sour; among the states of mind it is anger. [If] anger [causes harm, it] harms the liver; sadness dominates anger. [If] wind [causes harm, it] harms the sinews; dryness dominates wind. [If] sour [flavor causes harm, it] harms the sinews; acrid [flavor] dominates sour [flavor].

---

① interior/ɪnˈtɪərɪə/n. 内部,里面
② sinew/ˈsɪnjuː/n. 腱,肌腱
③ greenish/ˈɡriːnɪʃ/adj. 稍带绿色的,淡绿的,有一点绿的

南方生热,热生火,火生苦,苦生心,心生血,血生脾,心主舌。其在天为热,在地为火,在体为脉,在脏为心,在色为赤,在音为徵,在声为笑,在变动为忧,在窍为舌,在味为苦,在志为喜。喜伤心,恐胜喜;热伤气,寒胜热;苦伤气,咸胜苦。

中央生湿,湿生土,土生甘,甘生脾,脾生肉,肉生肺,脾主口。其在天为湿,在地为土,在体为肉,在脏为脾,在色为黄,在音为宫,在声为歌,在变动为哕①,在窍为口,在味为甘,在志为思。思伤脾,怒胜思;湿伤肉,风胜湿;甘伤肉,酸胜甘。

西方生燥,燥生金,金生辛,辛生肺,肺生皮毛②,皮毛生肾,肺主鼻。其在天为燥,在地为金,在体为皮毛,在脏为肺,在色为白,在音为商,在声为哭,在变动为咳,在窍为鼻,在味为辛,在志为忧。忧伤肺,喜胜忧;热伤皮毛,寒胜热;辛伤皮毛,苦胜辛。

北方生寒,寒生水,水生咸,咸生肾,肾生骨髓,髓生肝,肾主耳。其在天为寒,在地为水,在体为骨,在脏为肾,在色为黑,在音为羽,在声为呻,在变动为栗③,在窍为耳,在味为咸,在志为恐。恐伤肾,思胜恐;寒伤血,燥胜寒;咸伤血,甘胜咸。

---

① 哕(yuě):打呃。
② 皮毛:人的皮肤和毛发。泛指人体的浅表部分。
③ 栗:哆嗦,发抖。

The South generates heat; heat generates fire; fire generates bitter [flavor]; bitter [flavor] generates the heart; the heart generates the blood; the blood generates the spleen①. The heart rules the tongue. In heaven this is heat; on the earth it is fire; in man's body it is the vessels. Among the depots it is the heart; among the colors it is red; among the tones it is *zhi*; among the voices it is laughing; among the movements [indicating] changes it is anxiety; among the orifices it is the tongue; among the flavors it is bitter; among the states of mind it is joy. [If] joy [causes harm, it] harms the heart; fear dominates joy. [If] heat [causes harm, it] harms the qi; cold dominates heat. [If] bitter [flavor causes harm, it] harms the qi; salty [flavor] dominates bitter [flavor].

The center generates dampness; dampness generates soil; the soil generates sweet [flavor]; sweet [flavor] generates the spleen; the spleen generates the flesh; the flesh generates the lung. The spleen rules the mouth. In heaven it is dampness; on earth it is soil; in man's body it is the flesh. Among the depots it is the spleen; among the colors it is yellow; among the tones it is *gong*; among the voices it is singing; among the movements [indicating] changes it is hiccup②; among the orifices it is the mouth; among the flavors it is sweet; among the states of mind it is pensiveness③. [If] pensiveness [causes harm, it] harms the spleen; anger dominates pensiveness. [If] dampness [causes harm, it] harms the flesh; wind dominates dampness. [If] sweet [flavor causes harm, it] harms the flesh; sour [flavor] dominates sweet [flavor].

The West generates dryness; dryness generates metal; metal

---

① spleen/spliːn/ *n*. 脾，脾脏
② hiccup/'hɪkʌp/ *n*. 打嗝
③ pensiveness/'pensɪvnɪs/ *n*. 沉思，冥想

generates acrid [flavor]; acrid [flavor] generates the lung; the lung generates skin and body hair; skin and body hair generate the kidneys. The lung rules the nose. In heaven it is dryness; on the earth it is metal; on man's body it is skin and body hair. Among the depots it is the lung; among the colors it is white; among the tones it is *shang*; among the voices it is weeping; among the movements [indicating] changes it is coughing; among the orifices it is the nose; among the flavors it is acrid; among the states of mind it is anxiety. [If] anxiety [causes harm, it] harms the lung; joy dominates anxiety. [If] heat [causes harm, it] harms the skin and the body hair; cold dominates heat. [If] acrid [flavor causes harm, it] harms the skin and the body hair; bitter [flavor] dominates acrid.

The North generates cold; cold generates water; water generates salty [flavor]; salty [flavor] generates the kidneys; the kidneys generate the bones and the marrow①; the marrow generates the liver. The kidneys rule the ears. In heaven it is cold; on the earth it is water; in man's body it is the bone. Among the depots it is the kidneys; among the colors it is black; among the tones it is *yu*; among the voices it is groaning②; among the movements [indicating] changes it is shivering③; among the orifices it is the ear; among the flavors it is salty; among the states of mind it is fear. [If] fear [causes harm, it] harms the kidneys; pensiveness dominates fear. [If] cold [causes harm, it] harms the blood; dryness dominates cold. [If] salty [flavor causes harm, it] harms the blood; sweet [flavor] dominates salty [flavor].

① marrow/'mærəu/ *n*. 髓,骨髓
② groan/grəun/ *v*. 呻吟,叹息
③ shivering/'ʃɪvərɪŋ/ *n*. 颤抖

故曰：天地者，万物之上下也；阴阳者，血气之男女也^①；左右者，阴阳之道路也；水火者，阴阳之征兆也^②；阴阳者，万物之能始也^③。故曰：阴在内，阳之守也；阳在外，阴之使也。

帝曰：法阴阳奈何？

岐伯曰：阳胜则身热，腠理闭，喘粗为之俯仰^④，汗不出而热，齿干以烦冤^⑤，腹满死，能冬不能夏^⑥。阴胜则身寒，汗出，身常清^⑦，数栗而寒，寒则厥，厥则腹满死，能夏不能冬。此阴阳更胜之变，病之形能也^⑧。

帝曰：调此二者奈何^⑨？

岐伯曰：能知七损八益^⑩，则二者可调；不知用此，则早衰之节也。年四十，而阴气自半也，起居衰矣；年五十，体重，耳目不聪明矣；年六十，阴痿，气大衰，九窍不利，下虚上实，涕泣俱出矣。故曰：知之则强，不知则老，故同出而异名耳。智者察同，愚者察异^⑪，愚者不足，智者有余。有余则耳目聪明，身体轻强，老者复壮，壮者益治^⑫。

---

① 血气之男女：王冰注云："阴主血，阳主气。阴生女，阳生男。"

② 征兆：征候，先兆。

③ 能始：元始，根源。王冰注："谓能为变化之生成之元始。"

④ 俯仰：举动，举止。此处指喘急憋气，身体摆动的形状。

⑤ 烦冤：烦躁愤懑。

⑥ 能(nài)：受得住。

⑦ 清：同"凊"，寒。

⑧ 能：通"态"。

⑨ 调(tiáo)：协调，调和。

⑩ 七损：女子月事贵在时下。因女性以七年为生命节律变化周期。八益：男子精气贵在充满。因男性以八年为生命节律变化周期。

⑪ 同：此处指健康说。异：此处指疾病衰老说。察同：在未病之时，注意摄生。察异：到发病以后才知调养。

⑫ 益治：更为安好。

Hence it is said: As for heaven and earth, they are the above and the below of the myriad beings, as for yin and yang, they are the male-female [couple] of blood and qi. As for left and right, they are the paths of yin and yang. As for water and fire, they are the signs of yin and yang. As for yin and yang, they are the beginning of the myriad beings. Hence it is said: The yin is inside, it is the guardian① of the yang; the yang is outside, it is employed by the yin."

[Huang] Di: "In what way can yin and yang be considered as laws?"

Qi Bo: "When yang dominates, the body is hot and the interstice structures close. Rough panting② makes one bend down and up. No sweat flows and one is hot. The teeth are dry and [patients] experience vexation③ and grievance④. If there is [a feeling of] fullness in the abdomen⑤ [this indicates imminent⑥] death. It can be endured in winter; it cannot be endured in summer. When yin dominates, the body is cold and sweat flows. The body is permanently cool. One shivers⑦ frequently and feels cold. In case of cold, receding [qi] results. When receding [qi] occurs, there is [a feeling of] fullness in the abdomen and [this indicates imminent] death. This can be endured in summer; it cannot be endured in winter. These are the changes in the alternating⑧ domination of yin

---

① guardian/ˈɡɑːdɪən/ n. 保护者,保卫者
② pant/pænt/ v. 喘气,喘息
③ vexation/vekˈseɪʃn/ n. 烦恼,苦恼
④ grievance/ˈɡriːvns/ n. 委屈,苦衷,牢骚,不满,怨恨
⑤ abdomen/ˈæbdəmən/ n. 下腹,腹部
⑥ imminent/ˈɪmɪnənt/ adj. (尤指不愉快的事件)即将发生的,临近的,逼近的
⑦ shiver/ˈʃɪvə/ v. 颤抖(尤指因寒冷或恐惧),哆嗦
⑧ alternating/ˈɔːltɜːnətɪŋ/ adj. 交替的,更迭的

and yang, [and their associated] disease manifestations①. "

[Huang] Di: "How are these two harmonized?"

Qi Bo: "If one knows of the seven injuries and eight benefits, then the two can be harmonized. If one does not know to employ these [principles], then the term of weakening will come early. At the age of forty, the yin qi has decreased to half of its own [former amount]; one's daily activities weaken. At the age of fifty, the body feels heavy; the ears and the eyes are no longer clear. At the age of sixty, the yin [reaches a state of] limpness②; the qi is severely weakened and the nine orifices are no [longer] freely passable. Below is depletion③; above is repletion④. Snivel⑤ and tears both flow. Hence it is said: If one knows these [principles], then one remains strong; if one does not know these [principles], then one turns old. Hence, the origin is identical, but the names are different. Those who know, they investigate the identical; those who are ignorant, they investigate the different. The ignorant have not enough; those who know, they have surplus⑥. If one has surplus, then ears and eyes are clear; the body is light and the limbs are strong. Those who are old become strong again; those who are strong can be treated [with] even better [results].

---

① manifestation/ˌmænɪˈfesteɪʃn/ n. 显示,表现(形式)
② limpness/ˈlɪmpnɪs/ n. 柔弱,疲倦
③ depletion/dɪˈpliːʃn/ n. 损耗,减损,耗尽
④ repletion/rɪˈpliːʃn/ n. 充满,饱食
⑤ snivel/ˈsnɪvl/ n. 鼻涕
⑥ surplus/ˈsɜːpləs/ n. 剩余,盈余,过剩

是以圣人为无为之事，乐恬淡之能，从欲快志于虚无之守，故寿命无穷，与天地终。此圣人之治身也①。

天不足西北，故西北方阴也，而人右耳目不如左明也。地不满东南，故东南方阳也，而人左手足不如右强也。

帝曰：何以然？

岐伯曰：东方阳也，阳者其精并于上②，并于上则上明而下虚，故使耳目聪明而手足不便也。西方阴也，阴者其精并于下，并于下则下盛而上虚，故其耳目不聪明而手足便也。故俱感于邪③，其在上则右甚，在下则左甚，此天地阴阳所不能全也，故邪居之。

故天有精，地有形，天有八纪④，地有五里⑤，故能为万物之父母。清阳上天，浊阴归地。是故天地之动静，神明为之纲纪，故能以生长收藏，终而复始。惟贤人上配天以养头，下象地以养足⑥，中傍人事以养五脏⑦。天气通于肺，地气通于嗌⑧，风气通于肝，雷气通于心，谷气通于脾，雨气通于肾。六经为川⑨，肠胃为海，九窍为水注之气。以天地为之阴阳，阳之汗，以天地之雨名之；阳之气，以天地之疾风名之。暴气象雷⑩，逆气象阳，故治不法天之纪，不用地之理，则灾害至矣。

---

① 治身：修身，养生。
② 并：聚合。
③ 邪：中医学上指一切致病因素为邪，如风寒暑湿之气。
④ 八纪：指立春、立夏、立秋、立冬、春分、秋分、夏至、冬至八个大节气。一说，同"八维"，指四方和四隅的全称。四隅：《尔雅·释宫》云："西南隅谓之奥，西北隅谓之屋漏，东北隅谓之宦，东南隅谓之窔"。
⑤ 五里：指东南西北中五个方向的分布。里，应作"理"。
⑥ 象：效法，仿效。
⑦ 傍：依傍。人事：日常饮食和情志。
⑧ 嗌(yì)：咽喉。
⑨ 六经：即太阳、阳明、少阳、太阴、少阴、厥阴，为气血运行的道路。
⑩ 暴气：忿怒暴躁之气。

Hence, the sages have acted on the basis of 'no intervention'. They have enjoyed their ability to be peaceful and tranquil. They have followed their desires and their mind was pleased, maintaining absolute emptiness. Hence, [the fact that] their lifespan has no limit, and will end only with heaven and earth, this is [a result of the way] how the sages ordered their body.

Heaven is not sufficiently present in the North-West. Hence the North-West is yin, and the ears and the eyes of man on the right are not as clear as on the left. The earth is incomplete in the South-East. Hence the South-East is yang, and the hands and feet of man on the left are not as strong as on the right."

[Huang] Di: "Why is this so?"

Qi Bo: "The East is yang. As for the yang, its essence① collects above. When it collects above, then the above is brilliant and there is depletion below. Hence, this lets the ears and eyes be clear, while the hands and feet do not move comfortably. The West is yin. As for the yin, its essence collects below. When it collects below, then there is abundance② below and there is depletion above. Hence, the ears and eyes are not clear, while the hands and feet move comfortably. Hence, whenever one is affected by evil, if it happens above, then it is serious on the right. If it happens below, then it is serious on the left. These are locations where the yin and yang of heaven and earth cannot be complete. Hence, the evil resides there.

The fact is, heaven has the essence; the earth has the physical appearance. Heaven has the eight arrangements; the earth has the five structures. Hence, [heaven and earth] can be father and mother of the myriad beings. The clear yang rises towards heaven;

---

① essence/'esns/ n. 精髓,精华;本质
② abundance/ə'bʌndəns/ n. 丰富,充足,充裕

the turbid yin returns to the earth. The fact is, the movement and resting of heaven and earth, the spirit brilliance sets up their fundamental principles. Hence, they are able to pass through generation, growth, gathering, and storage and when the end is reached, to start anew. Only the exemplary① men correspond to heaven above to nourish the head, follow the image of the earth below to nourish the feet, side with the affairs of man in the middle to nourish the five depots. The qi of heaven communicates with the lung; the qi of the earth communicates with the throat; the qi of the wind communicates with the liver; the qi of thunder communicates with the heart; the qi of valleys communicates with the spleen; the qi of rain communicates with the kidneys. The six conduits are streams; the intestines② and the stomach are the sea. The nine orifices are where qi flows like water. One takes heaven and earth for yin and yang: the sweat of yang, this is how one names the rain of heaven and earth; the qi of yang, this is how one names the swift③ wind of heaven and earth. Violent qi resembles thunder. Qi moving contrary [to its regular course] resembles yang. Hence, if treatment does not take the arrangements of heaven as law and if it does not employ the structures of the earth, then catastrophe④ and harm will arrive.

---

① exemplary/ɪɡˈzemplərɪ/ adj. 模范的，值得效法的，值得推崇的
② intestine/ɪnˈtestɪn/ n. [通常作复数]肠
③ swift/swɪft/ adj. 迅速的，敏捷的，快的
④ catastrophe/kəˈtæstrəfɪ/ n. 突如其来的大灾难或大灾祸

故邪风之至，疾如风雨，故善治者治皮毛，其次治肌肤，其次治筋脉，其次治六腑，其次治五脏。治五脏者，半死半生也。故天之邪气，感则害人五脏；水谷之寒热，感则害于六腑；地之湿气，感则害皮肉筋脉。

故善用针者，从阴引阳，从阳引阴。以右治左，以左治右。以我知彼，以表知里，以观过与不及之理。见微得过，用之不殆。

善诊者，察色按脉，先别阴阳。审清浊，而知部分①；视喘息，听音声，而知所苦；观权衡规矩②，而知病所主；按尺寸③，观浮沉滑涩，而知病所生。以治无过，以诊则不失矣。

故曰：病之始起也，可刺而已；其盛，可待衰而已。故因其轻而扬之④，因其重而减之⑤，因其衰而彰之⑥。形不足者，温之以气⑦；精不足者，补之以味。其高者，因而越之⑧；其下者，引而竭之⑨；中满者⑩，泻之于内；其有邪者，渍形以为汗⑪；其在皮者，汗而发之；其慓悍者，按而收之⑫；其实者，散而泻之。审其阴阳，以别柔刚。阳病治阴，阴病治阳。定其血气，各守其乡，血实宜决之⑬，气虚宜掣引之⑭。

---

① 部分：部位，所处的位置。王冰注："部分，谓藏府之位可占候处。"
② 权衡规矩：指四时不同脉象，即春弦中规，夏洪中矩，秋毛中衡，冬沉中权。
③ 尺寸：指尺脉和寸脉。中医切脉三部位名，桡骨茎突处为关，关前为寸，关后为尺。
④ 轻：指病邪轻浅，病在表。扬：用轻宣疏散方法驱邪外泄。
⑤ 重：指病邪重深，病在里。减：以攻泻方法祛除病邪。
⑥ 衰：病气衰。彰：同"障"，防。病衰则为之防，防其复作也。
⑦ 温：温补，用温性药物补养正气。
⑧ 越之：使用涌吐方法。张介宾云："越，发扬也，谓升散之，吐涌之。"
⑨ 竭之：使用通便方法。张介宾云："竭，祛除也，谓涤荡之，疏利之。"
⑩ 中满：胸腹胀满。
⑪ 渍形以为汗：即"清以为汗"，用辛凉解肌之法。
⑫ 慓悍：姚止庵说："慓悍者，发越太过，如虚阳外浮，真阴不足之类。按者，抑而下也，抑而下降，使之收敛以归于原也。"
⑬ 决：分泄。
⑭ 气虚宜掣引之：气虚宜升提。"提之上升，如手掣物也。"

The fact is, the arrival of evil wind is fast like wind and rain. Hence, those who are experts in treatment, they treat [a disease as long as it is in] the skin and the body hair. Next are those who treat [a disease when it is in] the muscles and skin. Next are those who treat [a disease when it is in] the sinews and vessels. Next are those who treat [a disease when it is in] the six palaces. Next are those who treat [a disease when it is in] the five depots. When it comes to treating the five depots, the [chances of the patient's] death and survival are half and half. The fact is, if man is affected by the evil qi of heaven, then this harms his five depots. If one is affected by the cold or heat of water and grains, then this harms the six palaces. If one is affected by the dampness qi of the earth, then this harms the skin, the flesh, the sinews, and the vessels.

Hence, those who know well how to use the needles, from the yin they pull the yang and from the yang they pull the yin. With the right they treat the left and with the left they treat the right. From this they know that; from the exterior they know the interior. By observing the structures of excess and inadequacy, they see the minute① and notice the excess. When they apply the [needles], there will be no failure.

Those who know well how to diagnose, they inspect the color and press the vessels. First they distinguish yin and yang. They investigate what is clear and turbid and know the section. They observe [the patient's] panting and breathing, they listen to the tones and voices and they know what one is suffering from. They observe the weight and the beam, the circle and the square and they know which [qi] rule the disease. They press at the foot-long section and at the inch, they observe [whether the movement in the

---

① minute/maɪˈnjuːt/ *adj*. 微小的，琐细的

vessels] is at the surface or in the depth, smooth or rough, and they know the location where the disease has emerged. [The fact that] in their treatment they commit no mistakes, this is because in their diagnosis they do not miss [the point].

Hence it is said: When a disease begins to emerge, one can pierce① and [the disease] ends. When it abounds②, one must wait until it weakens and [the disease, when pierced,] ends. Hence, after it has become light, scatter it. After it has become heavy, eliminate it. After it has become weak, let it shine [again]. When the physical appearance has insufficiencies, warm it with qi. When the essence has insufficiencies, supplement③ it with flavor. When it is on high, trace [it] and disperse it. When it is down below, pull and eliminate it. In case of central fullness, drain④ it inside. When there is an evil, soak the physical appearance to induce⑤ sweating. Those in the skin, cause sweating and effuse them. Those that are fierce, press and collect them. Those that are replete, disperse and drain them. Investigate their yin and yang [association], to distinguish soft and hard [medication]. In case of yang diseases, treat the yin; in case of yin diseases, treat the yang. Stabilize⑥ blood and qi, so that each keeps its native place. When the blood is replete, one must open it; when the qi is depleted, one must pull it.

----

① pierce/pɪəs/ v. (指尖物)刺入,刺穿
② abound/əˈbaʊnd/ v. 非常多,大量存在
③ supplement/ˈsʌplɪmənt/ v. 补充,增补
④ drain/dreɪn/ v. 耗尽,排干,流干
⑤ induce/ɪnˈdjuːs/ v. 引起,引发,激发
⑥ stabilize/ˈsteɪbɪlaɪz/ v. 使稳定,使稳固,使稳定平衡

【推荐阅读】

一、中文版本

郭霭春主编.黄帝内经素问校注.北京：人民卫生出版社,1992 年。

人民卫生出版社.黄帝内经素问.北京：人民卫生出版社,1963 年。

姚春鹏译注.黄帝内经.北京：中华书局,2012 年。

（清）张志聪著.黄帝内经集注.北京：中医古籍出版社,2015 年。

二、英文译本

Bertschinger，Richard. 2015. *Essential Texts in Chinese Medicine*：
The Single Idea in the Mind of the Yellow Emperor. Philadelphia，
PA：Singing Dragon.

Ni，Maoshing. 2011. *The Yellow Emperor's Classic of Medicine*：*A
New Translation of the Neijing Suwen with Commentary*. Boston，
Massachusett：Shambhala.

Unschuld，Paul U. 2003. *HUANG DI NEI JING SU WEN*：*Nature*，
Knowledge，*Imagery in An Ancient Chinese Medical Text*.
Berkeley & Los Angeles，London：University of California Press.

Unschuld，Paul U. & Hermann Tessenow in collaboration with
Zheng Jinsheng. 2011. *Huang Di Nei Jing Su Wen*：*An Annotated
Translation of Huang Di's Inner Classic — Basic Questions*.
Berkeley and Los Angeles，CA. ：University of California Press.

Unschuld，Paul U. 2016. *Huang Di Nei Jing Ling Shu*：*The Ancient
Classic on Needle Therapy*：*The Complete Chinese Text with an
Annotated English Translation*. Oakland，CA：University of
California Press.

Veith，Ilza. 1972. *The Yellow Emperor's Classic of Internal
Medicine*. Berkeley and Los Angeles：University of California
Press.

Yang，Mingshan. 2019. *The Yellow Emperor's Classic of Medicine*：*Essential Questions*. New Jersey：World Scientific.

Zhu，Ming. 2001. *The Medical Classic of the Yellow Emperor*. Beijing：Foreign Languages Press.

李照国英译，刘希茹今译.《黄帝内经·素问》（*Yellow Emperor's Canon of Medicine*：*Plain Conversation*）.西安、北京、广州、上海：世界图书出版公司，2005 年。

周春才，韩亚洲.《黄帝内经》养生图典（汉英）.北京：海豚出版社，1997 年。

第十三单元 　《楚辞》

【导言】

楚辞为战国时期兴起于中国南方楚国（今湖南、湖北一带）的一种诗歌样式，最早见于西汉前期。初由西汉末年刘向汇编成集，定名《楚辞》，收入屈原、宋玉及汉代淮南小山、东方朔、王褒、刘向等人的辞赋计十六篇，后王逸增入己作《九思》，成十七篇，成为后世通行本。《楚辞》"皆书楚语，作楚声，纪楚地，名楚物"（黄伯思《东观余论》）为中国文学史上第一部浪漫主义诗歌总集，位列经、史、子、集四部中集部之首，全书以屈原作品为主，因其代表作《离骚》，其体例被称为"楚辞体"或"骚体"。在中国诗史上《诗》《骚》并称，为中国古典诗歌的两大源头。与因《国风》而称为"风"的《诗经》相对，后人以"风骚"代指诗歌，称诗人为"骚人"。

屈原（约前 339—约前 278 年），名平，字原，战国楚人，曾任楚怀王左徒、三闾大夫。因主张彰明法度，举贤授能，联齐抗秦而受怀王稚子子兰及靳尚谮毁而革职，后被放逐，在流放途中仍然忧国忧民，上下求索，写下了大量诗篇，后感无力挽救楚之危亡，无法实现其政治理想，遂投汨罗江而死。屈原是中国诗史上的一位伟大的爱国主义诗人，是中国浪漫主义文学的奠基人，被誉为"中华诗祖""辞赋之祖"。

刘向所辑《楚辞》和王逸《楚辞章句》原书已佚。通常认为，宋代洪兴祖所撰《楚辞补注》的篇章内容上承《楚辞章句》，较为完整地保留了《楚辞》原貌，现通行版本基本依其为据。宋代以后，《楚辞》校勘、训诂、韵读、文论等著述繁多，影响较大者还有《楚辞集注》（朱熹）、《楚辞通释》（王夫之）、《山带阁注楚辞》（蒋骥）等。近代以来的相关代表性著作有《屈原研究》（郭沫若）、《楚辞校补》（闻一多）、《楚辞新义》（闻一多）、《楚辞概论》（游国恩）、《楚辞论文集》（游国恩）、《楚辞注疏长编》（游国恩）、《屈原赋校注》（姜亮夫）、《屈赋通笺》（刘永济）、《笺屈余义》（刘永济）等。

《楚辞》在海外，特别是在日本、朝鲜、越南等"儒学—中华文化圈"，流传时间较早，但其西传则相对较晚。十六世纪以利玛窦为代表的耶稣会士来华,包括《楚辞》的中国经典开始西传。1879 年《中国评论》(*China Review*)杂志发表庄延龄(Edward H. Parker)英译的《离骚》,此为现今所知最早的英译文。自 1883 年起,翟理斯(Herbert A. Giles)在其《古文选珍》(*Gems of Chinese Literature*)等著作中,选译了《卜居》《渔父》和《九歌》中的《山鬼》《东皇太一》《云中君》《国殇》《礼魂》《卜居》等,其 1901 年出版的《中国文学史》辟专节译介《楚辞》。1916 年,英国汉学家阿瑟·韦利(Arthur Waley),在其《中国诗选》(*Chinese Poems*)翻译了《九歌》与《离骚》,1918 年又增译《国殇》,收入《汉诗 170 首》(*A Hundred and Seventy Chinese Poems*),之后,韦利又英译了《大招》,并于 1955 年出版个人楚辞研究专著《九歌:古代中国的萨满》(*The Nine Songs:A Study of Shamamism in Ancient China*)。1947 年,纽约约翰戴书局出版白瑛(Robert Payne)译编的《白马集》,其中收录《九歌》《九章》和《离骚》等篇目。国内也有许多学者先后翻译过《楚辞》,如林文庆、杨宪益夫妇、孙大雨、许渊冲等。

离骚(节选)^①

帝高阳之苗裔兮^②,朕皇考曰伯庸^③。

摄提贞于孟陬兮^④,惟庚寅吾以降^⑤。

皇览揆余初度兮^⑥,肇锡余以嘉名^⑦。

名余曰正则兮^⑧,字余曰灵均^⑨。

纷吾既有此内美兮^⑩,又重之以修能^⑪。

扈江离与辟芷兮^⑫,纫秋兰以为佩^⑬。

---

① 中文原文参校[宋]洪兴祖撰,白化文等点校.楚辞补注.北京:中华书局,1983 年。离骚:遭遇忧患。《史记》:"离骚者,犹离忧也……屈平之作《离骚》,盖自怨生也。"一说"离别愁思"。汉王逸注:"离,别也;骚,愁也;经,径也。言己放逐离别,中心愁思,犹陈直径,以风谏君也。"

② 帝:始生之祖,在夏商周三代,称已死的君主为帝。高阳:颛顼有天下,号高阳。苗裔:指遥远祖先的子孙后代,植物的茎叶为苗,衣服最下面的襟为裔。

③ 朕:我。(上古时第一人称,至秦始皇 26 年诏定为皇帝自称。)皇考:对亡父的尊称。

④ 摄提:"摄提格"的省称,岁阴名,古代岁星纪年法中的十二辰之一,相当于干支纪年法中的寅年。贞:正(与偏斜相对)。孟陬(zōu):夏历正月的别名,正月为陬,又为孟春月,故称。王逸注:"孟,始也。贞,正也。于,於也。正月为陬。"

⑤ 惟:语助词。庚寅:屈原出生的日子。降(古音 hóng):诞生,降生。

⑥ 皇:对先代的敬称。亦作皇考的省称。览揆(kuí):观察衡量。初度:始生之年时;度:诞生。

⑦ 肇:开始,创始。锡:通"赐",赐予。

⑧ 正则:公正而有法则。正,平也。则,法也。

⑨ 灵均:灵善而均调。王逸注:"灵,神也。均,调也。"

⑩ 纷:盛多貌,众多貌。内美:内在的美好德性。

⑪ 重(chóng):加上,表示更进一层。修能:卓越才能,"能",通"耐";一说美好的仪态、容貌,"能",通"态"。王逸注:"修,远也。言己之生,内含天地之美气,又重有绝远之能,与众异也。"

⑫ 扈(hù):披;带。江离:亦作"江蓠",香草名,又名"蘼芜"。辟芷(zhǐ):幽香的芷草。芷:香草名,即白芷。一说,生长在幽僻处的芷草。

⑬ 纫(rèn):本义为绳索,此处作动词,搓,捻;一作"纽"。秋兰:秋日的兰草。佩,佩戴,装饰,象征自己的德性。

汨余若将不及兮①,恐年岁之不吾与②。
朝搴阰之木兰兮③,夕揽洲之宿莽④。

日月忽其不淹兮⑤,春与秋其代序⑥。
惟草木之零落兮⑦,恐美人之迟暮⑧。
不抚壮而弃秽兮⑨,何不改乎此度⑩?

---

① 汨(yù):疾行,快速。王逸注:"汨,去貌,疾若水流也。"不,一作弗。
② 言我念年命汨然流去,诚欲辅君,心中汲汲,常若不及。又恐年岁忽过,不与我相待,而身老耄也。
③ 搴(qiān):拔取。阰(pí):山名。
④ 揽:采摘。洲:江河中的陆地。宿莽:经冬不死的草。
⑤ 忽:迅速。淹:逗留,挽留。
⑥ 代序:时序更替。王逸注:"代,更也;序,次也。"
⑦ 惟:思虑。零落:凋谢。草曰零,木曰落。王逸注:"零、落,皆堕也。草曰零,木曰落。"
⑧ 美人:指楚怀王。迟暮:比喻晚年。
⑨ 抚:趁着。壮:通"庄",美;一说,年德盛曰壮。秽:污浊;肮脏。
⑩ 此度:现行的政治法度。

Encountering Sorrow (Excerpt)

Translated by David Hawkes[①]

Scion[②] of the High Lord[③] Kao Yang，

Po Yung was my father's name.

When She T'i pointed to the first month of the year，

On the day *keng yin* I passed from the womb.

My father，seeing the aspect[④] of my nativity[⑤]，

Took omens[⑥] to give me an auspicious[⑦] name.

The name he gave me was True Exemplar[⑧]；

The title he gave me was Divine Balance.

Having from birth this inward beauty，

I added to it fair[⑨] outward adornment[⑩]：

I dressed in selinea and shady[⑪] angelica[⑫]，

And twined[⑬] autumn orchids[⑭] to make a garland[⑮].

---

① 译文选自 Hawkes, D. 1959. trans. from Birch, Cyril. ed. 1965. *Anthology of Chinese Literature：From early times to the fourteenth century*. New York：Grove Press，INC.，pp. 51 – 62。

② scion/ˈsaɪən/ *n*. （尤指贵[皇]族的）子孙，后裔

③ lord/lɔːd/ *n*. 贵族，勋爵，君主

④ aspect/ˈæspekt/ *n*. 星位，星象命运

⑤ nativity/nəˈtɪvɪtɪ/ *n*. 出生，诞生；算命天宫图

⑥ omen/ˈəumen/ *n*. 预兆，兆头

⑦ auspicious/ɔːsˈpɪʃəs/ *adj*. 吉利的，吉祥的，有前途的

⑧ exemplar/ɪgˈzemplə/ *n*. 模范，标本，榜样

⑨ fair/feə/ *adj*. 比较好，比较令人满意的

⑩ adornment/əˈdɔːnmənt/ *n*. 装饰

⑪ shady/ˈʃeɪdɪ/ *adj*. 遮阳的，背阴的，成荫的，在背阴处的

⑫ angelica/ænˈdʒelɪkə/ *n*. 白芷（一种有香味的植物，用于烹调及医药）

⑬ twine/twaɪn/ *v*. 捻，搓，编，卷

⑭ orchid/ˈɔːkɪd/ *n*. 兰，兰花

⑮ garland/ˈgɑːlənd/ *n*. 花环，花冠

Swiftly I sped，as in fearful pursuit，

Afraid Time would race on and leave me behind.

In the morning I gathered the angelica on the mountains；

In the evening I plucked① the sedges② of the islets③.

The days and months hurried on，never delaying；

Springs and autumns sped by in endless alternation：

And I thought how the trees and flowers were fading and falling，

And feared that my Fairest's beauty would fade too.

Gather the flower of youth and cast out④ the impure！

Why will you not change the error of your ways？

---

① pluck/plʌk/ v. 采,摘

② sedge/sedʒ/ n. 莎草,苔草

③ islet/ˈaɪlɪt/ n. 小岛

④ cast out 赶出,逐出

乘骐骥以驰骋兮①,来吾道夫先路②。

昔三后之纯粹兮③,固众芳之所在④。
杂申椒与菌桂兮⑤,岂维纫夫蕙茝?⑥
彼尧舜之耿介兮⑦,既遵道而得路⑧。
何桀纣之猖披兮⑨,夫唯捷径以窘步⑩。

惟夫党人之偷乐兮⑪,路幽昧以险隘⑫。
岂余身之惮殃兮⑬,恐皇舆之败绩⑭!
忽奔走以先后兮⑮,及前王之踵武⑯。
荃不察余之中情兮⑰,反信谗而齌怒⑱。

———————

① 骐骥:骏马,喻贤智。
② 来:招。道:通"导",引导。先路:指圣王之道。
③ 三后:三个君主或诸侯。古代天子、诸侯皆称后。此处指禹、汤、文王。纯粹:纯正不杂,精纯完美。至美曰纯,齐同曰粹。引申指德行完美无缺。
④ 众芳:草木的香气,比喻各种贤能的人。王逸注:"众芳,喻群贤。"
⑤ 杂:混合,掺杂。申椒:香木名,即大椒。菌桂:香木名,像竹子一样圆的桂树。
⑥ 维:仅,只。纫:绳索,一作"纽"。蕙、茝(zhǐ),皆香草,比喻贤者。
⑦ 耿介:光大圣明。王逸注:"耿,光也;介,大也。尧舜所以有光大圣明之称者,以循用天地之道,举贤任能,使得万事之正也。"
⑧ 遵:循。路:大道。
⑨ 何:何等,多么。猖披:衣不系带,散乱不整貌。谓狂妄偏邪。王逸注:"猖披,衣不带之貌。"
⑩ 捷径:原意指歧出的小路,喻不循正轨,贪便图快的做法。王逸注:"捷,疾也;径,邪道也。"窘步:急步。王逸注:"窘,急也……欲涉邪径,急疾为治。"
⑪ 党人:朋党,同伙。偷乐:贪图享乐,一作"苟且偷安"。
⑫ 幽昧:昏暗不明。险隘:比喻艰难险阻。王逸注:"险隘,谕倾危也。"
⑬ 惮:提难,畏惧。殃:祸患;灾难。
⑭ 皇舆:国君所乘的高大车子,多借指王朝或国君。王逸注:"皇,君也。舆,君之所乘,以喻国也。"败绩:指事业的败坏、失利。王逸注:"绩,功也。"
⑮ 忽:迅速,急匆匆的样子。王逸注:"忽,疾也。"奔走:急行。先后:前后。
⑯ 前王:已故帝王,先王。踵(zhǒng)武:跟着别人的脚步走。比喻继承前人的事业。王逸注:"踵,继也。武,迹也。"
⑰ 荃(quán):香草名,即菖蒲,多喻君主。察:一作"揆"。中情:内心真诚;中,一作"忠"。
⑱ 齌(jì)怒:疾怒,暴怒。王逸注:"齌,疾也。言怀王不徐徐察我忠信之言,反信谗言而疾怒己也。"

余固知謇謇之为患兮①,忍而不能舍也②。

指九天以为正兮③,夫唯灵修之故也④。

初既与余成言兮⑤,后悔遁而有他⑥。

余既不难夫离别兮⑦,伤灵修之数化⑧。

---

① 謇謇(jiǎn):忠贞,正直。王逸注:"謇謇,忠贞貌也。"
② 舍:停留;止息。王逸注:"舍,止也。言已知忠言謇謇谏君之过,必为身患,然中心不能自止而不言也。"
③ 指:意思上所指。王逸注:"指,语也。"九天:谓天之中央与八方。正:通"证",凭证。
④ 灵修:泛指君主,亦指贤德明哲的人。此处指楚怀王。王逸注:"灵,神也。修,远也。能神明远见者,君德也,故以谕君。"
⑤ 初:起始;开端。成言:订约,成议。
⑥ 悔遁:翻悔而改变主意。
⑦ 难(nàn):畏惧;担心。离别:比较长久地跟人或地方分开。王逸注:"近曰离,远曰别。"
⑧ 数(shuò)化:总是改变,反复无常。数:屡次。化:变化,改变。

I have harnessed① brave coursers② for you to gallop③ forth with：

Come，let me go before and show you the way！

'The three kings of old were most pure and perfect：

Then indeed fragrant flowers had their proper place.

They brought together pepper and cinnamon④；

All the most-prized blossoms were woven in their garlands.

Glorious and great were those two，Yao and Shun，

Because they had kept their feet on the right path.

And how great was the folly⑤ of Chieh and Chou，

Who hastened by crooked⑥ paths，and so came to grief.

'The fools enjoy their careless pleasure，

But their way is dark and leads to danger.

I have no fear for the peril⑦ of my own person，

But only lest the chariot of my lord should be dashed⑧.

I hurried about your chariot in attendance⑨，

Leading you in the tracks of the kings of old.'

But the Fragrant One refused to examine my true feelings：

He lent ear，instead，to slander⑩，and raged against⑪ me.

---

① harness/'hɑːnɪs/ v. 给……上挽具，驾驭

② courser/'kɔːsə/ n. 骏马，战马

③ gallop/'gæləp/ v. 疾驰，飞奔

④ cinnamon/'sɪnəmən/ n. 肉桂，牡桂

⑤ folly/'fɔlɪ/ n. 愚行，荒唐事，危险的蠢行

⑥ crooked/'krukɪd/ adj. 弯曲的，不老实的，不正当的

⑦ peril/'perɪl/ n. 严重危险

⑧ dash/dæʃ/ v. 猛撞，撞击，碰撞

⑨ in attendance 护理，卫护，服侍

⑩ slander/'slɑːndə/ n. 诽谤，诋毁，中伤

⑪ rage against sb. 对(某人)大发脾气，动怒

How well I know that loyalty brings disaster；

Yet I will endure：I cannot give it up.

I called on the ninefold heaven to be my witness，

And all for the sake of the Fair One，and no other.

There once was a time when he spoke with me in frankness；

But then he repented① and was of another mind.

I do not care，on my own count，about this divorcement②，

But it grieves me to find the Fair One so inconstant③.

---

① repent/ˈriːpənt/ v. 后悔，懊悔

② divorcement/dɪˈvɔːsmənt/ n. 分离

③ inconstant/ɪnˈkɒnstənt/ adj. 易变的，反复无常的

余既滋兰之九畹兮①，又树蕙之百亩②。

畦留夷与揭车兮③，杂杜衡与芳芷④。

冀枝叶之峻茂兮⑤，愿竢时乎吾将刈⑥。

虽萎绝其亦何伤兮⑦，哀众芳之芜秽⑧。

众皆竞进以贪婪兮⑨，凭不厌乎求索⑩。

羌内恕己以量人兮⑪，各兴心而嫉妒⑫。

忽驰骛以追逐兮⑬，非余心之所急。

老冉冉其将至兮⑭，恐修名之不立⑮。

---

① 滋：栽种；培植。王逸注："滋，蒔也。"畹(wǎn)：古代地积单位。或以三十亩为一畹，或以十二亩为一畹，或以三十步为一畹，说法不一；王逸注："十二亩为畹。"
② 树：种植；栽种。蕙(huì)：香草名。所指有二：一指薰草，俗称佩兰。古人佩之或作香焚以避疫。二指蕙兰。叶似草兰而稍瘦长，暮春开花，一茎可发八九朵，气逊于兰，色也略淡。亩：我国地积单位，市亩的通称。周制，六尺为步(或曰六尺四寸、八尺)，百步为亩；秦时以五尺为步，二百四十步为亩；汉因秦制；唐以广一步，长二百四十步为亩；清以五方尺为步，二百四十步为亩；今一亩等于六十平方丈，合 6.6667 公亩。
③ 畦(qí)：分畦种植(五十亩为畦)。留夷：香草名。一说，即芍药。王逸注："留夷，香草也。"揭车：香草名。
④ 杜衡：亦作"杜蘅"，即杜若。文学作品中常用以比喻君子、贤人。芳芷：香草名。王逸注："杜蘅、芳芷，皆香草也。"
⑤ 冀：希望，盼望。峻：高大。茂：草木繁盛。
⑥ 竢(sì)：一作"俟"，等待。刈(yì)：割取。王逸注："刈，获也。草曰刈，谷曰获。"
⑦ 萎绝：枯谢。
⑧ 众芳：此处指各种芳草。芜秽：亦作"芜薉""芜濊"，荒芜，谓田地不整治而杂草丛生。
⑨ 竞：竞相，争相，争着。贪婪：贪得无厌，不知足。王逸注："爱财曰贪，爱食曰婪。"
⑩ 凭：满足。王逸注："凭，满也。楚人名满曰凭。"不厌：不满足。厌，通"餍"。求索：寻找，搜寻。
⑪ 羌：句首助词。恕(shù)：体谅，按照自己的情况来推测别人的情况。量：思量，考虑。
⑫ 兴心：打定主意，存心。嫉妒：忌妒。王逸注："害贤为嫉，害色为妒。"
⑬ 忽：迅速。王逸注："忽，疾貌。"驰骛：疾驰，奔腾。王逸注："言极疾也。"追逐：追求，逐取。
⑭ 老：年岁大。与"幼"或"少"相对。王逸注："七十曰老。"冉冉：渐进貌，形容时光渐渐流逝。
⑮ 修名：美好的名声。立：确定，决定。王逸注："立，成也。"

朝饮木兰之坠露兮,夕餐秋菊之落英①。

苟余情其信姱以练要兮②,长顑颔亦何伤③?

揽木根以结茝兮④,贯薜荔之落蕊⑤。

矫菌桂以纫蕙兮⑥,索胡绳之纚纚⑦。

---

① 落英:落花,一说为初生之花。

② 苟:假如,如果,只要。余情:谓充沛的情趣。姱:美丽,美好。练要:谓精诚专一,操守坚贞。

③ 顑颔:因饥饿而面黄肌瘦的样子。

④ 揽:一作"擥",持,执持,拉住。木根:树根。

⑤ 贯:累,连续。薜荔:香草,缘木而生。蕊:花蕊,花朵。

⑥ 矫:使曲的变直。菌桂:香木名。

⑦ 索:搓,作成绳索。胡绳:香草名。纚纚(sǎ):长而下垂貌。

I had tended many an acre of orchids,

And planted a hundred rods① of melilotus②;

I had raised sweet lichens③ and the cart-halting flower,

And asarums④ mingled with fragrant angelica,

And hoped that when leaf and stem were in fullest bloom,

When the time had come, I could reap a fine harvest.

Though famine should pinch⑤ me, it is small matter;

But I grieve that all my blossoms should waste in rank weeds⑥.

All others press forward in greed and gluttony⑦,

No surfeit⑧ satiating⑨ their demands:

Forgiving themselves, but harshly judging others;

Each fretting⑩ his heart away in envy and malice⑪.

Madly they rush in the covetous⑫ chase,

But not after that which my heart sets store by⑬.

For old age comes creeping and soon will be upon me,

And I fear I shall not leave behind an enduring name.

In the mornings I drank the dew that fell from the magnolia⑭;

---

① rod/rɔd/n. 平方杆(等于30.25平方码或272.25平方英尺,25.30平方米)

② melilotus/melɪˈləutəs/n. 草木樨属

③ lichen/ˈlaɪkən/n. 苔藓,地衣

④ asarum/ˈæsərəm/n. 细辛属植物

⑤ pinch/pɪntʃ/v. 使紧缺,节制

⑥ rank weeds 丛生的杂草

⑦ gluttony/ˈɡlʌtnɪ/n. 贪吃或贪饮

⑧ surfeit/ˈsɜːfɪt/n. 过量,过度(尤指饮食)

⑨ satiate/ˈseɪʃɪeɪt/v. 使(某人)充分满足(而不再需要某物)

⑩ fret/fret/v. 使苦恼,使发愁,使烦躁

⑪ malice/ˈmælɪs/n. 敌意,恶意,怨恨

⑫ covetous/ˈkʌvətəs/adj. 妄想的,强烈渴望获得或占有的

⑬ set store by 重视,珍视

⑭ magnolia/mæɡˈnəulɪə/n. 木兰

At evening ate the petals that dropped from chrysanthemums[①].

If only my mind can be truly beautiful，

It matters nothing that I often faint for famine.

I pulled up roots to bind the valerian[②]

And thread the fallen clusters of the castor[③] plant；

I trimmed sprays[④] of cassia[⑤] for plaiting[⑥] melilotus，

And knotted the lithe[⑦]，light trails[⑧] of ivy.

---

① chrysanthemum/krɪˈsænθəməm/n. 菊花
② valerian/vælˈlɪərɪən/n. 缬草（花呈粉红色或白色，气味浓郁）
③ castor/ˈkɑːstə/n. 蓖麻
④ spray/spreɪ/n.（树或花草的）小枝（带叶和花的）
⑤ cassia/ˈkæsɪə/n. 肉桂，肉桂属植物
⑥ plait/plæt/v. 将（发、草等）编成辫
⑦ lithe/laɪð/adj. 柔软的，易弯（曲）的
⑧ trail/treɪl/n. 长而松松挂着的某物，沿着……拉或跟在后面的某物

謇吾法夫前修兮①，非世俗之所服②。
虽不周于今之人兮③，愿依彭咸之遗则④。
长太息以掩涕兮⑤，哀民生之多艰⑥。
余虽好修姱以鞿羁兮⑦，謇朝谇而夕替⑧。

既替余以蕙纕兮⑨，又申之以揽茝⑩。
亦余心之所善兮，虽九死其犹未悔。
怨灵修之浩荡兮⑪，终不察夫民心。
众女嫉余之蛾眉兮⑫，谣诼谓余以善淫⑬。

固时俗之工巧兮⑭，偭规矩而改错⑮。
背绳墨以追曲兮，竞周容以为度⑯。

---

① 謇(jiǎn)：助词，多用于句首；一说"艰难"。法：仿效，效法。前修：前代贤人。
② 世俗：俗人，普通人。服：用，佩带。
③ 周：合，适合。
④ 彭咸：殷贤大夫，谏其君不听，自投水而死。遗则：前代留传下来的法则、榜样。王逸注："遗，余也。则，法也。"
⑤ 太息：亦作"大息"，大声长叹，深深地叹息。掩涕：掩面流泪。
⑥ 民生：人生。艰：困苦，艰难。
⑦ 虽：通"唯"，唯有，只有。修姱(kuā)：洁美。洪兴祖补注："姱，好也。"鞿(jī)羁(jī)：马缰绳和络头，比喻束缚。王逸注："鞿羁，以马自喻。缰在口曰鞿，革络头曰羁，言为人所系累也。"
⑧ 谇(suì)：谏净，谏劝。王逸注："谇，谏也。"替：废弃。
⑨ 蕙纕：香草作的佩带，系之以示芳洁忠正。
⑩ 申：重复；一再。茝(chǎi)：香草名，即白芷。
⑪ 浩荡：无常不定。一说，荒唐。
⑫ 众女：比喻群小、谗人。蛾眉：蚕蛾触须细长而弯曲，因以比喻女子美丽的眉毛，在此指诗人自己的美好品质。
⑬ 谣诼(zhuó)：造谣毁谤。淫：邪恶，奸邪。
⑭ 时俗：世俗，流俗。工巧：善于取巧。王逸注："以言佞臣巧于言语，背违先圣之法。"
⑮ 偭(miǎn)：违背。规矩：规和矩，校正圆形和方形的两种工具，引申为法度、规则。改错：改变措施。改：变更，更改。错：通"措"。
⑯ 竞：争着，争相。周容：迎合讨好。度：法度，规范；一说为态度。

忳郁邑余侘傺兮^①，吾独穷困乎此时也^②。
宁溘死以流亡兮^③，余不忍为此态也^④。

鸷鸟之不群兮^⑤，自前世而固然。

---

① 忳（tún）：忧郁；烦闷。郁邑：郁悒，忧愁，苦闷。王逸注："郁邑，忧也。邑，一作悒。"侘傺（chà chì）：失意而神情恍惚的样子。

② 穷困：困难之极，处境窘迫。

③ 溘（kè）死：忽然而死。流亡：随流水消逝。

④ 不忍：不能忍受，不愿意。

⑤ 鸷（zhì）鸟：凶猛的鸟，如鹰鹖之类。不群：离群索居，喻不与小人为伍。

I take my fashion from the good men of old:

A garb① unlike that which the rude world cares for;

Though it may not accord with present-day manners,

I will follow the pattern that Peng Xian has left.

Heaving② a long sigh, I brush away my tears,

Grieving for man's life, so beset③ with hardships.

Though goodness and beauty were my bit④ and bridle,

I was slandered⑤ in the morning and cast off⑥ that same evening.

Yet, though cast off, I would wear my orchid girdle;

I would pluck⑦ some angelicas to add to its beauty;

For this it is that my heart takes most delight in,

And though I died nine times, I should not regret it.

What I do resent is the Fair One's waywardness⑧:

Because he will never look to see what is in men's hearts.

All your ladies were jealous of my delicate beauty;

In their spiteful⑨ chattering they said I was a wanton⑩.

Truly this generation are cunning⑪ artificers⑫,

---

① garb/gɑːb/ n. 服装,服装式样(尤指某类人穿的)

② heave/hiːv/ v. 发出(叹息,呻吟等)

③ beset/bɪ'set/ v. 被……包围,为……困扰

④ bit/bɪt/ n. 马勒,嚼子(放在嘴里的金属制马勒,用于控制约束和驾驭牲畜)

⑤ slander/'slɑːndə/ v. 诽谤,造谣中伤,诋毁

⑥ cast off 丢弃,遗弃,抛弃

⑦ pluck/plʌk/ v. 采,摘,拔

⑧ waywardness/'weɪwədnɪs/ n. 难以捉摸或反复无常,不稳定

⑨ spiteful/'spaɪtful/ adj. 怀恨的,心眼坏的,怀有恶意的

⑩ wanton/'wɔntən/ n. 放荡的人,不道德的人(尤指女子)

⑪ cunning/'kʌnɪŋ/ adj. 狡猾的,狡诈的,诡诈的

⑫ artificer/ɑː'tɪfɪsə/ n. 技师,工匠

From square and compass turn their eyes and change the true measurement，

Disregard the ruled line to follow their crooked fancies①；

To emulate② in flattery is their only rule.

But I am sick and sad at heart and stand irresolute③：

I alone am at a loss in this generation.

Yet I would rather quickly die and meet dissolution④

Before I ever would consent to ape⑤ their behaviour.

Eagles do not flock like birds of lesser species；

So it has ever been since the olden⑥ time.

---

① fancy/ˈfænsɪ/n. 奇想，反复无常的怪想，怪念头
② emulate/ˈemjuleɪt/v. 效法，同……竞争，尽力赶上
③ irresolute/ɪˈrezəluːt/adj. 优柔寡断的，犹豫不决的
④ dissolution/ˌdɪsəˈluːʃn/n. 消亡，死亡
⑤ ape/eɪp/v. 盲目模仿
⑥ olden/ˈəuldən/adj. 古时的，往昔的

何方圆之能周兮^①，夫孰异道而相安^②。
屈心而抑志兮^③，忍尤而攘诟^④。
伏清白以死直兮^⑤，固前圣之所厚^⑥。

悔相道之不察兮^⑦，延伫乎吾将反^⑧。
回朕车以复路兮^⑨，及行迷之未远^⑩。
步余马于兰皋兮^⑪，驰椒丘且焉止息^⑫。
进不入以离尤兮^⑬，退将复修吾初服^⑭。

制芰荷以为衣兮^⑮，集芙蓉以为裳^⑯。
不吾知其亦已兮^⑰，苟余情其信芳^⑱。
高余冠之岌岌兮^⑲，长余佩之陆离^⑳。

---

① 周：合，合适。
② 相安：相处平安，没有矛盾。王逸注："言何所有圜凿受方枘而能合者？谁有异道而相安耶？言忠佞不相为谋也。"
③ 屈心：屈抑心愿。抑志：抑制自己的志向。
④ 尤：过失，罪愆。攘诟：容忍耻辱；一说为除去耻辱。
⑤ 伏：抱持，怀。清白：谓品行纯洁，没有污点。死直：为正道而死。
⑥ 固：坚持。厚：注重。
⑦ 悔：后悔，悔恨。相（xiàng）道：观察、选择道路。不察：不察知，不了解。
⑧ 延伫：久立，久留。反：返回。
⑨ 复路：回到过去的路。
⑩ 及：乘，趁。行迷：赶往迷途。
⑪ 步：漫步，徐行。兰皋（gāo）：长兰草的河岸。
⑫ 椒丘：尖削的高丘；一说，生有椒木的丘陵。王逸注："土高四堕曰椒丘。"止息：休息，住宿。
⑬ 进：进仕，指在政治上有所作为。不入：不得入。离尤：遭罪，遇祸。
⑭ 初服：未入仕时的服装，与"朝服"相对。
⑮ 制：裁剪。芰（jì）荷：指菱叶与荷叶。衣：上衣。
⑯ 芙蓉：荷花的别名。洪兴祖补注："《本草》云：其叶名荷，其华未发为菡萏，已发为芙蓉。"裳（cháng）：古代称下身穿的衣裙，男女皆服。毛传："上曰衣，下曰裳。"
⑰ 不吾知：不理解我。亦已：算了。
⑱ 苟：假如，如果，只要。芳：芳香，亦泛指香气，与下文"泽"相对。
⑲ 岌岌（jí）：高耸的样子。
⑳ 佩：古代系于衣带的装饰品，常指珠玉、容刀、帨巾、觿之类，此处指佩剑。陆离：长剑低昂貌，长的样子。

芳与泽其杂糅兮^①，唯昭质其犹未亏^②。

忽反顾以游目兮^③，将往观乎四荒^④。
佩缤纷其繁饰兮^⑤，芳菲菲其弥章^⑥。
民生各有所乐兮，余独好修以为常^⑦。
虽体解吾犹未变兮^⑧，岂余心之可惩^⑨！

---

① 泽：光亮，润泽。王逸注："泽，质之润也。一说，泽，应作"殬"，腐朽发臭之物。"杂糅：混杂糅合。

② 唯：独，仅，只有；一说，其为语首助词，亦写作"惟""维"。昭质：明洁的品质。亏：歇，消失。

③ 反顾：回顾，回头看。游目：纵目，放眼观看。

④ 四荒：四方荒远之地。

⑤ 佩：指前文所言包括各种香草在内的佩饰。缤纷：繁盛的样子。繁饰：众多的彩饰，盛饰。

⑥ 菲菲：香气盛。王逸注："菲菲，犹勃勃，芬香貌也。"弥：益，更加。章：显著。

⑦ 好修：喜爱修饰仪容。借指重视道德修养。

⑧ 体解：分解人的肢体，古代酷刑之一。王逸注："虽遭支解，亦不能变。"

⑨ 惩：戒惧；一说，鉴戒；另一说，克制，制止。

How can the round and square ever fit together?

How can different ways of life ever be reconciled①?

Yet humbling one's spirit and curbing② one's pride,

Bearing blame humbly and enduring insults,

But keeping pure and spotless and dying in righteousness:

Such conduct was greatly prized by the wise men of old.

Repenting, therefore, that I had not conned③ the way more closely,

I halted, intending to turn back again —

To turn about my chariot and retrace my road

Before I had advanced too far along the path of folly④.

I walked my horses through the marsh's⑤ orchid-covered margin;

I galloped to the hill of pepper-trees and rested there.

I could not go in to him for fear of meeting trouble,

And so, retired, I would once more fashion my former raiment⑥.

I made a coat of lotus and water-chestnut⑦ leaves,

And gathered lotus petals to make myself a skirt.

I will no longer care that no one understands me,

As long as I can keep the sweet fragrance of my mind.

Higher towered the lofty⑧ hat on my head,

The longest of girdles dangled from my waist.

---

① reconcile/'rekənsaɪl/v 使符合,使一致

② curb/kɜːb/v. 抑制,勒住,束缚

③ con/kɔn/v. 精读,研究、探究或仔细检查

④ folly/'fɔlɪ/n. 愚蠢,愚行,荒唐事

⑤ marsh/mɑːʃ/n. 沼泽,湿地

⑥ raiment/'reɪmənt/n. 衣服,服饰,衣裳

⑦ water-chestnut 欧菱,野菱,刺菱(原产欧亚大陆和非洲的漂浮水生植物,长带四个尖儿的坚果状果实,可作为池塘或水缸的装饰物)

⑧ lofty/'lɔftɪ/adj. 高耸的,极高的

Fragrance and richness mingled in sweet confusion,
The brightness of their lustre① has remained undimmed.

Suddenly I turned back and let my eyes wander.
I resolved to go and visit all the world's quarters②.
My garland's crowded blossoms, mixed in fair confusion,
Wafted③ the sweetness of their fragrance far and wide.
All men have something in their lives that gives them pleasure:
With me the love of beauty is my constant joy.
I could not change this, even if my body were dismembered④;
For how could dismemberment ever hurt my mind?

---

① lustre/ˈlʌstə/ n. 轻柔的光泽,光彩,光亮
② quarter/ˈkwɔrtə/ n. 方位,象限,地区
③ waft/wɔft/ v. 使飘荡
④ dismember/dɪsˈmembə/ v. 肢解,拆开,分成几部分

女嬃之婵媛兮①，申申其詈予②。

曰："鲧婞直以亡身兮③，终然殀乎羽之野④。

汝何博謇而好修兮⑤，纷独有此姱节⑥。

薋菉葹以盈室兮⑦，判独离而不服⑧。

众不可户说兮⑨，孰云察余之中情⑩？

世并举而好朋兮⑪，夫何茕独而不予听⑫？"

依前圣以节中兮⑬，喟凭心而历兹⑭。

济沅湘以南征兮⑮，就重华而陈词：⑯

"启《九辩》与《九歌》兮⑰，夏康娱以自纵⑱。

───────────

① 女嬃(xū)：古代楚人称姐姐为嬃。王逸注："女嬃，屈原姊也。"婵媛：牵引，情思牵萦，因内心关切所显示出的牵连不已的样子。

② 申申：反复不休。詈(lì)：骂，责备。

③ 婞(xìng)直：倔强，刚直，固执不听劝告。亡身：杀身，丧身；一说，应作"忘身"，不顾生命。

④ 终然：终于。殀(yǎo)：短命而死。羽：羽山，地名。

⑤ 博謇：知无不言，正直之极。

⑥ 姱节：美好的节操。

⑦ 薋(cí)：草多貌，引申为把草积聚起来。菉(lù)：草名，即荩草，一名"王刍"。葹(shī)：植物名，亦名枲(xǐ)耳。

⑧ 判：分别。离：分别，指与众不同。不服：不佩带。

⑨ 户说：挨家挨户地说服。

⑩ 中情：内心的真诚；一说，隐藏在心中的思想或情感。

⑪ 并举：相互荐举。好朋：好结成朋党。王逸注："相与朋党，并相荐举。"

⑫ 茕(qióng)独：孤独，不合群。不予听：不听从我。

⑬ 前圣：古代圣贤。节中：折中，取正。

⑭ 喟(kuì)：叹息。凭心：胸怀愤懑。历兹：经受了这般遭遇。

⑮ 济：渡河。沅(yuán)湘：沅水和湘水的并称。沅，指湖南省西部沅江。古代也叫沅水。上游称清水江，源出贵州省云雾山，自湖南省黔城镇以下始名沅江。东北流经黔阳、常德到汉寿入洞庭湖；湘，即湘江，源出广西，注入湖南省，为湖南省最大的河流。南征：南行。

⑯ 重(chóng)华：虞舜的美称；一说，舜目重瞳，故名，后亦用以代称帝王。

⑰ 启：夏启，大禹之子，夏朝君主；一说，开启。《九辩》：夏乐名。《九歌》：古代乐曲，相传为禹时乐歌。王逸注："《九辩》《九歌》，禹乐也。言禹平治水土，以有天下……故九州岛之物，皆可辩数。"

⑱ 夏康：夏代君王太康的省称。太康为启之子，以游乐放纵而失国。王逸注："夏康，启子太康也。"一说"康娱"连文。康娱自纵，以致丧乱。夏：大。康娱：逸乐，安乐。自纵：放纵自己。

不顾难以图后兮^①，五子用失乎家巷^②。

羿淫游以佚畋兮^③，又好射夫封狐^④。

固乱流其鲜终兮^⑤，浞又贪夫厥家^⑥。

---

① 顾难：有两种解释，一是回顾最初取得天下之不易，二是不顾及后来的灾难。

② 五子：夏太康昆弟五人；一说，太康的五个儿子。用：因而，因此。家巷：亦作"家衖（xiàng）"，家乡，闾里。巷，里中道。

③ 羿（yì）：传说中夏有穷氏之国君，因夏民以代夏政，善射，不修民事，为家臣寒浞所杀。淫游：荒淫游乐。佚畋（tián）：亦作"佚田"，田猎无节制。佚：放逸，恣纵。畋：打猎。

④ 封狐：大狐。

⑤ 乱流：放纵恣行。鲜（xiǎn）终：少有善终。

⑥ 浞（zhuó）：传说夏时有穷氏后羿之相。羿不理政事，浞遂杀羿自立。厥：代词，其。家（gū）：古时对女子的尊称，此处指羿的妻室。

Then came my maidens with sobbing and sighing,

And over and over expostulated① with me:

'Kun in his stubbornness took no thought for his life,

And perished, as result, upon the moor② of Yü.

Why be so lofty③, with your passion for purity?

Why must you alone have such delicate adornment④?

Thorns, king-grass, curly-ear hold the place of power:

But you must needs⑤ stand apart⑥ and not speak them fair.

'You cannot go from door to door convincing everybody;

No one can say, "See, look into my mind!"

Others band together and like to have companions:

Why should you be so aloof⑦ and not take our advice?'

I look to the sages of old for inward guidance:

So, sighing, with a bursting heart, I endure these trials.

I crossed the Yüan and Hsiang and journeyed southward

Till I came to where Ch'ung Hua was and made my plaint⑧
to him

'In the Nine Variations and Nine Songs of Ch'i

The house of Hsia made revelry⑨ and knew no restraint,

Taking no thought for the troubles of the morrow⑩:

---

① expostulate/ɪkˈspɒstʃuleɪt/ v. (向某人)提抗议,(与某人)讲道理或争论,(尤指)规劝,劝诫
② moor/mɔː/ n. 漠泽,高沼,荒野,旷野(尤指石南丛生者)
③ lofty/ˈlɒftɪ/ adj. (指思想、目标等)高尚的,崇高的;傲慢的,自以为是的
④ adornment/əˈdɔːnmənt/ n. 装饰,装饰品
⑤ must needs 偏偏,偏要
⑥ stand apart 离开,远离,脱离
⑦ aloof/əˈluːf/ adj. 冷淡,疏远,淡漠
⑧ plaint/pleɪnt/ n. 抱怨,哀诉,诉苦
⑨ revelry/ˈrevlrɪ/ n. 狂欢,作乐
⑩ morrow/ˈmɒrəu/ n. 翌日,次日,第二天

And so it was that Wu Kuan made rebellion in his house.

Yi loved idle roaming and hunting to distraction，

And took delight in shooting at the mighty foxes.

But foolish dissipation① has seldom a good end：

And Han Cho covetously② took his master's wife.

---

① dissipation/ˌdɪsɪˈpeɪʃn/ *n*. 浪费，挥霍，放荡，消遣，娱乐
② covetously/ˈkʌvɪtəslɪ/*adv*. 妄想地，贪心地，贪婪地

浇身被服强圉兮①,纵欲而不忍②。

日康娱而自忘兮③,厥首用夫颠陨④。

夏桀之常违兮⑤,乃遂焉而逢殃⑥。

后辛之菹醢兮⑦,殷宗用而不长⑧。

汤禹俨而祗敬兮⑨,周论道而莫差⑩。

举贤而授能兮⑪,循绳墨而不颇⑫。

皇天无私阿兮⑬,览民德焉错辅⑭。

夫维圣哲以茂行兮⑮,苟得用此下土⑯。

瞻前而顾后兮,相观民之计极⑰。

夫孰非义而可用兮⑱,孰非善而可服⑲。

---

① 浇(ào):即过浇,传说为夏代寒浞之子。被(pī)服:负恃,信奉。强圉(yǔ):强壮多力。

② 不忍:不收敛。

③ 自忘:忘怀自身安危。

④ 用:因此,因而。颠陨:坠落,跌落。

⑤ 夏桀:夏朝末代君王,名履癸,暴虐荒淫。汤起兵伐桀,败之于鸣条,流死于南巢。常违:
屡背正道。

⑥ 逢殃:遭遇祸患。

⑦ 后辛:殷纣王;辛,纣王之名。菹(zū)醢(hǎi):亦作"葅醢",肉酱,此处指古代把人剁成肉
酱的酷刑,后亦用以泛指处死。

⑧ 殷宗:殷人的宗祀,指殷朝。

⑨ 汤禹:商汤与夏禹。俨:恭敬庄重,庄严。祗(zhī)敬:恭敬。

⑩ 论道:谋虑治国的政令。

⑪ 授能:任用有才能的人。

⑫ 循:顺着,遵从。绳墨:木工画直线用的工具,比喻规矩,法度。颇:偏颇,不平正。

⑬ 皇天:对天及天神的尊称。私阿(ē):偏爱,曲意庇护。

⑭ 民德:指有德之人。错辅:安排辅助,错,通"措"。

⑮ 维:同"唯",独。圣哲:指超人的道德才智,亦指具有这种道德才智的人,并亦以称帝王。
茂行:盛德之行,德行充盛。

⑯ 苟得:才得到;苟:于是。用:享有,拥有。下土:四方,天下。

⑰ 计极:最根本的规律。王逸注:"计,谋也;极,穷也。"

⑱ 非义:不义,不合乎道义。用:任用。

⑲ 服:行,行事。

　　阽余身而危死兮①,览余初其犹未悔②。
　　不量凿而正枘兮③,固前修以菹醢④。"

---

① 阽(diàn):危险,临近危险。危死:濒临死亡。
② 初:初心,本心。其:指代诗人自己。
③ 量:量度。凿(záo):榫眼。枘(ruì):榫头。
④ 前修:前贤。

'Cho's son, Chiao, put on his strong armour①

And wreaked② his wild will without any restraint.

The days passed in pleasure; far he forgot himself,

Till his head came tumbling③ down from his shoulders.

Chieh of Hsia all his days was a king most unnatural④,

And so he came finally to meet with calamity⑤.

Chou cut up and salted the body of his minister;

And so the days were numbered of the House of Yin.

'Tang of Shang and Yü of Hsia were reverent⑥ and respectful;

The House of Zhou chose the true way without error,

Raising up the virtuous and able men to government,

Following the straight line without fear or favour.

High God in Heaven knows no partiality⑦;

He looks for the virtuous and makes them his ministers.

For only the wise and good can ever flourish

If it is given them to possess the earth.

'I have looked back into the past and forward to later ages,

Examining the outcomes of men's different designs.

Where is the unrighteous man who could be trusted?

Where is the wicked man whose service could be used?

Though I stand at the pit's mouth and death yawns⑧ before me,

---

① armour/'ɑːmə/ n. (旧时)甲胄,盔甲,铁甲
② wreak/riːk/ v. 发泄
③ tumble/'tʌmbl/ v. 倒下,坠落
④ unnatural/ʌn'næʧrəl/ adj. 反常的,极残酷的,极邪恶的
⑤ calamity/kəl'æmətɪ/ n. 灾祸,灾难
⑥ reverent/'revərənt/ adj. 虔敬的,恭敬的
⑦ partiality/ˌpɑːʃɪ'ælətɪ/ n. 偏袒,偏见
⑧ yawn/jɔːn/ v. 打哈欠,张开,裂开

I still feel no regret at the course I have chosen.

Straightening the handle，regardless of the socket's① shape：

For that crime the good men of old were hacked② in pieces.'

---

① socket/'sɔkɪt/ *n*. （天然的或人造的）承物凹座，窝（用以容纳某物或某物可在其中转动），
插口

② hack/hæk/ *v*. 劈，砍

曾歔欷余郁邑兮①,哀朕时之不当②。
揽茹蕙以掩涕兮③,沾余襟之浪浪④。
跪敷衽以陈辞兮⑤,耿吾既得此中正⑥。
驷玉虬以乘鹥兮⑦,溘埃风余上征⑧。

朝发轫于苍梧兮⑨,夕余至乎县圃⑩。
欲少留此灵琐兮⑪,日忽忽其将暮⑫。
吾令羲和弭节兮⑬,望崦嵫而勿迫⑭。
路曼曼其修远兮⑮,吾将上下而求索⑯。

① 曾：屡次,不断地。歔欷：悲泣,叹息。郁邑：苦闷,忧愁。
② 时：时机,机遇。不当：不适当,不合宜。
③ 茹：柔弱,柔软。王逸注："茹,柔耎也。"蕙：香草名,所指有二：一指熏草,俗称佩兰,古人佩之或作焚以避疫;二指蕙兰,叶似草兰而稍瘦长,暮春开花,一茎可发八九朵,气逊于兰,色也略淡。
④ 襟：衣的前幅。浪浪：泪流不止的样子。
⑤ 敷衽(rèn)：解开襟衽,表示坦诚。
⑥ 耿：光明正大。王逸注："耿,明也。"中正：正道。
⑦ 驷：驾驭;乘。虬(qiú)：通"虬",传说中的一种无角龙。王逸注："有角曰龙,无角曰虬。"鹥(yì)：传说中的鸟名,凤凰之属。王逸注："鹥,凤皇别名也。"
⑧ 溘：依凭,附着;一说,忽然。埃风：卷着尘埃的大风。上征：上升,上天。
⑨ 发轫：拿掉支住车轮的木头,使车前进,借指出发,起程。轫：挡住车轮转动的横木。苍梧：向舜陈词的地方,据说舜死后葬在九嶷山,而九嶷山即在苍梧界内。
⑩ 县圃：传说中神仙居处,在昆仑山顶,亦泛指仙境。
⑪ 少留：稍微多停留一会儿。灵琐：国君宫门,神灵府宅。王逸注："灵以喻君。琐,门镂也,文如连琐,楚王之省合也。一云,灵,神之所在也。"
⑫ 忽忽：倏忽,急速,形容时间过得很快。
⑬ 羲(xī)和：古代神话传说中驾驭日车的神。王逸注："羲和,日御也。"弭(mǐ)节：放慢行驶速度;节,车行的节度。
⑭ 崦(yān)嵫(zī)：山名,在甘肃天水县西境,传说为日落的地方。迫：接近。
⑮ 曼曼：形容距离远或时间长。修远：道路长远,辽远。
⑯ 求索：寻找,搜寻。

Many a heavy sigh I heaved in my despair，

Grieving that I was born in such an unlucky time.

I plucked① soft lotus petals to wipe my welling② tears

That fell down in rivers and wet my coat front.

I knelt on my outspread skirts and poured my plaint out，

And the righteousness within me was clearly manifest③.

I yoked④ a team of jade dragons to a phoenix-figured car

And waited for the wind to come，to soar⑤ up on my journey.

In the morning I started on my way from Ts'ang-wu；

By evening I had arrived at the Hanging Garden.

I wanted to stay a while in those fairy precincts⑥，

But the swift-moving sun was dipping to the west.

I ordered His-ho to stay the sun-steeds'⑦ gallop，

To stand over Yen-tzu mountain and not go in；

Long，long had been my road and far，far was the journey：

I would go up and down to seek my heart's desire.

---

① pluck/plʌk/ v. 采，摘，拔

② well/wel/ v. 涌出，升到表面准备流出，从内部升起来或涌出

③ manifest/'mænɪfest/ adj. 显示，表明，证明

④ yoke/jəuk/ v. 给……套上轭

⑤ soar/sɔː/ v. 急速升入高空，翱翔

⑥ precinct/'priːsɪŋkt/ n. 围地（由明显界限，如墙划出的地方或围占地），范围

⑦ steed/stiːd/ n. 骏马，战马

【推荐阅读】

一、中文版本及注疏

陈子展. 楚辞直解. 江苏：江苏古籍出版社, 1988 年。

黄寿祺, 梅桐生合著. 楚辞全译. 贵阳：贵州人民出版社, 1984 年。

洪兴祖. 楚辞补注. 北京：中华书局, 1983 年。

姜亮夫. 楚辞今绎讲录. 北京：北京出版社, 1981 年。

金开诚等. 屈原集校注. 北京：中华书局, 1996 年。

李山. 楚辞选译. 北京：中华书局, 2005 年。

马茂元. 楚辞选. 北京：人民文学出版社, 1958 年。

梅桐生. 楚辞入门. 贵阳：贵州人民出版社, 1991 年。

汤炳正等. 楚辞今注. 上海：上海古籍出版社, 1996 年。

张正明. 楚文化史. 上海：上海人民出版社, 1988 年。

朱熹撰, 蒋立甫校点. 楚辞集注. 上海：上海古籍出版社, 2001 年。

二、英文译本

Birch，Cyril. 1965. *Anthology of Chinese Literature：From early times to the fourteenth century*. New York：Grove Press，INC.

Burton，W. 1984. *The Columbia Book of Chinese Poetry：From the Early Times to the 13th Century*. New York：Columbia University Press.

Hawkes，David. 1985. *The Songs of the South：An Ancient Chinese Anthology of Poems by Qu Yuan and Other Poets*. Harmondsworth：Penguin Books Ltd.

Hawkes，D. tr. 1959. *Ch'u Tz'u：The Songs of the South*. Oxford：Oxford University Press.

Lin，W. Q. tr. 1935. *The Li Sao，an Elegy on Encountering Sorrows*. Shanghai：The Commercial Press.

Payne，R. tr. 1947. *The White Pony，an Anthology of Chinese*

Poetry from the Earliest Times to the Present Day. Sydney：G. Allen & Unwin.

Sun，D. Y. 1996. *Selected Poems of Chu Yuan*. Shanghai：Shanghai Foreign Language Education Press.

Waley，A. 1955. *The Nine Songs：A Study of Shamanism in Ancient China*. Sydney：G. Allen & Unwin.

Yang，G. & Yang，X. Y. 1953. *Li Sao and Other Poems of Ch'u Yuan*. Beijing：Foreign Language Press.

许渊冲译.《楚辞：汉英对照》.北京：中国对外翻译出版公司,2008 年。

卓振英英译,陈器之、李奕今译.《楚辞》.长沙：湖南人民出版社, 2006 年。

第十四单元 《乐府诗集》

【导言】

"乐府"原为官署之名,初设于秦,汉武帝时重建,负责制作乐谱,收集歌词和训练音乐人才。后世将乐府官署所搜集整理的诗歌称为"乐府诗",简称"乐府",所收多为优秀的民歌和后世文人仿此形式所作的诗,是继《诗经》《楚辞》而起的一种新诗体。

北宋郭茂倩所编《乐府诗集》为中国历代各种乐府诗最为完备的一部重要总籍,现存 100 卷,5000 余首,分为郊庙歌辞、燕射歌辞、鼓吹曲辞、横吹曲辞、相和歌辞、清商曲辞、舞曲歌辞、琴曲歌辞、杂曲歌辞、近代曲辞、杂歌谣辞和新乐府辞等 12 大类。《乐府诗集》中所收《孔雀东南飞》是我国古代最长的叙事诗,与《木兰诗》合称"乐府双璧";《孔雀东南飞》《木兰诗》和唐代韦庄《秦妇吟》并称"乐府三绝"。《木兰诗》中女英雄木兰从军的故事在中国早已家喻户晓。

《乐府诗集》的编者郭茂倩(1041—1099 年),字德粲,宋代郓州须城(今山东东平)人,其祖父郭劝为莱州通判,父郭源明为太常博士。郭茂倩曾于宋神宗元丰七年(1084 年)任河南府法曹参军,所编《乐府诗集》解题考据精博,为其后各代学者所重视。《乐府诗集》版本以宋代浙江刻本为最早,元代有至正元年集庆路儒学刊本,明代有明末毛晋汲古阁刊本,系据元本雕造,后毛晋之子毛扆又据宋本对其进行挖改,故"汲古阁本早印本传世少而后印本则文字佳",清代仅对汲古阁本进行过翻刻,后收入《四部丛刊》。1955 年,文学古籍刊行社出版了傅增湘藏宋本影印《乐府诗集》本,2010 年,人民文学出版社重新影印出版。1979 年,中华书局以文学古籍刊行社本为底本,参考汲古阁本及其他本子出了点校本。

乐府诗英译始于十九世纪末,大多散见于中国诗歌选译本之中。主要译者及收录乐府诗的主要英文译本有:翟理斯(Herbert A. Giles)的《古今诗选》(*Chinese Poetry in English Verse*,1898),阿瑟·韦利(Arthur Waley)的《中国诗一百七十首》(*A Hundred and Seventy Chinese Poems*,1918)、《中国诗选译续集》(*More Translations from*

the Chinese，1919）、《中国诗集》（*Chinese Poems*，1946）等，柏芝
（Cyril Birch）的《中国文学选集》（*Anthology of Chinese Literature*，
1965），弗洛德山姆（J. D. Frodsham）的《汉魏晋南北朝诗选》（*An
Anthology of Chinese Verse：Han Wei Chin and the Northern and
Southern Dynasties*，1967），柳无忌和欧文·罗郁正（Wu-Chi Liu，
Irving Yucheng Lo）合编的《葵晔集》（*Sunfolwer Splendor：Three
Thousand Years of Chinese Poetry*，1975），唐安石（John A. Turner）
编译的《中诗金库》（*A Golden Treasury of Chinese Poetry*，1976），华
兹生（Burton Watson）编译的《哥伦比亚中国诗集》（*The Columbia
Book of Chinese Poetry*，1984），比雷尔（Anne Birrel）翻译的《玉台新
咏》（*Chinese Love Poetry-New Songs from a Jade Terrace*，1995），宇
文所安（Stephen Owen）编译的《中国早期古诗解读》（*The Making of
Early Chinese Classical Poetry*，2006）等。

木兰诗①

唧唧复唧唧，木兰当户织②。

不闻机杼声，唯闻女叹息③。

问女何所思，问女何所忆④。

女亦无所思，女亦无所忆。

昨夜见军帖，可汗大点兵⑤，

军书十二卷，卷卷有爷名⑥。

阿爷无大儿，木兰无长兄⑦。

愿为市鞍马，从此替爷征⑧。

东市买骏马，西市买鞍鞯⑨，

南市买辔头，北市买长鞭⑩。

---

① 原文选自［宋］郭茂倩编.《乐府诗集》，北京：中华书局，1979 年版，1998 年重印。

② 唧（jī）唧：织布机的声音。当户：对着门户。

③ 机杼（zhù）：指织机。杼，织梭。

④ 忆：思念，惦记。

⑤ 军帖（tiě）：征兵的文书。可汗（kè hán）：亦作"可罕"，古代鲜卑、突厥、回纥、蒙古等族最高统治者的称号。

⑥ 军书：军事文书。十二：形容数量多或程度深。爷：古义指父亲。

⑦ 阿爷：亦作"阿耶"，父亲。长兄：兄弟中排行最大者。

⑧ 为：为此，指代父从军。市：动词，意为"买"。从此：从此时或此地起；从这一道理或事实基础出发。

⑨ 鞍鞯（ān jiān）：鞍子和托鞍的垫子。

⑩ 辔（pèi）头：马笼头。

The Ballad of Mulan

Translated by Arthur Waley①

Click，click②，forever click，click；

Mulan sits at the door and weaves③.

Listen，and you will not hear the shuttle④'s sound，

But only hear a girl's sobs and sighs.

"Oh，tell me，lady，are you thinking of your love，

Oh，tell me，lady，are you longing for your dear?"

"Oh no，oh no，I am not thinking of my love，

Oh no，oh no，I am not longing for my dear."

But last night I read the battle-roll⑤；

The Khan⑥ has ordered a great levy⑦ of men.

The battle-roll was written in twelve books，

And in each book stood my father's name.

My father's sons are not grown men，

And of all my brothers，none is older than me.

Oh let me to the market to buy saddle and horse，

And ride with the soldiers to take my father's place.

In the eastern market she's bought a gallant⑧ horse，

---

① 译文选自 Waley, A. 1946. Trans. *Chinese Poems*. London：George Allen and Unwin Ltd. pp.113 - 115。ballad/'bæləd/ n . 歌谣，诗歌，谣曲，(尤指)叙事歌谣

② click/klɪk/ v . 发卡嗒声

③ weave/wiːv/ v . (用手工或机器)编，织

④ shuttle/'ʃʌtl/ n . (织机的)梭，梭子

⑤ roll/rəul/ n . 花名册

⑥ Khan/kɑːn/ n . 可汗(古代土耳其、鞑靼、蒙古、突厥各族最高统治者的尊称)

⑦ levy/'levɪ/ n . 征兵

⑧ gallant/'gælənt/ adj . 健壮的

In the western market she's bought saddle and cloth.

In the southern market she's bought snaffle[①] and reins,

In the northern market she's bought a tall whip.

---

① snaffle/'snæfl/ *n*. 马衔铁

旦辞爷娘去，暮宿黄河边①。

不闻爷娘唤女声，但闻黄河流水鸣溅溅②。

旦辞黄河去，暮至黑山头③。

不闻爷娘唤女声，但闻燕山胡骑鸣啾啾④。

万里赴戎机，关山度若飞⑤。

朔气传金柝，寒光照铁衣⑥。

将军百战死，壮士十年归⑦。

归来见天子，天子坐明堂⑧。

策勋十二转，赏赐百千强⑨。

---

① 爷娘：亦作"爷孃"，父母。
② 但：古义为"只"。溅（jiān）溅：流水声，水疾流貌。
③ 黑山：今北京市昌平县境内的天寿山。
④ 燕山：在河北平原北侧，东西走向。胡：古代对北方少数民族的称呼。胡骑（jì）：胡人的骑兵，亦泛指胡人军队。啾啾（jiū）：鸟兽虫的鸣叫声。
⑤ 戎（róng）机：军事行动，战争。关山：关隘山岭。度，越过。
⑥ 朔（shuò）气：北方的寒气。朔，北方。金柝（tuò）：行军用的刁斗，铜制有柄的三脚锅，白天用来做饭，晚上用来报更。一说金为刁斗，柝为木柝。李善注："金，谓刁斗也。卫宏《汉旧仪》曰：昼漏尽，夜漏起，城门击刁斗，周庐击木柝。"寒光：指清冷的月光。铁衣：古代战士穿的带有铁片的铠甲。
⑦ 将军：官名。春秋时通称军将为将军。战国时始为武将名。汉代皇帝左右的大臣称大将军、车骑将军、前将军、后将军、左将军、右将军等；临时出征的统帅有别加称号者，如楼船将军、材官将军等。魏晋南北朝时，将军有各种不同的职权和地位，如中军将军、龙骧将军等，多为临时设置而有实权，如骁骑将军、游击将军等，则仅为称号。唐十六卫、羽林、龙武、神武、神策等军，均于大将军下设将军之官。宋、元、明多以将军为武散官。明代的总兵官有挂印带将军号的。此外，宋、元、明亦称殿廷武士为将军。清代的将军有三种：一为宗室爵号之一，如镇国将军、辅国将军等。二为驻防各地的八旗最高长官，专由满族人充任。内地各省将军（如江宁、广州、成都等将军），掌驻防军事及旗籍民事；在边疆地区（如黑龙江、吉林、伊犁），将军即为全区的最高军事和行政长官。三为临时出征的统帅，如扬威将军、靖逆将军等。太平天国朝内官职，丞相最高，以次为检点、指挥、将军。
⑧ 天子：古以君权为神所授，故称君王为天子，此处即前文所言"可汗"。明堂：古代帝王宣明政教的地方。凡朝会、祭祀、庆赏、选士、养老、教学等大典，都在此举行。
⑨ 策勋：记功勋于书之上。十二：古义为虚指，非数字 12，形容功劳极高。转：勋级每升一级叫一转，十二转为最高的勋级。百千：形容数量多。强，有余。

可汗问所欲,木兰不用尚书郎①;
愿驰千里足,送儿还故乡②。

---

① 尚书郎:官名。东汉之制,取孝廉中之有才能者入尚书台,在皇帝左右处理政务,初入台称守尚书郎中,满一年称尚书郎,三年称侍郎。魏晋以后尚书各曹有侍郎、郎中等官,综理职务,通称为尚书郎。
② 千里足:千里马。儿:古代年轻女子的自称,亦指对年少男子的称呼。

In the morning she stole from her father's and mother's house;

At night she was camping by the Yellow River's side.

She could not hear her father and mother calling to her by her name,

But only the voice of the Yellow River as its waters hissed[1] and swirled[2] through the night.

At dawn they left the River and went on their way;

At dusk they came to the Black Water's side.

She could not hear her father and mother calling to her by her name,

She could only hear the muffled[3] voices of foreign horsemen riding on the hills of Yen.

A thousand leagues[4] she tramped[5] on the errands[6] of war,

Frontiers[7] and hills she crossed like a bird in flight.

Through the northern air echoed the watchman's[8] tap;

The wintry light gleamed on coats of mail[9].

The captain had fought a hundred fights, and died;

The warriors in ten years had won their rest.

They went home; they saw the Emperor's face;

The Son of Heaven was seated in the Hall of Light.

---

① hiss/hɪs/ v. 发出"嘶"声

② swirl/swɜːl/ v. 打旋，旋转

③ muffled/ˈmʌfld/ adj. 隐约的，听不太清的

④ league/liːg/ n. 里格(旧时长度单位，约 3 英里或 4.8 公里)

⑤ tramp/træmp/ v. 步行经过(某一地区)(尤指长途且疲惫不堪)

⑥ errand/ˈerənd/ n. 差使

⑦ frontier/ˈfrʌntɪə/ n. 边疆，边陲，边境，国境

⑧ watchman/ˈwɒtʃmən/ n. 巡夜者，看守人

⑨ coat of mail 甲胄(一种装甲外衣，由铠甲、链相互联接的环或重叠的金属片制成)

Then spoke the Khan and asked her what she would take.

"Oh, Mulan asks not to be made

    A Counsellor at the Khan's court;

I only beg for a camel that can march

    A thousand leagues a day,

To take me back to my home."

爷娘闻女来,出郭相扶将①。

阿姊闻妹来,当户理红妆②;

小弟闻姊来,磨刀霍霍向猪羊③。

开我东阁门,坐我西阁床④,

脱我战时袍,着我旧时裳,

当窗理云鬓,对镜帖花黄⑤。

出门看火伴,火伴皆惊惶⑥。

同行十二年,不知木兰是女郎⑦。

雄兔脚扑朔,雌兔眼迷离⑧;

双兔傍地走,安能辨我是雄雌⑨?

---

① 郭:外城,古代在城的外围加筑的一道城墙。相:表示一方对另一方有所施为。扶将:扶持,搀扶。
② 阿姊:姐姐。理:梳理。红妆:指女子的盛妆。因妇女妆饰多用红色,故称。
③ 霍(huò)霍:象声词,此处指快速磨刀的声音。
④ 东阁:东厢的居室或楼房。
⑤ 云鬓(bìn):形容妇女浓黑而柔美的鬓发。帖:通"贴"。花黄:古代妇女的面饰,用金黄色纸剪成星月花鸟等形贴在额上,或在额上涂点黄色。
⑥ 火伴:古时兵制,十人为一火,火伴即同火的人,伙伴。
⑦ 十二:古义为虚指,非数字 12。女郎:年轻女子。
⑧ 扑朔,指雄兔脚毛蓬松。迷离,指雌兔眼睛眯缝。但在兔奔跑时即难辨其雌雄。一说,扑朔为四脚爬搔或跳跃貌。后以"扑朔迷离"形容事物错综复杂,不易看清真相。
⑨ 傍(bàng)地走:贴着地面跑。走:古义为跑。

When her father and mother heard that she had come，

They went out to the wall and led her back to the house.

When her elder sister heard that she had come，

She went to the door and rouged[①] her face afresh[②].

When her little brother heard that his sister had come，

He sharpened his knife and darted[③] like a flash

Towards the pigs and sheep.

She opened the gate that leads to the eastern tower，

She sat on her bed that stood in the western tower.

She cast aside her heavy soldier's cloak[④]，

And wore again her old-time dress.

She stood at the window and bound her cloudy hair；

She went to the mirror and fastened her yellow combs[⑤].

She left the house and met her messmates[⑥] on the road；

Her messmates were startled[⑦] out of their wits[⑧].

They had marched with her for twelve years of war

And never known that Mulan was a girl.

For the male hare sits with its legs tucked[⑨] in，

And the female hare is known for her bleary[⑩] eye；

But set them both scampering[⑪] side by side，

And who so wise could tell you "This is he"?

---

① rouge/ruːʒ/ v. 用胭脂搽

② afresh/əˈfreʃ/ adv. 重新装扮

③ dart/dɑːt/ v. 猛冲，狂奔

④ cloak/kləuk/ n. 披风，斗篷

⑤ comb/kəum/ n. 发插(用以使头发固定或作头饰)

⑥ messmate/ˈmesmeit/ n. (军队等的)共餐伙伴，同食者

⑦ startle/ˈstɑːtl/ v. 使(人或动物)惊吓或吓一跳

⑧ out of one's wits 不知所措

⑨ tuck/tʌk/ v. 缩进，收缩，收起并折起

⑩ bleary/ˈblɪərɪ/ adj. (指视力)模糊的(尤因疲倦所致)，蒙蒙眬眬的

⑪ scamper/ˈskæmpə/ v. 奔跑，蹦蹦跳跳

【推荐阅读】

一、中文版本及注疏

韩宁.鼓吹横吹曲辞研究.北京：北京大学出版社,2009 年。

梁海燕.舞曲歌辞研究.北京：北京大学出版社,2009 年。

雷家骥.史诗三首笺证.台北：兰台出版社,2009 年。

刘万章.木兰歌注.长沙：商务印书馆,1940 年。

尚丽新.《乐府诗集》版本研究.北京：中国社会科学出版社,2012 年。

王传飞.相和歌辞研究.北京：北京大学出版社,2009 年。

王福利.郊庙燕射歌辞研究.北京：北京大学出版社,2009 年。

张馨露.木兰诗详解.台北：致知学术出版社,2015 年。

张煜.新乐府辞研究.北京：北京大学出版社,2009 年。

二、英文译本

Birch，Cyril. 1965. *Anthology of Chinese Literature*. New York：Grove Press.

Frodsham，J. D. and Hsi Ch'eng. 1967. *An Anthology of Chinese Verse：Han Wei Chin and the Northern and Southern Dynasties*. Oxford：Oxford University Press.

Giles，Herbert A. 1898. *Chinese Poetry in English Verse*. London：B. Quaritch.

Liu，Wu-Chi，& Irving Yucheng Lo. 1975. *Sunfolwer Splendor：Three Thousand Years of Chinese Poetry*. Norwell，MA：Anchor Press.

Owen，Stephen. 2006. *The Making of Early Chinese Classical Poetry*. Cambridge，Mass：Harvard University Press.

Turner，John A. 1976. *A Golden Treasury of Chinese Poetry*. Toronto：Public Library.

Waley，Arthur. 2016. *A Hundred and Seventy Chinese Poems*.

South Yarra: Leopold Classic Library.

Waley, Arthur. 2012. *More Translations from the Chinese*, Lexington: HardPress Publishing.

Watson, Burton. 1984. *The Columbia Book of Chinese Poetry*. New York, NY: Columbia University Press.

第十五单元　《李太白集》

【导言】

李白(公元701—762年)字太白,一生经历了唐开元盛世和安史之乱。5岁时,随父李客回绵州昌隆县(今四川江油),15岁起致力于文学创作,26岁离川,到各地漫游,途中创作了大量诗歌,开始名扬海内。42岁时,经道士吴筠举荐进京,奉唐玄宗之召供奉翰林。在长安三年间,遭太监高力士等人的毁谤,赐金放还。离开长安后,又开始全国各地游历之旅。安史之乱爆发后,56岁的李白隐居庐山。唐肃宗时,奉江陵大都督永王璘之邀加入其幕府,后因此受连累流放夜郎(今贵州东部),途中获赦。62岁客死安徽当涂县令李阳冰处。

李白为盛唐浪漫诗派的代表,一生创作了大量诗文,有"诗仙"之美誉。唐代李阳冰编成《草堂集》十卷,为最早的李白诗文集,现已散佚。传世的诗文集注有南宋杨齐贤注《李翰林集》,元代萧士赟删补杨注而成的《分类补注李太白集》,明代胡震亨的《李诗通》等。清代王琦注《李太白文集》是李白诗文合注,为历代最完备者。

最早将唐诗系统翻译成英文者为英国汉学家翟理斯(Herbert A. Giles)。其《古今诗选》(1898)收录英译唐诗101首,《中国文学史》(1901)中有其英译的《长恨歌》等唐诗;1922年,翟理斯的《古文选珍》在上海出版修订扩展版;1935年,翟理斯与韦利合译的《中国诗歌选》由上海商务印书馆出版。在欧美享有"中国古诗专家"之美誉的英国汉学家克莱默·宾(L. Cranmer-Byng)的汉诗选译本《玉琵琶》自1909年初版以来,再版、重印多达30余次;英国汉学家弗莱彻(William B. Fletcher)的《英译唐诗选》(1919)译有唐诗181首,《英译唐诗选续集》(1925)译有唐诗105首;英国汉学家、文学翻译家阿瑟·韦利(Arthur Waley)所翻译的中国文学作品大多为唐诗,主要包括《中国古诗选译》(1916)、《中国古诗170首》(1918),以及《中国古诗选译续集》(1919)。1913年,美国诗人庞德(Ezra Pound)在为美国东方学家范诺罗萨(Emest Francisco Fenolosa)整理遗稿时发现其唐诗和《诗经》英译稿,庞德择出其中17首诗加以润色,于1915年在威尼斯以《华夏集》为题出版,其中有李白的《长干行》等唐诗 14 首;美国诗人威特·宾纳(Witter Bynner)与江亢虎合作,以《玉山》为题将《唐诗三百首》译成英文于 1929 年出版,此为《唐诗三百首》的首个英译本。日本留美学者小畑熏良(Shigeyoshi Obata)的《李白诗集》(1922)是首部李白诗歌英译专集。

　　二战后唐诗英译的代表人物为葛瑞汉(A. C. Graham)和唐安石(John Turner)。葛瑞汉的《晚唐诗选》(1965),曾被列入"联合国教科文组织代表作品集中国系列丛书";唐安石的《中诗金库》(1976)亦为该时期唐诗英译之代表作;阿瑟·库柏(Arthur Cooper)的《李白与杜甫》(1979)中有多首李白与杜甫的诗作译文;宇文所安(Stephen Owen)的《初唐诗》(1977)、《盛唐诗》(1981),及《晚唐诗:827—860》(2006)均为影响巨大的唐诗译作。

将进酒①

君不见黄河之水天上来，
奔流到海不复回。
君不见高堂明镜悲白发②，
朝如青丝暮成雪③。
人生得意须尽欢，
莫使金樽空对月。
天生我材必有用，
千金散尽还复来。
烹羊宰牛且为乐，
会须一饮三百杯④。
岑夫子，丹丘生⑤，
将进酒，杯莫停。
与君歌一曲，
请君为我倾耳听。
钟鼓馔玉不足贵⑥，
但愿长醉不复醒。

---

① 选自(清)王琦注《李太白全集》(中华书局，1977年版)。将(qiāng)：请。将进酒：汉乐府旧题。该诗大约作于唐玄宗天宝十一年(公元752年)，距诗人被唐玄宗"赐金放还"已达八年。此间李白与岑征曾多次应邀赴嵩山元丹丘家做客。
② 高堂：父母。
③ 青丝：指黑发。雪：指白发。
④ 会须：正应当，适逢需要。
⑤ 岑(cén)夫子：指岑征。丹丘生：元丹丘。二人均为李白好友。
⑥ 钟鼓：钟和鼓，指富贵人家宴会时用的乐器。馔(zhuàn)玉：珍美如玉的食品。钟鼓馔玉：泛指豪门贵族的奢华生活。

The Feast of Life

Translated by W.J.B. Fletcher①

Seest thou② not the Yellow River coming from the Sky,

Downward to the Ocean flowing, never turning back?

How thy③ hair to grey is growing, sadly in yon④ mirror spy —

Snow at eve⑤ that but this morning showed so glossy⑥ black!

Would you taste this life so fleeting⑦, quickly snatch at⑧ every boon⑨,

Leaving not the golden goblet⑩ glinting⑪ empty to the moon.

Heaven has given me these talents; yea⑫, and gave them not in vain.

Lo⑬! A thousand golden ducats⑭ lavished⑮ greet the world again!

These roasted sheep and oxen slain⑯ for someone make a feast.

Our meeting here shall swallow down three hundred cups at least.

Now, friends, the wine is ready: I prithee⑰ no delay.

---

① 英文译文选自 Fletcher，W.J.B. trans. *Gems of Chinese Verse Translated into English Verse*，Shanghai：The Commercial Press，1919。

② thou/ðaʊ/ *pron.* [古用法,用作第二人称单数动词的主体,＝you]汝,你

③ thy/ðaɪ/ *pron.* [古用法,thou 的物主代词]你的

④ yon/jɒn/ *pron.* [古、方]在那边的东西或人

⑤ eve/iːv/ *n.* [古]傍晚

⑥ glossy/ɡlɒsɪ/ *adj.* 平滑的,有光泽的

⑦ fleeting/ˈfliːtɪŋ/ *adj.* 飞逝的,短暂的

⑧ snatch at/snætʃ/ *v.* 抓住

⑨ boon/buːn/ *n.* [旧用法]请求,恩惠

⑩ goblet/ˈɡɒblɪt/ *n.* (玻璃、金属等的)高脚(酒)杯

⑪ glint/ɡlɪnt/ *v.* 闪闪发光

⑫ yea/jeɪ/ *adv.* [古用法]＝yes

⑬ lo/ləʊ/ *interj.* [古用法＝look]看！瞧！

⑭ ducat/ˈdʌkət/ *n.* 曾在欧洲通用的金币

⑮ lavish/ˈlævɪʃ/ *v.* 慷慨地给予,挥霍

⑯ slain/sleɪn/ *v.* [slay 的过去式]杀,宰杀

⑰ prithee/ˈprɪðɪ/ *interj.* [古用法]请,求求你

Incline① your ears to listen while I sing to you a lay②.

"Of music and dainties③ small reck④ do I make.

My bliss⑤ to be drunken，ne'er sober⑥ to wake.

---

① incline/ɪnˈklaɪn/ *v*. 使倾斜，屈（身），低（头）
② lay/leɪ/ *n*. ［古用法］供吟唱的诗，民歌，民谣
③ dainty/ˈdeɪntɪ/ *n*. ［通常用作复数］量少而味美的食物
④ reck/rek/ *n*. 介意，注意，留心
⑤ bliss/blɪs/ *n*. 洪福，极乐
⑥ sober/ˈsəʊbə/ *adj*. 清醒的，没有醉的

古来圣贤皆寂寞①,

惟有饮者留其名。

陈王昔时宴平乐②,

斗酒十千恣欢谑③。

主人何为言少钱,

径须沽取对君酌④。

五花马,千金裘⑤,

呼儿将出换美酒,

与尔同销万古愁⑥。

---

① 寂寞:寂静无声,沉寂。

② 陈王:指陈思王曹植。曹植于太和六年(232年)封为陈王,其所作《名都篇》有云:"归来宴平乐,美酒斗十千。"平乐:观名,在洛阳西门外,为汉代富豪显贵的娱乐场所。

③ 恣(zì):放纵,无拘无束。谑(xuè):玩笑。

④ 径须:只管。沽(gū):通"酤",买。

⑤ 五花马:指名贵的马。一说马之毛色作五花纹,一说马的颈上毛修剪成五瓣。千金裘:《史记》:"孟尝君有一狐白裘,直千金,天下无双。"

⑥ 销:同"消"。

The sages of old have scarce left us a name,

The deep drinkers only recorded by fame.

When Ch'en Wang of old gave his feast at Pinglor,

A gallon① of wine each aroused their acclaim②.

The host shall ne'er say that too small is his store,

But buy the good vintage③ and lavishly④ pour.

This gallant⑤ bay⑥ charger⑦ and fur coat of mine,

Now let the boy take them and change them for wine.

The cares⑧ of the ages, though many and sore⑨,

Away will we scatter⑩, and know them no more."

---

① gallon/ˈɡælən/n. 加仑(液量单位,合 4.5 升)
② acclaim/əˈkleɪm/n. 欢呼,喝彩
③ vintage/ˈvɪntɪdʒ/n. 收获葡萄酿酒(的期间或季节),一个收获季节采得的葡萄(所酿制的酒)
④ lavishly/ˈlævɪʃlɪ/adv. 慷慨地,大方地
⑤ gallant/ˈɡælənt/adj. 豪侠,殷勤的男士,时髦男士
⑥ bay/beɪ/adj. 红棕色的(马)
⑦ charger/ˈtʃɑːdʒə/n. 军马,战马
⑧ care/keə/n. 忧虑,担心,操心,烦恼
⑨ sore/sɔː/adj. [旧用法]严重的,剧烈的
⑩ scatter/ˈskætə/v. 消除,摧毁,逐散

【推荐阅读】

一、中文版本及注疏

(唐)李白著,(清)王琦注. 李太白全集. 北京:中华书局,1977 年版,
1999 年重印。

二、英文译本

Ankenbrand,Frank. 1941. *Poems of Li Po,the Chinese Poet*,
Haddon Heights,New Jersey:W. L. Washburn.

Bynner,Witter,and Kiang Kang-hu. 1929. *The Jade Mountain,a
Chinese Anthology:Being Three Hundred Poems of the T'ang
Dynasty,618-906*. New York:A. A. Knopf.

Cooper,Arthur. 1973. *Li Po and Tu Fu*. Baltimore:Penguin
Books.

Curtiss,Florence Rising. 1952. *Translations from the Chinese T'ang
Dynasty Poets,A. D. 618-906*. New York.

Fletcher,W. J. B. 1919. *Gems of Chinese Verse Translated into
English Verse*,Shanghai:The Commercial Press.

Fletcher,W. J. B. 1933. *More Gems of Chinese Poetry*. Shanghai:
The Commercial Press.

Giles,H. A. 1898. *Chinese Poetry in English Verse*. London:
Bernard & Quaritch.

Giles,H. A. and Waley A. 1934. *Selected Chinese Verses*.
Shanghai:The Commercial Press.

Herdan,Innes. 1973,1979. *The Three Hundred T'ang Poems*.
Taipei:The Far East Book Co.,Ltd.

Jenyns,S. 1940. *Selections from the Three Hundred Poems of the
T'ang Dynasty*. London:John Murray.

Jenyns,S. 1944. *A Further Selection from the Three Hundred Poems of the T'ang Dynasty*. London: John Murray.

Obata, Shigeyoshi. *The Works of Li Po, the Chinese Poet*. New York, Dutton, 1922; London, Dent, 1923; Tokyo, 1935; reprinted, New York: Paragon Book Reprint Corp. , 1965.

Waley, Arthur. *A Hundred and Seventy Chinese Poems*. London, 1918; New York: A. A. Knopf, 1919, 2nd ed. , 1962.

Waley, Arthur. *Translations from the Chinese*. New York: Random House, 1919; New York, A. A. Knopf, 1941.

Waley, Arthur. *More Translations from the Chinese*. New York: A. A. Knopf, 1919; London, George Allen & Unwin Ltd. , 1920.

Waley, Arthur. 1930. *Poems from the Chinese*. London.

Waley, Arthur. 1950. *The Poetry and Career of Li Po*. London: Allen and Unwin; New York: Macmillan.

许渊冲. 中英文对照唐诗三百首. 北京: 中国对外翻译出版公司, 2006 年。

许渊冲. 李白诗选. 长沙: 湖南人民出版社, 2007 年。

第十六单元 《苏东坡集》

【导言】

　　苏轼（1037—1101 年），字子瞻，号东坡居士，四川眉山人，北宋著名文学家、书画家和美食家。苏轼天赋极高，博学多才，精通书画，善文学，工诗词，与欧阳修并称欧苏，为"唐宋八大家"之一，苏轼与他的父亲苏洵（1009—1066 年）、弟弟苏辙（1039—1112 年）皆以文学名世，世称"三苏"。

　　《苏东坡集》又名《苏文忠公全集》《东坡七集》，收录了苏轼一生的鸿篇巨著。苏轼作品集，历代有不同编法，主要有诗集、文集和诗文合集三种。苏轼诗有王十朋的《集注分类东坡诗》25 卷，有黄善夫刊本、《四部丛刊》影元刊本。编年注本有施元之、顾禧《注东坡先生诗》，清有查慎行《补注东坡编年诗》，冯应榴《苏文忠诗合注》，王文诰《苏文忠公诗编注集成》等。苏轼词较常见的有朱祖谋编年本《东坡乐府》三卷，龙榆生《东坡乐府笺》本。苏轼文最早的选本是南宋邱晔的《经进东坡文集事略》，有《四部丛刊》影宋刊本。明末茅维《苏文忠公全集》只有文和词。其诗文全刊本，宋代有《东坡集》《东坡后集》等。明成化四年程宗刊《苏文忠公全集》共 112 卷，有清末端方校印本和《四部备要》本等。

　　苏轼以其辉煌的成就吸引了国内外众多学者的译介。但除极少专门的苏轼作品选译本之外，大多数苏轼作品英文译作均散见于各种诗文选译本中。英译苏轼作品的主要译者及诗文集有：翟理斯（Herbert A. Giles）的《古文选珍》(*Gems of Chinese Literature*, 1884)、《古今诗选》(*Chinese Poetry in English Verse*, 1898)；阿瑟韦利的《汉诗 170 首》(*A Hundred and Seventy Chinese Poems*, 1918)；李高洁（Cyril Drummond Le Gros Clark）的《苏东坡文选》(*Selections from the Works of Su Tung-p'o*, 1932)；肯尼斯·雷克斯洛斯（Kenneth Rexroth）的《中国诗百首》(100 *Poems from the Chinese*, 1956)；艾林（Alan Ayling）和麦金托希（Duncan Mackintosh）的《中国词选》(*A Collection of Chinese Lyrics*, 1965)、《中国词选续编》(*A Further Collection of Chinese Lyrics*, 1969)；华兹生（Burton Watson）的《东坡

诗词选》(*Tung-P'o*: *Selections from a Sung Dynasty Poet*, 1965);刘若愚(James Liu)的《北宋六大词家(960—1126)》(*Major Lyricist of the Northern Sung*, 1974);柳无忌和罗郁正全编的《葵花集:三千年的中国诗歌》(*Sunflower Splendor*: *Three Thousand Years of Chinese Poetry*, 1975);刘师舜的中英对照《唐宋八大家文选》(*Chinese Classical Prose*: *the Eight Masters of the Tang-Sung Period*, 1979);杨宪益夫妇合译的《唐宋诗文选》(*Poetry and Prose of the Tang and Song*, 1984);朱莉·兰多(Julie Landau)的《春之外:宋词选集》(*Beyond Spring*: *Tz'u Poems of the Sung Dynasty*, 1994);叶维廉(Wai-Lim Yip)的《中国诗词选》(*Chinese Poetry*: *An Anthology of Major Modes and Genres*, 1997);戈登·奥赛茵(Gordon Osing)的《寒心未肯随春态:苏东坡诗词欣赏》(*Blooming Alone in Winter*: *Poems of Su Dong-po*, 1999)等。

前赤壁赋①

壬戌之秋②，七月既望③，苏子与客泛舟④，游于赤壁之下。清风徐⑤来，水波不兴⑥。举酒属客⑦，诵明月之诗⑧，歌窈窕之章⑨。少焉⑩，月出于东山之上，徘徊于斗牛之间⑪。白露横江⑫，水光接天。纵一苇之所如⑬，凌万顷之茫然⑭。浩浩乎如冯虚御风⑮，而不知其所止；飘飘乎如遗世独立⑯，羽化而登仙⑰。

于是饮酒乐甚，扣舷而歌之。歌曰："桂棹兮兰桨⑱，击空明兮溯流

---

① 选自《经进东坡文集事略》。宋神宗元丰五年(1082 年)，苏轼贬谪黄州(今湖北黄冈)时所作。后来他还写过一篇同题的赋，故称此篇为《前赤壁赋》，另外一篇为《后赤壁赋》。赤壁：实为黄州赤鼻矶，并非三国时期赤壁之战旧址，当地人因发音相近亦称之为赤壁。苏轼知道这一点，将错就错，借景以抒怀。
② 壬(rén)戌(xū)：宋神宗元丰五年，岁在壬戌，即公元 1082 年。
③ 既望：望日的次日，即农历每月十六日。周历以每月十五、十六日至廿二、廿三日为既望。后称农历十五日为望，十六日为既望。孔颖达疏："周公摄政七年二月十六日，其日为庚寅，既日月相望矣。于已望后六日乙未，为二月二十一日。"《释名·释天》："望，月满之名也。月大十六日，小十五日，日在东，月在西，遥相望也。"
④ 泛舟：行船，坐船游玩。
⑤ 徐：缓慢。
⑥ 兴：起，作。
⑦ 属(zhǔ)：通"嘱"，斟酒相劝。
⑧ 明月之诗：描写明月的诗。《诗经·陈风·月出》有"舒窈纠兮"之句，故称"明月之诗"。
⑨ 窈窕之章：《诗经·陈风·月出》诗首章为："月出皎兮，佼人僚兮，舒窈纠兮，劳心悄兮。""窈纠"同"窈窕"。
⑩ 少(shǎo)焉：少刻，一会儿。
⑪ 斗(dǒu)牛：也作"牛斗"。二十八宿中的斗宿和牛宿。
⑫ 白露横江：白茫茫的水气笼罩着江面。横江：横陈江上，横越江上。
⑬ 纵：任凭。一苇：一根芦苇，借指小船。孔颖达疏："言一苇者，谓一束也，可以浮之水上而渡，若桴筏然，非一根苇也。"后以"一苇"为小船的代称。如：往。
⑭ 凌：渡过，逾越。万顷：极为宽阔的江面。茫然：广阔无边的样子。
⑮ 浩浩：广大无际。冯虚御风：冯：乘。虚：太空。御：驾御。
⑯ 飘飘：轻盈舒缓，超尘脱俗的样子。
⑰ 羽化而登仙：道教把成仙称作"羽化"，认为成仙后能够飞升。
⑱ 棹(zhào)：船桨。

光①。渺渺兮予怀②,望美人兮天一方③。"

---

① 空明：特指月光下的清波。溯：逆流而上。流光：如水般流泻的月光。
② 渺渺兮予怀：我的心思飘得很远很远。渺渺：幽远的样子。
③ 美人：古指有德有才的人；一说指内心思慕的人。

Thoughts Suggested by the Red Wall: Summer

Translated by Herbert A. Giles[1]

In the year 1081[2], the seventh moon just on the wane[3], I went with a friend on a boat excursion[4] to the Red Wall. A clear[5] breeze was gently blowing, scarce enough to ruffle[6] the river, as I filled my friend's cup and bade[7] him troll[8] a lay[9] to the bright moon, singing the song of the *Modest*[10] *Maid*[11].

By-and-by, up rose the moon over the eastern hills, wandering between the Wain[12] and the Goat[13], shedding[14] forth her silver beams[15], and linking the water with the sky. On a skiff[16] we took our seats, and shot[17] over the liquid plain[18], lightly as though travelling through space, riding on the wind without knowing

---

① 英文译文选自：Giles, Herbert A. 1922. *Gems of Chinese Literature* (Revised and greatly enlarged). Shanghai: Kelly and Walsh, Limited, pp.175－176。

② 原文"壬戌"年为宋神宗元丰五年,即公元 1082 年,此处 1081 年为辛酉年。

③ wane/weɪn/*n*. 月亏(期)。on the wane:逐渐减弱,衰败,衰落

④ excursion/ɪkˈskɜːʃn/*n*. 短程旅行,远足

⑤ clear/klɪə/*adj*. 清澈的,透明的,爽朗的,晴朗的

⑥ ruffle/ˈrʌfl/*v*. 使起涟漪,使……起伏不平,弄皱

⑦ bade/beɪd/*v*. (bid 的过去式)吩咐(某人),告诉,邀请

⑧ troll/trəul/*v*. 轮唱,连续地唱,高声唱

⑨ lay/leɪ/*n*. 叙事诗,供吟唱的诗,民歌,民谣

⑩ modest/ˈmɒdɪst/*adj*. (尤指女子或其容貌或行为)端庄的,高雅的,正派的,纯洁的

⑪ maid/meɪd/*n*. 未婚的年轻女子,姑娘

⑫ Wain/weɪn/*n*. 北斗七星

⑬ Goat/gəut/*n*. Capricorn 摩羯宫(黄道第十宫),山羊座

⑭ shed/ʃed/*v*. 散发出(光等)

⑮ beam/biːm/*n*. (灯、灯塔、日月等的)光线、光束或其他射线

⑯ skiff/skɪf/*n*. 轻舟,小艇

⑰ shoot/ʃuːt/*v*. (指船或船中人)迅速穿过(某物)

⑱ plain/pleɪn/*n*. 平原,平坦、水平或开阔的区域

whither① we were bound②. We seemed to be moving in another sphere③, sailing through air like the Gods. So I poured out a bumper④ for joy, and, beating time⑤ on the skiff's side, sang the following verse:

With laughing oars⑥, our joyous prow⑦
Shoots swiftly through the glittering⑧ wave —
My heart within grows sadly grave⑨—
Great heroes dead, where are ye⑩ now?

---

① whither/'wɪðə/adv. 向何处
② bound/baund/adj. 去,准备去
③ sphere/sfɪə/n. 天体,行星体,[诗]天空
④ bumper/'bʌmpə/n. 干杯中的满杯,已满到边沿的一大杯
⑤ beat time 打拍子
⑥ oar/ɔː/n. 桨,桨手,划船者
⑦ prow/prau/n. 船首,船头
⑧ glittering/'glɪtərɪŋ/adj. 闪闪发光的
⑨ grave/greɪv/adj. 严肃的,沉重的
⑩ ye/jiː/pron. [古语]你,你们

客有吹洞箫者①,倚歌而和之②。其声呜呜然③,如怨如慕,如泣如诉。余音袅袅④,不绝如缕⑤。舞幽壑之潜蛟⑥,泣孤舟之嫠妇⑦。

苏子愀然⑧,正襟危坐⑨,而问客曰:"何为其然也?"客曰:"'月明星稀,乌鹊南飞。'此非曹孟德之诗乎? 西望夏口⑩,东望武昌,山川相缪⑪,郁乎苍苍,此非孟德之困于周郎者乎⑫? 方其破荆州,下江陵,顺流而东也⑬,舳舻千里⑭,旌旗蔽空,酾酒临江⑮,横槊赋诗⑯,固一世之雄也⑰,而今安在哉? 况吾与子渔樵于江渚之上⑱,侣鱼虾而友麋鹿,驾一叶之扁舟⑲,举匏樽以相属⑳。寄蜉蝣于天地㉑,渺沧海之一粟㉒。哀

---

① 洞箫:管乐器。简称箫。古代的箫以竹管编排而成,称为排箫。排箫以蜡蜜封底,无封底者称洞箫。后称单管直吹、正面五孔、背面一孔者为洞箫。发音清幽凄婉。

② 倚歌:以乐声为歌声伴奏。和(hè):以声相应,跟着唱或跟着唱腔伴奏。

③ 呜呜:歌咏声,吟咏声。又,象声词,多形容低沉的声响。

④ 袅袅(niǎo):形容声音延长不绝,宛转悠扬。

⑤ 不绝如缕:形容声音细微而连绵不断。缕:细丝。

⑥ 舞:使……飞舞。幽壑:深谷,深渊。蛟:古代传说中的一种龙,常居深渊,能发洪水。

⑦ 嫠(lí)妇:指寡妇。

⑧ 愀(qiǎo)然:神色变得严肃或不愉快。

⑨ 正襟危坐:整理好衣服,端正地坐着。形容严肃或拘谨。危坐:端坐。

⑩ 夏口:古地名,位于汉水下游入长江处,由于汉水自沔阳以下古称夏水,故名。

⑪ 缪(liáo):通"缭",缠绕,环绕。

⑫ 孟德之困于周郎:指汉献帝建安十三年(208年),吴将周瑜在赤壁之战中击败曹操号称八十万大军。周郎:周瑜二十四岁即为中郎将,故称"周郎"。

⑬ 方其破荆州,下江陵,顺流而东也:指建安十三年刘琮率众向曹操投降,曹军不战而占领荆州、江陵。方:当。荆州:辖南阳、江夏、长沙等八郡,今湖南、湖北一带。江陵:当时的荆州首府。

⑭ 舳(zhú)舻(lú):船头和船尾的并称,多泛指前后首尾相接的船。"舳"指船尾或船舵,"舻"指船头。《汉书·武帝纪》:"自寻阳浮江,亲射蛟江中,获之。舳舻千里,薄枞阳而出。"颜师古注引李斐曰:"舳,船后持柁处也。舻,船前头刺棹处也。言其船多,前后相衔,千里不绝也。"

⑮ 酾(shī)酒:斟酒。

⑯ 横槊(shuò):横执长矛。槊:长矛,古代的一种兵器。

⑰ 固:必,一定;原来,本来。

⑱ 渔樵(qiáo):捕鱼砍柴。江渚(zhǔ):江中小洲,亦指江边。

⑲ 扁(piān)舟:小船。

⑳ 匏(páo)樽:用葫芦做成的酒器。匏:葫芦。

㉑ 寄:寓托。蜉(fú)蝣(yóu):昆虫的一科,幼虫生活在水中一年至五、六年,成虫有翅两对,尾部有丝状物二或三条,成虫常在水面飞行,寿命很短,只有数小时至一星期左右。

㉒ 渺:微小。沧海:大海。粟:谷粒。未去皮壳者为粟,已春去糠则为米。

吾生之须臾,羡长江之无穷。挟飞仙以遨游,抱明月而长终①。知不可乎骤得,托遗响于悲风②。"

---

① 长终:永远。
② 遗响:余音。

My friend accompanied① these words upon his flageolet②, delicately③ adjusting its notes④ to express the varied emotions of pity and regret, without the slightest break in the thread of sound which seemed to wind⑤ around us like a silken skein⑥. The very monsters of the deep yielded to the influence of his strains⑦, while the boat-woman, who had lost her husband, burst into a flood of tears. Overpowered⑧ by my own feelings, I settled myself into a serious mood, and asked my friend for some explanation of his art. To this he replied, "Did not Ts'ao Ts'ao say:

The stars are few, the moon is bright,
The raven⑨ southward wings his flight.

"Westwards to Hsia-k'ou, eastwards to Wu-ch'ang, where hill and stream in wild luxuriance⑩ blend, — was it not there that Ts'ao Ts'ao was routed⑪ by Chou Yu? Ching-chou was at his feet: he was pushing down stream towards the east. His war-vessels stretched stem⑫ to stern⑬ for a thousand *li*: his banners darkened the sky. He

---

① accompany/əˈkʌmpənɪ/ *v*. 伴唱，伴奏
② flageolet/ˌflædʒəˈlet/ *n*. 六孔竖笛（一种有圆柱形吹口、四个指孔和两个拇指孔的小的长笛状乐器）
③ delicately/ˈdelɪkɪtlɪ/ *adv*. 优美地
④ note/nəut/ *n*. 音调，曲调
⑤ wind/waɪnd/ *v*. 袅袅上升，螺旋前进，盘旋而行
⑥ skein/skeɪn/ *n*. 丝球，线团，线球
⑦ strain/streɪn/ *n*. 奋力（极端的或极其费力的努力，操作或工作）
⑧ overpower/ˌəuvəˈpauə/ *v*. 征服，制服，压倒
⑨ raven/ˈreɪvn/ *n*. 渡鸦（较乌鸦大，羽毛黑色而有光泽，叫声嘶哑）
⑩ luxuriance/lʌkˈʃurɪəns/ *n*. 繁茂，繁盛
⑪ be routed/ruːtɪd/战败，大败，溃败
⑫ stem/stem/ *n*. 船头
⑬ stern/stɜːn/ *n*. 船尾

poured out a libation① as he neared Chiangling; and sitting in the saddle, armed *cap-à-pie*②, he uttered those words did that hero of his age. Yet where is he to-day?

"Now you and I have fished and gathered fuel together on the river eyots③. We have fraternized④ with the crayfish⑤; we have made friends with the deer. We have embarked⑥ together in our frail⑦ canoe; we have drawn inspiration together from the wine-flask⑧— a couple of ephemeridaes⑨, launched on the ocean in a rice-husk⑩! Alas, life is but an instant of Time. I long to be like the Great River which rolls on⑪ its way without end. Ah, that I might cling to some angel's wing and roam⑫ with him for ever! Ah, that I might clasp⑬ the bright moon in my arms and dwell with her for aye⑭! Alas, it only remains to me to enwrap these regrets in the tender melody⑮ of sound."

---

① libation/laɪˈbeɪʃn/ *n*. 酒,(旧时向神的)祭酒,奠酒

② cap-à-pie/kæpəˈpiː/ *adv*. 从头到脚,全身,全部

③ eyot/ˈeɪət/ *n*. 河心岛,湖泊中小岛,湖心岛,湖洲

④ fraternize/ˈfrætənaɪz/ *v*. 亲如兄弟,亲善

⑤ crayfish/ˈkreɪfɪʃ/ *n*. (淡水的)螯虾,小龙虾

⑥ embark/ɪmˈbɑːk/ *v*. 乘船,上船

⑦ frail/freɪl/ *adj*. 易打破或毁坏的,易碎的

⑧ flask/flɑːsk/ *n*. (装油、酒等的)细颈瓶

⑨ ephemerida/ɪˈfemərɪdə/ *n*. 蜉蝣目(昆虫)

⑩ husk/hʌsk/ *n*. (某些种子和果实的)外壳,外皮(尤指谷类的)

⑪ roll on 滔滔流动

⑫ roam/rəum/ *v*. 漫步,漫游

⑬ clasp/klɑːsp/ *v*. 紧抱,紧握

⑭ for aye 永远地

⑮ melody/ˈmelədɪ/ *n*. 曲子,曲调,美的音乐

苏子曰:"客亦知夫水与月乎? 逝者如斯①,而未尝往也。盈虚者如彼②,而卒莫消长也③。盖将自其变者而观之,则天地曾不能以一瞬。自其不变者而观之,则物与我皆无尽也,而又何羡乎! 且夫天地之间,物各有主。苟非吾之所有,虽一毫而莫取。惟江上之清风,与山间之明月。耳得之而为声,目遇之而成色。取之无禁,用之不竭。是造物者之无尽藏也④,而吾与子之所共适⑤。"客喜而笑,洗盏更酌⑥。肴核既尽⑦,杯盘狼籍⑧。相与枕藉乎舟中⑨,不知东方之既白⑩。

---

① 逝者如斯:流逝的像这江水。语出《论语·子罕》:"子在川上曰:'逝者如斯夫,不舍昼夜。'"逝:往,流逝。斯:此,指水。

② 盈虚:指月亮的圆缺。

③ 卒:最终。消长(zhǎng):增减。

④ 无尽藏(zàng):佛教用语,指无穷无尽的宝藏。

⑤ 共适:共享。适:享用。原为"共食"。《释典》谓六识以六入为养,其养也胥谓之食,目以色为食,耳以声为食,鼻以香为食,口以味为食,身以触为食,意以法为食。清风明月,耳得成声,目遇成色。故曰"共食"。易以"共适",则意味索然。当时有问轼"食"字之义,轼曰:"如食吧之'食',犹共享也。"轼盖不欲以博览上人,故权词以答,古人谦抑如此。

⑥ 洗盏(zhǎn)更(gēng)酌(zhuó):清洗酒杯,再次饮酒。

⑦ 肴(yáo)核:荤菜和果品。

⑧ 狼籍(jí):凌乱。"籍"通"藉"。

⑨ 枕藉(jiè):相互枕着,靠着。

⑩ 既白:已经显出白色,意为"天亮"。

"But do you forsooth① comprehend," I enquired, "the mystery of this river and of this moon? The water passes by but is never gone; the moon wanes only to wax once more. Relatively speaking, Time itself is but an instant of time; absolutely speaking, you and I, in common with② all matter, shall exist to all eternity③. Wherefore④ then the longing of which you speak?

The objects we see around us are one and all⑤ the property of individuals. If a thing does not belong to me, not a particle⑥ of it may be enjoyed by me. But the clear breeze blowing across this stream, the bight moon streaming over yon hills, — these are sounds and sights to be enjoyed without let or hindrance⑦ by all. They are the eternal gifts of God to all mankind, and their enjoyment is inexhaustible⑧. Hence it is that you and I are enjoying them now."

My friend smiled as he threw away the dregs⑨ from his wine-cup and filled it once more to the brim⑩. And then, when our feast was over, amid the litter⑪ of cups and plates, we lay down to rest in the boat; for streaks⑫ of light from the east had stolen upon us unawares⑬.

---

① forsooth/fə'su:θ/v. 真的,当然,的确
② in common with 与……一样
③ eternity/ɪ'tɜ:nətɪ/n. 永恒,不朽,来世
④ wherefore/'weəfɔ:/adv. 何以
⑤ one and all 全部,全都
⑥ particle/'pɑ:tɪkl/n. 粒子,极小量
⑦ hindrance/'hɪndrəns/n. 妨害,妨碍
⑧ inexhaustible/ˌɪnɪg'zɔ:stəbl/adj. 无穷尽的,用不完的
⑨ dreg/dreg/n. 残滓,渣滓
⑩ to the brim 斟满,充满
⑪ litter/'lɪtə/n. 乱扔的杂物,(尤指在公共场所乱扔的)垃圾
⑫ streak/stri:k/n. 条纹,痕迹
⑬ unawares/ˌʌnə'weəz/adv. 没想到,不知不觉地,不料

【推荐阅读】

一、中文版本及注疏

陈迩冬选注.苏轼诗选.北京：人民文学出版社,1984 年。

孔凡礼点校.苏轼文集.北京：中华书局,1986 年。

徐英才.英译唐宋八大家散文精选.上海：上海外语教育出版社, 2011 年。

曾枣庄.苏轼评传.成都：四川人民出版社,1981 年。

郑孟彤等.苏东坡诗词文译释.哈尔滨：黑龙江人民出版社,1984 年。

钟来茵.苏东坡三部曲.上海：上海文汇出版社,1998 年。

二、英文译本

Clark, Cyril D. L. G. 1932. *Selections from the Works of Su Tung-p'o*. London: Jonathan Cape.

Giles, Herbert A. 1922. *Gems of Chinese Literature* (Revised and greatly enlarged). Shanghai: Kelly and Walsh, Limited.

Landau, Julie. 1994. *Beyond Spring: T'zu Poems of the Sung Dynasty*. New York: Columbia University Press.

Liu, James. 1974. *Major Lyricist of the Northern Sung*. Princeton: Princeton University Press.

Liu Shih Shun. 1979. *Chinese Classical Prose: The Eight Masters of the T'ang-Sung Period*. Renditions Press.

Liu, Wu-chi and Irving Lo, eds. 1975. *Sunflower Splendor: Three Thousand Years of Chinese Poetry*. Bloomington: Indiana University Press.

Owen, Stephen. 1997. *An Anthology of Chinese Literature: Beginnings to 1911*. W. W. Norton & Co Inc (Np).

Pollard, David. 2000. *The Chinese Essay*. New York: Columbia University Press.

Rexroth，Kenneth. 1959. 100 *Poems from the Chinese*. New York： New Directions.

Waley，Arthur. 1918. *A Hundred and Seventy Chinese Poems*. Kessinger Publishing.

Watson，Burton. 1965. *Su Tung-P'o*： *Selections from a Sung Dynasty Poet*，New York：Columbia University Press.

Yang Xianyi & Gladys Yang. 1984. *Poetry and Prose of the Tang and Song*. Chinese Literature.

Yip，Wai-Lim. 1997. *Chinese Poetry*： *An Anthology of Major Modes and Genres*. Duke University Press.

主要参考文献

Birch，Cyril. 1965. *Anthology of Chinese Literature*，*From Early Times to the Fourteenth Century*. New York：Grove Press，Inc.

Fletcher，W.J.B. 1919.（trans.）*Gems of Chinese Verse*. Shanghai：Commercial Press Limited.

Giles，Herbert A.（trans.）1888. *Chuang Tzu*：*Mystic*，*Moralist*，*and Social Reformer*. London：Bernard Quaritch.

Giles，Herbert A. 1922. *Gems of Chinese Literature*（Revised and greatly enlarged）. Shanghai：Kelly and Walsh，Limited

Giles，Lionel. 1910.（trans.）*Sun Tzǔ on the Art of War*. London：Luzac and Company.

Knoblock，John.（trans.）1927. *The Works of Hsüntze*. London：Probsthain's Oriental Series 16.

Legge，James. 1861. T*he Chinese Classics*：*The Works of Mencius*. Oxford：Clarendon Press.

Legge，James. 1876. *The She King*；*or*，*The Book of Ancient Poetry*，*Translated in English Verse*，*with Essays and Notes*. London：Trübner & Co.

Legge，James. 1991. *The Chinese Classics*. Taipei：SMC Publishing Inc.

Mair，Victor. 1994. *The Columbia Anthology of Traditional Chinese Literature*.

Waley，A.（Trans.）1946. *Chinese Poems*. London：George Allen and Unwin Ltd.

Watson，Burton. 1969.（trans）*Records of the Grand Historian*. New York：Columbia University Press.

蔡尚思编.中国文化史要论(人物·图书).长沙：湖南人民出版社,1979 年。

曹操等注,杨丙安校理.十一家注孙子校理.北京：中华书局,1999 年。

陈鼓应.庄子今注今译(最新修订版).北京：商务印书馆,2007 年版。

曹伯韩.国学常识.北京：生活·读书·新知三联书店,2008 年。

程俊英、蒋见元.诗经注析.北京：中华书局,1999 年。

[宋]郭茂倩编.乐府诗集.北京：中华书局,1979 年版,1998 年重印。

郭朋.坛经校释.北京：中华书局,1983 年。

韩兆琦译注.中华经典藏书·史记.北京：中华书局,2007 年。

胡道静主编.国学大师论国学.上海：东方出版中心,1998 年。

[唐]李白著,[清]王琦注.李太白全集.北京：中华书局,1977 年版,1999 年重印。

梁启超.国学入门书要目及其读法.饮冰室合集：专集七十一.北京：中华书局,
    1989 年。

梁启超.要籍解题及其读法.长沙：岳麓书社,2010 年。

林光明.六祖坛经及其英译.台北：嘉丰出版社,2004 年。

吕叔湘编.中诗英译比录.北京：中华书局,2002 年。

钱基博.国学必读.上海：上海古籍出版社,2011 年。

钱穆.国学概论.北京：商务印书馆,1997 年。

屈万里.屈万里全集·古籍导读.上海：上海辞书出版社,2015 年。

任继愈.老子绎读.北京：北京图书馆出版社,2006 年版。

阮元校刻.十三经注疏(附校勘记).北京：中华书局,1980 年。

汪辟疆.汪辟疆文集.上海：上海古籍出版社,1985 年。

王先谦.荀子集解.北京：中华书局,1988 年版。

杨伯峻.孟子译注.北京：中华书局,1984 年。

朱熹.楚辞集注.上海：上海古籍出版社,1979 年。

朱熹.四书章句集注.北京：中华书局,1983 年。

朱熹.论语集注.北京：北京图书馆出版社,2001 年。

图书在版编目(CIP)数据

汉英对照国学经典选读/俞森林主编.—上海:上海三联书店,2023.6
ISBN 978 - 7 - 5426 - 7884 - 3

Ⅰ.①汉… Ⅱ.①俞… Ⅲ.①国学-推荐书目-中国-汉、英 Ⅳ.①Z835

中国版本图书馆 CIP 数据核字(2022)第 187126 号

汉英对照国学经典选读

主　　编 / 俞森林

责任编辑 / 殷亚平
装帧设计 / 徐　徐
监　　制 / 姚　军
责任校对 / 王凌霄

出版发行 / 上海三联书店
　　　　　 (200030)中国上海市漕溪北路 331 号 A 座 6 楼
邮　　箱 / sdxsanlian@sina.com
邮购电话 / 021 - 22895540
印　　刷 / 上海惠敦印务科技有限公司

版　　次 / 2023 年 6 月第 1 版
印　　次 / 2023 年 6 月第 1 次印刷
开　　本 / 640 mm × 960 mm　1/16
字　　数 / 350 千字
印　　张 / 25.25
书　　号 / ISBN 978 - 7 - 5426 - 7884 - 3/Z·139
定　　价 / 98.00 元

敬启读者,如发现本书有印装质量问题,请与印刷厂联系 021 - 63779028